ECONOMIC ISSUES AND POLITICAL CONFLICT: US–LATIN AMERICAN RELATIONS

Butterworths Studies in International Political Economy will present new work, from a multinational stable of authors, on major issues, theoretical and practical, in the international political economy.

General Editor

Susan Strange, Professor of International Relations, London School of Economics and Political Science, England

Consulting Editors

Ladd Hollist, Director, Program for International Political Economy Research, University of Southern California, USA

Karl Kaiser, Director, Research Institute of the German Society for Foreign Affairs, Bonn, and Professor of Political Science, University of Cologne, West Germany

William Leohr, Graduate School of International Studies, University of Denver, USA

Joseph Nye, Professor of Government, Harvard University, USA

Forthcoming titles

War, Trade and Regime Formation
Japan and Western Europe: Conflict and Cooperation
Defence, Technology and International Integration
International Political Economy – A Text

Published titles

The East European Economies in the 1970s (Nove, Höhmann and Seidenstecher)
The Political Economy of New and Old Industrial Countries (Saunders)
France in the Troubled World Economy (Cohen and Gourevitch)

Economic Issues and Political Conflict: US–Latin American Relations

Edited by
Jorge I. Domínguez
Center for International Affairs, Harvard University

Butterworth Scientific
London   Boston   Durban   Singapore   Sydney   Toronto   Wellington

This book was written under the auspices of the Center for
International Affairs, Harvard University.

First published 1982

© Butterworth & Co (Publishers) Ltd 1982

British Library Cataloguing in Publication Data

Economic issues and political conflict
   (Butterworths studies in international
   political economy)
   1. Economic development – Political aspects
   2. Latin America – Economic conditions – 1945-
   I. Domínguez, Jorge I.
   330.98′003   HC125
   ISBN 0-408-10807-X

Photoset by Butterworths Litho Preparation Department
Printed in England by Redwood Burn Ltd, Trowbridge, Wiltshire

Preface

This book is the result of a somewhat unusual joint endeavor. Some of the authors have been studying Latin American countries for some time; other authors have been principally interested in global issues or in US foreign policy but had not done much previous work on Latin America. We found our scholarly interests and relations evolving in ways not unlike those we sketch for Latin American countries and for the United States in the pages that follow. The Latin Americanists among us believed it important to address issues of concern within as well as outside the countries of the region. The globalists among us found that understanding and working on Latin American countries had become important for their own scholarly concerns. The inclusion of Latin America in world affairs was thus paralleled by the inclusion of the Latin Americanists and the globalists on each other's research agenda. And so this project was born.

We have benefited from each other's suggestions and criticisms and from discussions at the Center for International Affairs at Harvard University, with which all of us have had varying degrees of association over the years. We thus dedicate this book to the Center that has supported our work, in part or in full, through the years.

This original research was supported by the Center for International Affairs at Harvard University and it was funded by the Office of Long Range Assessments and Research of the US Department of State. The authors alone bear responsibility for findings, conclusions and all other statements. We are very grateful for the support we have received. We were especially pleased because the scholarly independence and integrity of the work was a common objective of both the authors and the donor. Unfettered and impartial research serves the interests of all. In particular, we wish to thank Kenneth Roberts for his support and assistance in facilitating our work.

Ann Stibal and Andrée Brown provided their customary superb and cheerful assistance in getting this book actually done.

Jorge I. Domínguez
September 1981

Contents

1 Introduction   Jorge I. Domínguez (Center for International Affairs, Harvard University)   1

2 Business nationalism: Latin American national business attitudes and behavior toward multinational enterprises   Jorge I. Domínguez (Center for International Affairs, Harvard University)   16

3 Public policy, foreign investment and implementation style in Mexico   Merilee S. Grindle (Department of Political Science, Brown University)   69

4 Venezuelan foreign economic policy and the United States   Janet Kelly Escobar (Universidad Simón Bolívar, Caracas)   107

5 Latin American industrial exports and trade negotiations with the United States   John S. Odell (Center for International Affairs, Harvard University)   142

6 The transformation of US–Latin American technology transfer relations: the first stage   Debra Lynn Miller (Barnard College, Columbia University)   168

7 The costs and benefits of paying more attention to Latin America   Robert L. Paarlberg (Department of Political Science, Wellesley College, and Center for International Affairs, Harvard University)   208

Index   238

Introduction

Jorge I. Domínguez*

Relations between Latin America and the United States have changed substantially in recent years. Many of the issues that gripped the imagination of peoples, scholars and public officials have been settled. The Cuban missile crisis, the Dominican intervention, the efforts of Ernesto (Che) Guevara, the status of the Panama Canal – these and other political and military issues dominated the agenda of US–Latin American relations for many years. They now belong to the past. Newer 'Cold War' issues have arisen as a result of revolutions in Nicaragua and Grenada and of civil war in El Salvador, and of US–Cuban conflicts over them. They will demand ingenuity and attention for some time, but they seem unlikely to dominate so exclusively the inter-American agenda – especially the relations between the US and the larger Latin American countries – in the future as they did in the past. Yet politics remains at the core of the inter-American agenda, both in the relations among countries, and in decision-making within countries. This is no longer just the politics of the Cold War or of counter-insurgency but also the politics of economic relations. This shift results from a series of changes in the international system and in the countries of the western hemisphere.

1.1 The evolution of US–Latin American economic relations

The relative weight of the United States in the international economic system has changed, permanently altering US–Latin American relations. The consequences of allied victory – with Latin American participation – in World War II had had the paradoxical effect of reducing the scope of international action of the major Latin American countries. Europe and Japan lay in ruins, and were unable to provide alternatives to US primacy. The Cold War led to a bipolar international system where Latin America's interests were found readily on the US side. Political and military relations were tightened. The Inter-American Treaty of Reciprocal Assistance and the Charter of the Organization of American States formalized the evolving ties

* Center for International Affairs, Harvard University.

between Latin America and the United States. While the aim of these agreements was to present a unified western hemisphere in the confrontation with the Soviet Union, an unintended consequence was to reduce Latin American options beyond the hemisphere.

From a Latin American perspective, the US established a loose hegemony over the region. This hegemony had two basic rules: client states would be loyal to the US in foreign affairs – Latin American voting in the United Nations until the late 1950s is spectacular evidence of this loyalty; secondly, the flow of goods and capital between the US and Latin America would be relatively open and unimpeded. Within these two rules, there was considerable freedom of action. The United States did not dominate the internal affairs of most of these countries, unless they threatened to break the rules. The goal of US policy was to ensure that loyalty to anti-communism and to capitalism prevailed in the region.

The United States went on to build a new international economic order, with the consent of the Europeans, the opposition of the Soviets, and the resignation of the Latin Americans. The Latin American countries, at best reluctant partners in this new system, proceeded to violate many of the new rules while paying formal obedience to them. Contrary to the North Atlantic trend toward tariff reductions to facilitate trade, Latin American governments raised import tariffs to protect infant industries, sacrificing international trade for the sake of protected economic growth at home. Contrary to rules of monetary stability, Latin American governments financed a part of their economic growth by printing paper money. They ran huge government deficits, induced very high rates of inflation, and engaged in periodic and massive currency devaluations. Some Latin American countries opposed US policies toward the oceans, seeking to expand their jurisdiction up to 200 miles to exploit ocean resources for their own development. Latin American governments never fully subscribed to US preferences on private foreign investments. They insisted on their right to regulate foreign-owned firms as if they were national, not multinational, firms and, at times, to expropriate them.

In fact, the violations tended to be minor. In the field of investment, the violations were often merely rhetorical because most governments wanted to increase such investment. Concerning the oceans, violations were necessarily minor because Latin American countries lacked the naval power to prevail. The General Agreement on Tariffs and Trade (GATT) had provisions that avoided confrontation over some Latin American violations of free trade rules. The International Monetary Fund, under US leadership, often imposed austerity measures on Latin American governments that had the effect of inducing the violation of other rules. In the political and military fields, violations of US primacy were either crushed (Guatemala in 1954) or truly exceptional (Cuba after 1959).

The US-supported anti-communist policy succeeded too well. In 1965,

US armed forces landed in the Dominican Republic to prevent a second Cuban revolution there even though none was occurring as such. The Dominican intervention is best understood as deriving from a broader US policy under President Lyndon Johnson to make the world everywhere safe for itself, from the Caribbean to Southeast Asia, even if it required the force of arms. Elsewhere in Latin America, the fear of communism, successfully transmitted by the US to Latin American elites, became the overriding ideological reason for opposing social change at home. The desire to combat communism contributed to the spread of a national security state mentality in many Latin American countries. There is, it should be added, no direct cause and effect between the US government's policies and the emergence of authoritarian regimes in Latin America in the 1960s; but the US did add to the development of an intellectual and international policy milieu that facilitated the rise of leviathans to power in Brazil, Argentina, Uruguay and Chile. Despite high human costs, one result was the emergence of much stronger states in Latin America, more competent to implement policies at home and abroad. They were ready to become not just objects of but also subjects in international politics.

As the dreams of political and military hegemony turned into the nightmare of authoritarian rule along with violations of human rights, the structure of the international economic order broke down, too. The power of the United States has declined considerably since 1945 compared to the power of others in the international system. The US share of world trade and investment fell as Europe and Japan recovered. The international monetary system was transformed in the 1970s as the US devalued the dollar relative to other major currencies and became unable alone to shape the rules and behavior of the international monetary system. The international energy system perhaps witnessed the most dramatic changes in the 1970s as power passed from the industrial consumers to the oil producers. International practices concerning the oceans have changed markedly, with the new 200-mile economic jurisdiction zone reflecting rather more closely the historic preferences of the Latin Americans. The United States no longer had the unilateral ability to determine the nature of the international regimes, that is, to set the norms, rules and behaviors in key areas in the international economic system.

Latin American countries have not been passive actors. They, too, have changed. In addition to the stronger states most of them now have, several of the larger countries are no longer easily classified merely as economically underdeveloped, even though they still face formidable problems if their development potential is to be fulfilled. They now have large, dynamic modern sectors in their societies, economies and polities, pressing their governments for further changes and, in turn, impinging on international relations. Mexico, Brazil and Argentina have grown as industrial exporters. Both the governments and the modern business sectors now seek to flex their muscles in world arenas, no longer limited to an inter-American setting. Moreover, all of the major Latin American countries have benefited from increases in trade with, and in direct investments from, European countries and Japan. Latin American countries deal with international financial centers throughout the world, and they seek technology wherever it is cost-effective. Venezuela and Mexico, in particular, have received windfalls from the increases in the world price of the energy they export. In short, the trends that broke down the US-built international economic order have also transformed the international economic relations, and the internal economies, of most Latin American countries.

Changes occurred as well at the level of inter-American relations. Many of the long-standing issues between the United States and the larger Latin American countries, especially those of a military or territorial nature, have now been settled. Political questions pertaining to communism or guerrillas that might have come to the Organization of American States have also faded in importance in the larger Latin American countries, although they still matter in four northern Central American countries.

A telling example of the change was the Latin American response to the Reagan administration's early policies in 1981 toward the civil war in El Salvador. Most of the South American countries quietly declined to be enlisted in an 'anti-Soviet crusade' over El Salvador (in part, perhaps, because the military governments of Argentina and Brazil have had excellent trade relations with the USSR). The Venezuelan government, which supported the government of El Salvador's Junta President José Napoleón Duarte as did the US, disassociated itself from the US government's Cold War language and broader policy implications. Mexico opposed US policy in El Salvador more actively, providing some political support to the more moderate elements of the Salvadorean opposition. In contrast to the Reagan administration, both Venezuela and Mexico continued to assist the Nicaraguan revolutionary government. And, most important of all, all the major Latin American governments retained their own foreign policy agenda: US policies toward El Salvador were no substitute for other US policies toward Latin America. The major Latin American countries continued to focus on the consequences for them of changes in US economic policy and of international economic relations.

Inter-American relations are characterized by the paradox of successful relations. Because so many disputes have been successfully settled, scholars or public officials may minimize or neglect the policies and mechanisms that made such settlements possible. On the other hand, long-standing economic issues have now made their way to the top of the inter-American agenda, as a result of changes in internal circumstances that have repercussions for international affairs. For example, the industrialization processes in several of the larger Latin American countries have led governments and private businessmen to be more concerned about technology transfers. Governments and industries seek to promote the export of manufactured products, which leads at times to disputes with importing countries. The evolution of private and state-owned national industrial firms, as well as multinational firms operating in the same countries, shapes the pattern of relations among business enterprises and governments. The changes within the western hemisphere have cleaned the inter-American slate of the debris of the Cold War (except in Central America) at about the same time that Latin American governments in the larger countries are ready and interested to press new economic disputes.

Other changes followed as a consequence. Several leading Latin American states, such as Mexico or Venezuela, have become keenly interested in the politics of North–South international relations bargaining. Trade, technology, debt, or nationality of firm ownership are global issues, not just inter-American ones. The waning of certain issues of exclusive interest to the Americas has made it possible for several Latin American countries to pay sustained and serious attention to worldwide politics and economics. The new internal political and economic changes in these countries have pushed their governments in the same direction. Thus the stakes of Latin America's foreign economic relations and of its internal politics lead these governments on to global engagement.

Because Latin American governments, alone or in concert, lack the resources to alter international regimes over these key areas, they have not relied on global bargaining alone to achieve the ends of their foreign economic policies. Instead, they learned from their own experiences in the post-World War II era that actions of national governments within their own boundaries could often be portrayed as no more than minor violations of an international regime so that retaliation from major powers might be constrained or avoided. These actions, however, were often enough to achieve many important goals of economic policy. Moreover, the international circumstances of the 1970s and early 1980s had changed. What had once been violations of otherwise strong international regimes, now would be sovereign state actions in issue areas where the international regime had broken down or had been greatly weakened. The norms, rules and behaviors were no longer so clear, or clearly adhered to by the industrial countries, in trade, technology transfer, or foreign investment regulation, for example. The national actions of Latin American governments therefore contributed to the erosion of already weakening international regimes. In turn, Latin American governments succeeded in many cases, notwithstanding their objectively more limited power compared to the major industrial countries, precisely because the international regime was already weakened.

The targets of many of the new government policies were national and multinational business firms active in Latin American industrial affairs. The emergence of these firms is yet another major change in the international and internal environment of the major Latin American countries. There have been business firms of both types, of course, in the histories of Latin American countries. What was new was the simultaneous impact of Latin American industrialization, on the one hand, and the spread and growth of both national and multinational firms in the industrial sectors. Government policies thus sought to increase the bargaining power of national firms, or of the local subsidiaries of multinational firms located in a country, with parent firms or with firms located in other countries, and to affect technology transfer transactions, the firm's likelihood of imports of raw materials or intermediate goods, the propensity to export semi-manufactured and manufactured products, the local content of production, the nationality of the equity of the firm, and a host of other issues affecting business behavior and the international relations of governments and firms. Strong Latin American states were effective in shaping economic behavior to suit their ends thanks in part to the changes in the international system.

Latin American governments also broke with the liberal ideology that had often portrayed contemporary economic relations only as technical non-political questions. They deliberately recognized their political content and acted accordingly. Industrial trade has enlivened protectionist demands; Latin American governments have assisted the exports of firms located in their countries. Technology is often owned by foreign-based private enterprises and transferred to Latin American private firms, but Latin American governments have sought to change the relationship between foreign suppliers and national recipients to promote their vision of economic development. Multinational enterprises, operating across national boundaries, multiply contacts with political consequences. National businessmen who may have welcomed multinational firms discovered eventually that these may also generate industrial competition; so governments have discriminated in favor of national firms to help them compete. Governments sought to regulate all of these economic activities within their borders, including those that were internationally generated. The net effect has been the politicization of what appeared to be technical and non-political.

Modern economic relations are inherently dynamic. They tend to grow out of and to resist confinement within national borders, and are likely to become internationalized. Military force or subversion are less able to handle disputes in these issue areas. Thus the exercise of leverage, the settlement of disputes, and the management of conflict in modern economic relations require subtle planning and foresight.

1.2   Latin America as an issue in US policy

All of these changes have affected how the United States government thinks about Latin American issues. For example, the problem of accommodating industrial exports from less developed countries cannot be understood primarily in geographic terms. US policy must take into account not only such exports from Latin America but also similar ones from South Korea, Singapore or Taiwan. To be sure, one still needs to understand the patterns of regional economic and political variation or the regional linkages among economic, political or military questions; these may still have geographic dimensions. But often the issues are global and policy must be made to face up to global concerns. The US government had been used to thinking about Cold War issues in a global framework, but often thought about Latin American economic issues as specific national or regional problems. Now these, too, must be analyzed in a broader framework. Latin American countries are, indeed, important, but this is because several of them are among the most important less developed countries in many lively issues of global politics and because some are the emerging industrial powers of the twenty-first century, not because they are Latin American.

If it is correct that some issues should be thought of as less distinctly Latin American in the future, then a policy of 'giving high priority to Latin America' may misallocate US government resources. And yet, countries and their governments are not just disembodied sets of issue areas. Governments may be competent, wise, efficient and just – or the very opposite of these things. One thing that seems likely is that they are not withering away. So policy needs to be made toward particular governments, even if the content of policy may no longer just be government-specific. Policies may have to be attuned to issue areas, with the content varying in degree from government to government. How much priority, then, should be accorded to relations with a particular government to cope with the tension between the need for worldwide policies and the realities of government-to-government policy? For example, should Latin American industrial exports be treated different-ly, because they come from Latin America, than any other industrial exports to the US?

Latin America's weight, we argue, must now be assessed more by issue area and by country rather than by taking the entire region as a whole. All governments will be more effective if they are aware of the global dimen-sions of policy by issue area. US government policy-making may also be more effective if it is recognized that both Latin American countries and the United States may often benefit from dealing with each other more at a sustained sub-presidential level where expertise by issue and by country is greater. High presidential attention often entails very high risks. Among these are inappropriate links among policies and problems, lack of expertise over specific problems, and quick changes in presidential attention. The Reagan administration's changing attention and policy toward El Salvador in its first months in office in 1981 is but one example of this long-standing policy syndrome. This book's authors do not entirely agree, however, on the conditions under which high presidential priority may still be beneficial to the US or to Latin American countries, or on the proper amount of policy tension between presidential and sub-presidential levels. In addition, some of the book's authors would prefer routine treatment and ambiguities to remain as an ordinary aspect of policy while others believe there may be a larger role for higher presidential priority and a greater need for policy consistency within issue areas.

There is yet another complexity. While the processes of change in inter-American relations are at the cutting edge of North–South international relations, and while Latin American countries are part of the so-called North–South dialogue, Latin America still sings a different tune. US–Latin American relations must be looked at within a North–South international relations framework, but only in part. The framework is necessary because Latin American countries have sought to be leaders of the Third World on many of these issues, and because some of the issues are of importance to many non-Latin American countries. But a North–South international relations framework is inadequate for studying some key issues in US–Latin American conflict and cooperation. For example, Mexico's importance in trade, investment and technology issues approximates or surpasses the significance of US relations with other advanced industrial countries, albeit in different form. Therefore, Latin American international relations are located near the meeting point of North–South and West–West.

Some Latin American countries are now well along in the voyage from the regional 'special relationship' of the past to a new 'special relationship' of the future, varying by issues and individual countries. The special relationship of the past involved weak Latin American elites seeking assistance from the United States in exchange for support for common international political and economic objectives. It also tended to emphasize Latin America's relationship with the United States to the exclusion of relations with other industrial countries. For the first time since Japan's industrialization, there is a new group of countries ready to break into the modern international industrial economy. Along with some East and Southeast Asian countries, these include the Latin American giants. Their new relationships are no longer exclusively oriented toward the United States; they now seek to diversify their international relations with countries the world over.

And yet, something 'special' will remain about the Latin American relationship with the US. First, the United States is the leading industrial country, and is still Latin America's main trade partner and source of foreign investment and technology. Thus the new vibrancy in the politics of modern economic relations will necessarily engage the US and the major Latin American countries. Second, there are persisting structures that change slowly, such as accumulated foreign investment stocks, technological routines and market access, or accustomed military relations. Third, the memories – political, bureaucratic, ideological, scholarly, and in elite and mass opinion – of past relations are likely both to sweeten and to poison the future relations between the United States and Latin America, facilitating cooperation on many issues while exacerbating conflict on others.

1.3 This book

This book has been based on several assumptions:

1. The international economic order built after World War II has changed enough to create new 'political space' that allows major Latin American governments, among others, to take actions within their boundaries that effectively alter economic behavior at home and further erode the international regimes over issue areas abroad.
2. While the US remains unquestionably the world's leading power, its relative economic decline in comparison to Western Europe and Japan has also created new options for Latin America.
3. The states of the larger Latin American countries have become stronger and more competent, and their economies have grown and industrialized, enabling them to act internationally in new ways.
4. The spread and growth of multinational firms, and of state and private national firms, in the largest Latin American countries create problems and opportunities for states: problems, because states feel the need to regulate them to avoid loss of control, and opportunities not only for further growth, but also to benefit from competition among firms and to pick firms that will be 'national champions'.
5. A focus on contemporary economic relations requires a study of the newly dynamic Latin American countries, such as Mexico and Venezuela, and of critical issue areas such as industrial exports to the United States, transfer of technology, and Latin American elite and mass attitudes toward US-based private foreign investment.
6. This focus touches upon a part of the efforts of some Latin American governments to assert their worldwide leadership in the western hemisphere, in the North–South dialogue, and among old industrial and newly industrial countries.
7. Contemporary economic relations are inherently political, global, and difficult to control by traditional means of statecraft: they regularly mix domestic and international affairs, leading to a tension between the global needs of policy and the government-to-government sensitivities of diplomacy.
8. The issues of the future of US–Latin American relations fit exclusively neither the framework of the old 'special relationship' nor that of North–South international relations; rather they show a mix of those two, along with some dimensions common to US relations with other industrial countries arising from the politics of global issues; this leads us to suggest a new 'special relationship' fraught with conflict, but also open to new opportunities for collaboration.

Ours is a study, then, of new elements in the political economy of international relations between the United States and Latin America with implications that go far beyond it. It is not just a study of US foreign economic policy toward Latin America, although one paper pays particular attention to US foreign policy-making and most address at least some matters of concern to the study of US policy. Nor is it principally a study of Latin American foreign policy, or even of the inter-American system, although much of what is said bears on these.

We focus on issue areas at the cutting edge of evolving international relations and on some of the countries most involved in seeking or effecting changes that affect these issue areas. The book is organized so as to study relationships among countries over particular issues in order to learn about both. Relations between governments and the private sector as well as between firms from various countries are also considered. The chapters on industrial exports, technology transfer and business disputes identify the major dimensions of each problem, and the patterns of change, conflict and resolution. They are sensitive to worldwide as well as to Latin American patterns. Each of them seeks to identify the policies of specific governments that have succeeded or failed to change outcomes in the patterns of industrial exports or technology transfer, or that have altered the pattern of coalition formation, as in the case of business disputes.

Domínguez (ch. 2) suggests that the attitudes and behavior of national business in Latin American countries shifted from the 1940s to the 1970s. In the aftermath of World War II, national and foreign-owned firms often perceived common interests and acted to support each other. That trans-national coalition has broken down in the areas of natural resources and utilities in all the major Latin American countries, where national business, primarily for political reasons, has often come to support the state's takeover of many foreign firms. The pattern differed in manufacturing. As direct foreign investment in manufacturing appeared, national business divided, with smaller businessmen taking the lead to advocate restrictions on the operations of foreign firms. As such investment increased, support for 'national bourgeois' policies spread to large firms. These policies select some foreign firms and exclude others. They also discriminate among firms according to nationality of ownership by manipulating access to fiscal incentives, credit, government purchases, and so forth. The emergence of a national bourgeois coalition serves the needs of national firms for a secure and predictable environment through the reduction of competition, and the interests of Latin American governments for more control over their economies.

Odell (ch. 5) argues that as Latin American industrialization led to manufactured exports, political disputes over such exports to the United States became more frequent. These conflicts have been salient and irritating in Latin American countries. Their governments have had little success in rolling back barriers to the US industrial market. The outcomes of these conflicts have been closer to the initial US objectives than to those of Latin American countries. The latter, however, sought to improve their position by mobilizing allies within the United States, by retaliating or threatening to do so, or, most effectively, by proposing technical alternatives to those the US government seemed to be ready to adopt.

Miller (ch. 6) discusses how the transfer of non-military proprietary technology became an increasingly contentious issue in international affairs during the 1960s and 1970s, and particularly so in inter-American relations. Latin American governments sought to change the rules and norms governing the transfer process to remedy what they perceived as unequal bargaining power in a supplier-skewed relationship. The internal strategies of national governments worked more effectively than their use of international organizations. The results of these policies have led to benefits (though more limited than Latin American governments have claimed) as well as to costs (though these are lower than multinational firms have alleged). Miller considers the various levels of bargaining over this issue: individual firms, national governments and legislation, bilateral international transactions, and negotiations in international conferences and organizations.

These three chapters, therefore, are concerned with international relations among governments and among private firms, and between governments and private firms. They also point to patterns of change and conflict that are critical in Latin America but have implications well beyond the region.

The chapters on Mexico, Venezuela and the United States explore the dimensions of politics best understood through close examination of a country's affairs. But each of the chapters, too, connects country-specific expertise with larger questions of international significance: the assessment of foreign investment regulation, the outcomes of bilateral relations in several economic issue areas, and the relative costs and benefits of policies and policy-making styles. Thus all of the papers explore both global issues and specific countries.

Grindle (ch. 3) analyzes the policies of one of the world's most experienced governments in its relations with private foreign investment. She focuses on the tension between the Mexican government's assertiveness in seeking to influence the impact of foreign investment on Mexico, on the one hand, and the increasing importance of Mexico for investments from the United States in recent decades, on the other hand. She discusses both long-term continuity in certain key policies, accounted for by persisting constraints on policy-making, and variations that result from changes of presidential administration as well as from Mexico's particular 'style' of policy implementation, which emphasizes wide executive discretion. This style has had the effect of increasing the central role of the government bureaucracy in the regulatory process while at the same time providing for flexibility and a good deal of variation from case to case.

Kelly (ch. 4) focuses on the long-term emergence of economic nationalism and its implications for Venezuelan foreign economic policy, especially toward the US. She shows that internal changes in Venezuela explained much of the impetus for policy changes in the areas of trade, investment, finance and oil during the past two decades. She notes a remarkable continuity both in the evolution of policies and in the persistence of outcomes consistent with US goals. The structure of the international system – political and economic – has sharply limited Venezuela's ability to have a real impact on foreign economic policy outcomes, notwithstanding economic nationalist preferences. Thus US–Venezuelan relations appear to be marked by coincidence over several major structural issues but also suspicion and conflict over specific policies where a more economically nationalist Venezuela seeks, with very limited success, greater control over policy outcomes.

Paarlberg (ch. 7) assesses the costs and benefits of according high presidential priority to Latin America or of according it routine priority. He considers the problems that high presidential priority would allegedly cure, such as inconsistency, incoherence, inertia, and the undue influence of private and bureaucratic interests at the expense of the national interest. He finds, however, that these presumed benefits do not often materialize, and that there may be severe costs in loss of expertise, improper linkages across issues, excessive politicization, often unsuspected inconsistencies, and opportunity costs. Thus he sketches a preferred tilt toward a sustained but sub-presidential treatment of relations between Latin American countries and the United States. He suggests that priority could be accorded to Latin America or to particular Latin American governments at an inappropriately high level. The result of that may be unsatisfactory to the United States, the particular Latin American countries, and broader requirements for the international system. He illustrates the general argument with a detailed case study of US–Jamaican relations.

Implications

In addition to each chapter's specific findings, the book contributes to the conceptual refinement of scholarly perspectives on the study of international relations in the western hemisphere[1]. The chapters provide little support for views emphasizing a high degree of harmony of interest between the United States and Latin America, or a cohesive, rational design, imperial or otherwise, in US policy toward Latin America. Nor is there much support for a study of inter-American relations that would focus exclusively, or even primarily, on bureaucratic politics within each government. Thus what have been called elsewhere the liberal, the bureaucratic or the orthodox dependency perspectives do not seem to be the more useful ways of thinking about inter-American relations.

On the other hand, there is evidence indicating that some dependency perspectives do shed considerable light on certain aspects of inter-American relations, and for some periods of time. This is so, for example, in some of the industrial trade and technology transfer disputes, in some of the coalition patterns formed by businessmen, and in aspects of US–Venezuelan and US–Mexican relations. Similarly, Paarlberg for the United States and Grindle for Mexico assess the importance of presidential terms of office in shaping the rhythm of policy.

All the authors discuss the existence of organizational ideologies in ministries, policy groups, agencies and private business firms. The interplay of politics and of interest groups also permeates the book. Kelly shows as well the impact of long-range rational, economic nationalist strategic thinking in Venezuela on the conduct of its foreign policy. These findings, therefore, suggest preferred strategies for further research on these issues and countries.

These chapters present some propositions about the efficacy of certain techniques in international affairs. Latin American states appear to have been most successful at achieving some of their goals over time when two conditions are present: the willingness to compromise on details without sacrificing major objectives, and the ability to be technically proficient in the handling of a dispute rather than simply relying on the politicization of an issue. Thus, although Mexican government policy toward foreign invest-ment has varied, there have been many Mexican governmental achievements over the long run that fulfill that government's policy priorities, as indicated by Grindle. Similarly, Odell notes that Brazil was most effective in handling industrial trade disputes because it has the technical expertise as well as the ability to bargain and to compromise politically. Paarlberg suggests that Jamaica may have benefited from this treatment even if it was less a shaper of events than a recipient of rewards from the initiatives of others.

In contrast, the politicization of issues so they receive high presidential priority in the United States, or the mere politicization of industrial trade disputes and of codes of technology transfer to the detriment of other strategies, are all associated with outcomes that might be considered less favorable to Latin America. Paarlberg notes the disadvantages faced by Latin America as a result of inappropriately high US presidential interest in the 1960s. Odell argues that the more technocratic strategies served Latin American countries best in industrial disputes. Miller notes that to some extent successful resolution of the technology transfer questions had been hindered by high levels of politicization caused by the North–South dialogue and technology transfer's role in it. Ideological politics, interna-tional organization politics, or presidential politics, perhaps paradoxically, are the arenas where Latin American countries are least likely to achieve the goals they seem to value most. They may win the votes about rhetoric at the UN General Assembly, but may not be able to shape international outcomes concerning implementation to serve their interests as they themselves identify them.

The essays in this book suggest ways to think about US policy toward these countries. An important and conflictual agenda has been highlighted. On the one hand, these countries matter to the United States: Venezuela's and Mexico's oil and their economies are very important, as are the more frequent and effective national bourgeois coalitions that alter the foreign investment climate in some countries. On the other hand, Latin American governments, public and private enterprises, are engaged in disputes with the US government, or with firms based in the United States. This is not a state of international bliss.

The chapters also suggest many ways in which the United States or US firms have or might have responded to these conflicts. There have been some compromises over industrial disputes. US firms have adopted a number of strategies, including increasing the local content of production or entering into joint ventures, to deal with changes in the foreign investment regimes and especially with government preference for firms that look 'national'. There is also a long tradition of collaboration, as well as conflict, between the US and Venezuela and the US and Mexico. In all of this, however, there has been no single recipe for US government success (as there seems to be for Latin American governments) in achieving US goals in inter-American relations. If compromise has met some US government goals in some of these issue areas, blunt political clout may have been essential for the US to achieve its goals in aspects of technology transfer relations. If detailed technical knowledge is critical in the industrial dispute issue area, far more emotional and symbolic issues clearly matter in the US–Venezuela relationship.

That is, perhaps, part of what it means for the United States to be a major world power, namely, that there is no quick-fix, not even a workable strategy consistent across issues and countries, that systematically maximizes governmental effectiveness. The United States often prevails simply because it remains the world's largest economy. Its economic power over technology, trade or investment rests on this persisting structural economic primacy (albeit declining in relative terms) rather than on generally shrewd tactics. The United States has a broad array of policy techniques at its disposal, but it lives in a world too complex for singular strategies. And yet, because the US remains the kind of world power that it is, it can still afford to muddle through policies riddled by inconsistencies and ambiguities. The United States' condition as a superpower may thus be defined in part as the ability to prevail often enough, even for wrong reasons, without knowing it or without knowing why or how to do it again, and even committing major mistakes.

Acknowledgements

I am grateful to my colleagues in the project, and to Van R. Whiting, Jr., and Donald Wyman, for their helpful criticism.

Notes

1 See Jorge I. Domínguez, 'Consensus and Divergence: The State of the Literature on Inter-American Relations in the 1970s'. *Latin American Research Review* **13** (1), 1978, pp. 87–126.

Business nationalism: Latin American national business attitudes and behavior toward multinational enterprises

Jorge I. Domínguez*

The participants in inter-American relations include governments and intergovernmental and non-governmental organizations; multinational enterprises are found among the latter. The attitudes and behavior of Latin American elite and mass publics toward these enterprises, and the constraints they may place on governments in their relations with such enterprises, are our central questions. This chapter will focus on the attitudes and behavior of national business elites toward multinational business, and especially toward those firms headquartered in the United States. When does national business prefer to behave as a part of a transnational alliance with foreign business and when does it join other national elites to constrain (a national bourgeois coalition) or to socialize (a statist coalition) foreign business?

2.1   The nature of the question

One view among some scholars of 'dependence' is that there is an alliance between foreign and national entrepreneurs in Latin America: 'Tied to the dominant class interests and dependent on world imperialism for the manufacture of some goods, for foreign currency, and for foreign capital, the national bourgeoisie has no choice other than to accept its condition as a dependent bourgeoisie.' Although national entrepreneurs might have preferred greater autonomy in an ideal world, and may have had a nationalist phase opposing some earlier links between dependent and metropolitan countries, national business has now 'chosen to play a secondary role in the ruling class', remaining 'captive to a network of imperialism'[1]. Similarly, an analysis of Argentine industrialists concluded that 'the assumption of conflict between national and foreign industrialists that might lead the former to play a nationalist-developmentalist role is incorrect. Foreign and national socioeconomic elites have been intertwined with each other either through financial, technological–economic, political, and/or ideological links'[2]. It has also been argued that the spread of transnational capitalism integrated the modern sectors in industrialized and in less industrialized

* Center for International Affairs, Harvard University.

countries and, consequently, led to the disintegration of economic sectors within the latter[3]. A discussion of Mexican development notes that, while many forms of direct dependence had been changed, new forms had led to a close interpenetration of foreign and national business: 'to confront foreign interest means often to confront our own interest'[4].

Even scholars and public officials who may reject a dependency perspective support the view that foreign and national enterprise have common interests because, 'in general, foreign investors are welcomed by the most progressive Latin American industrialists'[5]. Such investment 'has been and will continue to be important to the development of Latin American countries'[6]. Or, more bluntly, US national policy should be 'to provide maximum encouragement for private investment throughout the hemisphere'[7]. One core proposition seems to be shared by this liberal[8] modernization perspective: that direct private investment from the US to Latin America is compatible with the interests of all concerned in the long run, and that only mistakes and misunderstandings have posed problems along the way. Thus no fundamental conflicts exist to prevent the consolidation of a transnational bourgeois coalition when 'reasonable people' see the light.

On the other hand, I shall argue that a transnational coalition of foreign and national industrialists, in the aggregate, may be a passing phenomenon. The more typical pattern shows a long-term shift in the attitudes and behavior of a good portion of national business leading toward moderate conflict with multinational firms. Many national businessmen come to advocate policies to constrain the operation of multinational firms, often provoking international disputes between foreign and national governments.

2.2 The pattern of US investments

The pattern of United States investments in the main Latin American countries (Argentina, Brazil, Chile, Colombia, Mexico, Peru and Venezuela) has come to emphasize investments in manufacturing. (All references to Latin America are limited to these seven countries.) While their share of US worldwide manufacturing investments fell from 19.6% in 1955 to 13.0% in 1960, it remained essentially invariant thereafter (it was 13.8% in 1979). But, Latin America's share of all other US investments (mining and smelting, petroleum, utilities, agriculture and trade) has fallen precipitously[9]. These seven countries received 27.6% of all US non-manufacturing investments in 1955, and this fell steadily to only 7.2% in 1975 and 1979. Total US manufacturing investment in these Latin American countries grew exponentially (in current prices) during this quarter-century, whereas non-manufacturing investments remained stagnant from 1960 to 1975 (*Table 2.1*) – thus declining in real terms. These countries, therefore, experienced simultaneous processes of investment and divestment that altered their relationships with multinational firms.

There is also wide variation among Latin American countries. In 1955, Brazil led in US investments in manufacturing but trailed behind Venezuela and Chile in non-manufacturing investments. As the governments of Venezuela and Chile took over their petroleum and copper industries, Brazil became the leader in both types of investments with almost $5 billion in US manufacturing investments and $2.6 billion in non-manufacturing areas in 1979. Mexico was second in manufacturing (with about $3.4 billion in 1979) and fourth in non-manufacturing areas (with almost $1.2 billion in 1979). Brazil and Mexico together accounted for 72% of all US manufacturing investments and for 62% of total US investments in these seven countries in 1979.

Table 2.1 *Indices of the book value of US private direct investment in current prices (1955 = 100)*

	Manufacturing					Non-manufacturing				
	1960	1965	1970	1975	1979	1960	1965	1970	1975	1979
Argentina	93	268	335	319	573	120	174	236	180	390
Brazil	91	128	221	552	873	81	65	110	268	478
Chile	59	105	178	132	227	120	132	114	42	35
Colombia	153	267	392	633	972	157	173	218	126	142
Mexico	145	280	416	904	1271	122	129	178	225	350
Peru	152	343	400	722	722	148	157	214	376	570
Venezuela	305	420	783	1149	1778	175	181	164	102	85
All seven	117	211	322	608	929	140	147	160	156	221
All world	176	305	510	886	1322	168	233	357	600	848

Source: Computed from US, Department of Commerce, Office of Business Economics, *Survey of Current Business* **36** (8), August 1956, p. 19; **41** (8), August 1961, p. 22; **46** (9), September 1966, p. 34; **52** (11), November 1972, pp. 30–31; **56** (8), August 1976, p. 49; **60** (8), August 1980, p. 27.

These countries also differ in the speed of change (*Table 2.1*). US manufacturing investments rose most quickly in Venezuela and in Mexico from 1955 to 1979; between 1970 and 1975 there were sharp increases in Brazil and Mexico. Venezuela outstripped the long-term world trend for growth of US investments in manufacturing, and Mexico did so for the period since 1970. In non-manufacturing investments, however, the 1979 statistic shows a decline from a higher previous baseline in Chile, Colombia and Venezuela, and Chile's 1979 level was a third of its 1955 level. Growth of US investments in non-manufacturing areas in these seven countries lagged far behind the world trend.

There are differences, too, in the relative importance of US investments in manufacturing and in non-manufacturing areas (*Table 2.2*). In 1955, US

Table 2.2 *Ratio of manufacturing
to non-manufacturing US private
direct investment*

	1955	1975	1979
Argentina	1.06	1.88	1.56
Brazil	1.03	2.13	1.89
Chile	0.06	0.20	0.41
Colombia	0.28	1.42	1.93
Mexico	0.82	3.27	2.96
Peru	0.08	0.16	0.10
Venezuela	0.04	0.49	0.91
All seven	0.35	1.36	1.47
All world	0.49	0.73	0.77

Source: Computed from same sources as
        Table 2.1

investments in manufacturing already prevailed in Argentina and in Brazil, with Mexico not far behind; US investments in manufacturing in these three countries were a substantially higher proportion of US investments than in the world as whole. US investments in primary activities prevailed in the other four countries, where US investments in manufacturing were worth less than $60 million in each country. By 1979, US manufacturing investments had come to prevail in Mexico, Brazil, Argentina and Colombia, with Venezuela close to that mark. The seven countries surpassed the world pattern. US investments in manufacturing were secondary only in Chile and Peru: in Chile, because all US investments had been curtailed in the early 1970s, and in Peru because investments in the mining sector in the 1970s had outstripped investments in manufacturing.

A crude scale of US firms' penetration of the manufacturing sectors is shown in *Table 2.3*. The countries are arranged ordinally according to the total size of US private direct foreign investment in manufacturing in 1979, the ratio of such manufacturing to non-manufacturing investments in 1979, and the speed of change of these investments between 1970 and 1979. These ranks were then simply added to provide a rough comparison of penetration in manufacturing at the end of the 1970s. Mexico and Brazil rank at the top: US investments in manufacturing are very high, are increasing rapidly, and are far more important than other US investments. Chile and Peru rank consistently toward the bottom: US investments in manufacturing are comparatively low, changes are also very slow, and investments in non-manufacturing areas still predominate. Argentina, Colombia and Venezuela rank in between the two other sets.

A similar picture emerges from individual country data. The manufacturing share of all direct private foreign investment in Mexico in 1911, at the

Table 2.3 *Rank order of US private direct foreign investment weight[a]*

	Size of US investment in manufacturing in 1979	Ratio of US manufacturing to non-manufacturing investments in 1979	Speed of change in US manufacturing investments 1970–1979	Cumulative rank points
Mexico	6	7	6	19
Brazil	7	5	5	17
Venezuela	4	3	7	14
Colombia	3	6	4	13
Argentina	5	4	2	11
Peru	2	1	3	6
Chile	1	2	1	4

[a] The first three columns are ordinal scales. The second column is based on Table 2.2; the third column is based on Table 2.1. The last column adds the ranks in the three first columns. The higher numbers indicate the higher ranks. The Pearson product–moment correction between the first and second column is 0.68, between the first and the third, 0.57, and between the second and the third, 0.46.

Source: Computed from same sources as Table 2.1

outset of the revolution, was 4.5%[10], rising only to 7.1% at the close of the Cárdenas presidency in 1940. By 1955, manufacturing had come to account for 34.8%, and this share grew to 73.8% in 1970 and 77.5% in 1979. An index of non-manufacturing foreign investments in Mexico rose only to 149 in 1955 and to 177 in 1970 (1940 set at 100). The respective indices for all foreign investments in manufacturing were 1036 and 6509. Declines in non-manufacturing foreign investments occurred mainly in the electricity, transport and communications, and mining sectors where the state took over from private firms; rather substantial increases in direct foreign investments occurred in commerce (an index of foreign investments in commerce rose to 934 in 1955 and to 2775 in 1970). Of the 150 largest Mexican enterprises in 1972, 25 were state enterprises and 24 were in banking and insurance. Of the remaining enterprises, 57 had foreign equity participation while 44 were wholly nationally owned[11]. In sum, there was spectacular growth of foreign manufacturing investments but only more modest growth or net divestment in other sectors. Manufacturing predominated over all other foreign investments by 1970.

Private direct foreign investments in manufacturing in Brazil were 81.9% of total foreign investment in 1971 and 74.9% in 1974 (services grew most rapidly in the interim). Foreign investments in utilities and agriculture fell from 6.1% in 1971 to 4.2% in 1974[12]. Of the 100 largest Brazilian firms in 1972, a third were state enterprises, while the others divided evenly between foreign-owned majority and nationally owned majority firms (with a slight edge to the former). However, 45 of the top 100 had some foreign equity participation even if in a minority position and, by 1975, 80 of the top 100 private firms had foreign equity participation to some degree[13]. Foreign investment in industry predominated and, as in Mexico, the division of ownership between nationals and foreigners in the largest industrial firms gives an edge to the latter.

In Colombia, private direct foreign investments in manufacturing reached 50.1% of total foreign investment in 1971[14]. In Argentina, the number of foreign firms among the 100 largest enterprises rose from 14 in 1957 to 50 in 1966[15]. In Venezuela, foreign investments in industry increased 232% from 1962 to 1967[16]. These are consistent with the patterns outlined above: rapid increases of foreign investment in manufacturing, with foreign-owned firms occupying a large share of the commanding heights of the manufacturing sector.

2.3   Business nationalism – an argument

Private direct foreign investments in Latin America have an effect on the attitudes and behaviors of Latin American business elites. Patterns differ between manufacturing and non-manufacturing investments. These patterns are shaped, of course, by each country's own history. For example, the long-troubled history of US–Mexican relations may make Mexican businesses especially receptive to some nationalistic appeals, in turn shaping the content of attitudes and coalitions. In this chapter, however, more attention is paid to some more neglected cross-national processes that promote or hinder business nationalism.

Non-manufacturing investments

The pattern for non-manufacturing investments such as mining, petroleum, utilities and agriculture is better known[17]. At early stages of modernization, national governments and local elites tend to welcome private direct foreign investments in those non-manufacturing sectors where local capital re-sources are lacking or cannot be mobilized effectively, where the technology and managerial skills necessary for effective exploitation and production have not yet been learned, and where the output is typically exported so that access to foreign markets is critical. As time passes, the relative capital contribution of these foreign firms declines; many managerial and technolo-gical skills are standardized and learned. Access to foreign markets is not an issue in the case of telephones, electricity or railroads; so they become vulnerable sooner. In other non-manufacturing sectors, this factor's import-ance varies from case to case. As transnational enterprises lose their advantage, the pressures and possibilities for nationalization increase. (Nationalization is the transfer of predominant ownership from foreigners to nationals; socialization is its subset in which the state takes over predominant ownership.) The transfer is further affected by the terms of compensation and whether it was forced or voluntary.

The response of national business elites to nationalization of non-manufacturing foreign firms in primary production is almost wholly conditioned by political factors. These foreign firms had rarely competed with national business. They typically operated in sectors featuring only fully owned foreign firm subsidiaries. National business tended to believe that the foreign firms made a long-term positive contribution by purchasing goods and services from national business, and increasing disposable income in the host country, thus creating a market for national business firms. Foreign firms may have been taxed more heavily by host governments, relieving the pressure on national business. But foreign firms may also have increased the prevailing wage rate, pushing up costs for all business; foreign firms became the target of nationalists who called on the state to take them over, thereby weakening the protection of all capitalists against state interference.

A transnational coalition, therefore, may exist for a long time between foreign and national business. Its defining feature is the perception of a common interest leading to common action to defend the entire private sector regardless of the nationality of the firm in the face of government intervention. As these foreign firms lose their advantage and nationalist statist pressures increase, a political split often severs the transnational coalition. National business remains quite united, persuading itself and others that it is safe and prudent for the state to take over these foreign firms so long as this does not threaten the rest of the private sector. The shift of national business from the transnational to this limited statist coalition is often the determining factor in the timing of the state's takeover of foreign firms in natural resource industries. Weak governments may fear a divisive national debate over the takeover of an important part of the private sector. When national business shifts its allegiance, the social bases of the limited statist coalition are considerably strengthened and a state takeover may follow. This limited statist coalition includes – in addition to government officials and national business – the intellectuals, who articulate the need for statism and the expected beneficial consequences of socialization, as well as military officers, persuaded that national honor and security require government control over basic resources. Its defining feature is support for socialization limited by firm, sector, time and, above all, nationality of ownership.

Utilities are more vulnerable sooner than other non-manufacturing investments to nationalization or socialization because they may come into conflict with national business over fees for electricity, communications or transportation. A portion of the national business community may come rather more quickly to the view that the host government should take over these firms in order to subsidize the development of private industry and commerce.

There are two important limitations to this argument. First, it refers principally to large, existing investments, which do acquire political importance because of their extraordinary size in a national economy. More modest investments in the non-manufacturing sectors may not generate such political conflict. Moreover, it is possible that existing investments in a natural resource sector may be expropriated but that the government may still seek foreign direct investment to open up new areas of resource exploitation in that same sector. Thus, for example, existing mining or oil firms might be taken over even as a government, with national business support, advertises requests for bids from national or foreign firms for new concessions for mining and petroleum exploration and exploitation. While existing firms may have lost their competitive edge in capital, technology, management and access to markets, new firms (or old firms in new projects) may still have these advantages.

Secondly, because the commitment of national business to a limited statist coalition is so conditioned by political factors, that commitment is subject to partial change if the political conditions change. National business may come to argue that it should run these major non-manufacturing firms, and that facilities should be given for its gradual acquisition of partial or full control over them. Thus, in the long run, national business may move away from its support of socialization in these large non-manufacturing firms toward a policy of mere nationalization that would enhance its own role.

Manufacturing investments

The pattern in manufacturing differs from the outset. Private direct foreign investment in manufacturing is much less likely to stimulate the development of a statist coalition over the long run. The political visibility and long history, and hence the vulnerability, of for example petroleum in Mexico, Venezuela and Peru, or copper in Chile, are rarely matched by any manufacturing firm. While the contributions of manufacturing firms in capital, technology and market access in particular product lines may decline, such firms can innovate in other product lines and slough off the older ones. Thus each foreign firm – as opposed to the product line – may make a long-run case about its continuing contribution to national development. This leads also to differences among manufacturing sectors – but these lie beyond the scope of the present work. A statist coalition does, of course, make contrary arguments about negative balance of payments effects through profit repatriation, royalty payments and transfer prices; it becomes concerned over the foreign ownership of the more modern and dynamic sectors of industry. But statists are less successful in building up a large coalition to shape policy for the manufacturing sector than they are for the natural resources sectors. No Latin American country besides Cuba has deliberately shut itself off totally from private direct foreign investment in manufacturing. However, a statist coalition, including the military, may make some important differences to policy in the capital goods sector or in the steel industry.

Foreign investments in manufacturing, then, are much less threatened by a statist coalition, and governments often seek to channel private direct foreign investment away from natural resources and utilities toward manufacturing. But foreign firms are threatened from a different part of the political spectrum: the national bourgeois coalition. Small nationally owned business firms complain early on about unfair competition from large foreign firms that may drive them out of business. They claim that foreign firms in manufacturing may lead to excessive industrial concentration and oligopoly conditions, in which anti-competitive benefits accrue to foreigners rather than to nationals. Small firms call for government regulations such as differential access to credit facilities, national government purchase of goods and services ('buy national' legislation), prohibition of entry into sectors where national firms are already active, and forced partial divestment into joint ventures where foreign firm subsidiary equity must be sold relatively cheaply to national business.

Larger nationally owned firms, too, soon come to feel the pinch of competition, and respond to it in the same way as the smaller firms, albeit more gradually. National business cannot succeed alone; it combines with government officials willing to implement discriminatory policies against foreign firms, and with intellectuals who articulate the need for such policies. Military officers join the national bourgeois coalition on the grounds that the dynamic, commanding heights of the industrial economy, too, must remain in national hands. In this mature stage of the development of the national bourgeois coalition, local oligopolies are seen as desirable. Governments limit particular product markets to a small number of national firms to ensure their protected success against 'unfair' foreign firm competition by excluding trade or local subsidiary investment. Governments seek to reduce the number of producers in particular industries, favoring national firms whenever possible. The national bourgeois coalition, therefore, is far more conditioned by industrial factors than the statist coalition, even though politics is important to both.

The consequence of private direct foreign investment in manufacturing, then, is to split national business. In the beginning, small national firms lead the fight against foreign firms. The larger national firms may benefit early on from the enlarged national market, new technologies and joint ventures; the smaller national firms often lack the resources to attain these gains. Large national firms in manufacturing may belong for a long time to the transnational coalition independently of events in the natural resources area. The segments of national business whose production is complementary and retains links to foreign firms may remain transnationalist. But, as industrial competition rises, a majority of national business shifts to the national bourgeois coalition. Socialization is rarely the issue: national business distrusts socialization in the industrial sector. The defense of capitalism remains a common element within the private sector – the unbreakable, important, but residual bond of the transnational coalition. This is not a trivial agreement: it structures the political and the economic systems. Thus national and foreign firms continue to recognize common interests, and to act in concert, whenever there appears to be a serious threat to the structure of the capitalist economy. But outside of short-lived experiences (and short of revolution) this does not affect the daily or long-term conduct of public or private policies. These policies are, however, strongly shaped by the preferred discriminatory policies of the national bourgeois coalition. Nationalization is posed through joint ventures or fade-out provisions of investment where the terms are negotiated, albeit not always totally to the foreign firm's satisfaction. The hallmark of the national bourgeois coalition is advocacy and implementation of discriminatory national government policies to favor national firms.

This argument has implications for thinking about the proliferation of joint business ventures between nationals and foreigners. At one level, close, collaborative, friendly ties of mutual support are clearly established. At another level, there is an inherent conflict in many such arrangements. The bargaining clout of the national partner within a joint venture depends in part on the maintenance and spread of government discriminatory policies that provide the necessary incentives for the foreign partner to seek out and to accommodate the existing and future needs of the national partner. Therefore, the moderate conflict between national and foreign firms that has been sketched for the manufacturing sector may be reflected partially within joint ventures as well.

As in the case of clearly foreign or clearly national firms, all capitalists, including partners in joint ventures, believe in, require and support a market economy structure. But that issue is not ordinarily raised in the conduct of normal business. Instead, a more frequent issue, within joint ventures as well as among all types of firms, is the relative bargaining leverage among firms or among partners of different nationality. National partners depend on the foreigner for profits; but they depend on their relationship to, and the policies of, their own government for a politico-economic situation that allows them to be partners in the first place. Some foreign firms choose joint ventures with nationals because they prefer them. Many more enter them, however, because that is the only way for their business to prosper in a particular politico-economic environment. Thus discriminatory policies and a national bourgeois ideology may exist not only in clearly national firms but also among the national partners in joint ventures. National business-men engaged in joint ventures with foreign firms may derive strength within the venture from government regulations that, for example, may allocate credit or government purchases according to the national business share of equity in a firm. National partners might be considered veiled members of a national bourgeois coalition.

On the other hand, this argument should not be taken to imply that the state acts principally in response to national business pressure. The reasons for state action include the attitudes and behavior of the business community, but are not limited to them. For example, it is possible for the state to support nationalistic policies for reasons consistent with the military rather than the business goals that were sketched. It is also possible, at least in the short run, for the state to resist pressures from the business community for more nationalistic policies as the state pursues a strategy of promoting the internationalization of the economy with a view toward fostering efficiency and international competitiveness. National business policy preferences do not always prevail. National governments often are substantially independent of social forces. The explanations of state action are necessarily beyond the scope of this work except to note, of course, that the evidence to be presented does suggest a long-term correspondence between state policies and national business preferences.

Transnational and statist coalitions are most likely in countries with relatively little private direct foreign investment weight in manufacturing (see *Table 2.3*). In these, industrial business may remain quite united over time until manufacturing investments rise. National bourgeois coalitions are most likely in countries where such weight is high; there one can trace the breakdown in attitudes and behavior of the transnational coalition and the emergence of others. National bourgeois discriminatory policies are most likely in periods of rapid expansion of private direct foreign investments in manufacturing and least likely in periods of slower growth. National bourgeois coalitions may also prefer foreign loans to direct foreign investment, because the former imply less immediate loss of control, while the latter would add to the competition.

National business becomes a swing factor. Intellectuals, government officials, and manual workers, for example, may be virtually permanent supporters of some form of government intervention over foreign investment. National business is far more variable. Its shift from the transnational to either the statist or the national bourgeois coalition is an important determinant of national policy.

2.4 Variations in attitudes to expropriation: by class or by country?

In 1965, people in the metropolitan areas of Buenos Aires, Santiago, Mexico City and Caracas were asked directly about their views on expropriating 'foreign-owned industries, that is, having the government take over large corporations owned by foreigners'. Most had an answer. And yet these

Table 2.4 *Views on expropriation: differences between social classes (percentages)*[a]

'Would you favor or oppose expropriation of foreign-owned industries, that is, having the government take over large corporations owned by foreigners?'[a]

Attitudes	Buenos Aires			Caracas			Mexico City			Rio de Janeiro			Santiago		
	High	Mid	Low	High	Mid	Low	High	Mid	Low	High	Mid	Low	High	Mid	Low
(N)	(46)	(252)	(209)	(37)	(160)	(303)	(35)	(161)	(284)	(36)	(211)	(254)	(40)	(170)	(301)
Favor	22	25	41	11	24	34	60	62	55	33	38	42	35	47	60
Oppose	61	55	37	81	62	46	37	30	34	42	19	17	53	38	20
Don't know	17	20	22	8	14	20	3	8	11	25	43	41	12	15	20

[a] The 'high' socioeconomic level refers to those who can afford luxuries and live in good homes. The 'modest' level refers to those who have few luxuries and modest homes but no real deprivation. The 'low' level refers to those below the middle level down to completely impoverished. (N) refers to the number of respondents in each group.

Source: US Information Agency, Research and Reference Service, 'Latin American Attitudes toward the Alliance for Progress and the Role of Private Investment', World Survey III Series, R-206-65, December 1965, Table 14.

Table 2.5 *Views on expropriation: differences between small businessmen and manual workers (percentages)[a]*

'Would you favor or oppose expropriation of foreign-owned industries, that is, having the government take over large corporations owned by foreigners?'

Attitudes	Buenos Aires		Santiago		Mexico City		Caracas		Urban Brazil	
	Small business	Manual workers	Small business	Manual workers	Small business	Manual workers	Small business	Manual workers	Small business	Manual workers
(N)	(64)	(53)	(65)	(75)	(79)	(85)	(84)	(72)	(62)	(623)
Favor	33	55	48	71	61	58	32	28	45	46
Oppose	53	32	35	23	33	34	51	62	23	22
Don't know, other	14	13	17	6	6	8	17	10	32	32

[a] Differences between the answers given by small business and manual worker respondents were not statistically significant in chi-square tests (excluding 'don't knows' and others) for each country. The chi-square statistics were: 6.194, 4.675, 0.069, 0.904, and 0.018. Among small businessmen, differences in the answers given in Mexico City versus Caracas and Buenos Aires, and in urban Brazil versus Caracas and Buenos Aires, were significant; these chi-square statistics were: 9.965, 9.029, 8.291, and 7.730. Differences in the small businessmen's answers in Santiago versus Mexico City, Caracas, Buenos Aires and urban Brazil, in Caracas and Buenos Aires, and in urban Brazil and Mexico City, were not significant; these chi-square statistics were: 0.735, 4.344, 4.037, 0.855, 0.002 and 0.039. Among manual workers, differences in the answers given in Caracas versus Mexico City, Santiago, Buenos Aires and urban Brazil were significant; the chi-square statistics were: 14.587, 27.415, 11.379 and 32.850. Differences in manual workers' answers in Mexico City versus Buenos Aires and Santiago, in Santiago and Buenos Aires, and in urban Brazil versus Buenos Aires, Mexico City and Santiago, were not significant; the chi-square statistics were: 0.001, 2.863, 2.151, 0.407, 0.707 and 1.799. Statistical significance is reported at the .01 level for one degree of freedom in all cases.

Source: Secondary analysis of 1965 data from the US Information Agency's World Survey III for the four cities, and from its Brazil Alliance for Progress Study, both deposited at the Roper Center, Yale University.

answers did not reflect their most salient concerns. They were also asked: 'What, in your opinion, are the most important problems facing our country at the present time?' The answers to this question show an overwhelming concern with internal problems, with economic standard of living problems leading each list[18]. There was virtually no concern about multinational enterprises or private foreign investment in the responses to this open-ended question that tapped the respondents' own priorities.

Views on expropriation are presented in *Tables 2.4* and *2.5*. Consensus prevailed in Caracas and in Mexico City concerning expropriation: pluralities or majorities opposed such expropriation in Caracas across social class while majorities supported it in Mexico City (*Table 2.4*). The gap between the high and low groups was only 11% in Rio and 19% in Buenos Aires, with the poor more supportive of expropriation (though many expressed no opinion). Chileans were the people most sharply polarized by social class over the role of foreign firms: the gap between high and low groups was 25%, with fewer people lacking opinions than in Buenos Aires or Rio and with 60% of the poor supporting expropriation.

However, the more interesting differences are not those between social classes in the same country, but those between countries for the same social class. Differences in attitudes toward expropriation are statistically insignificant between small businessmen and manual workers within all countries (*Table 2.5*), although cross-class consensus is most pronounced in Mexico City, Caracas and urban Brazil. However, small businessmen in Mexico City and urban Brazil were significantly different in their more favorable views toward expropriation than their presumed class brethren in Caracas and Buenos Aires, while manual workers in Caracas were significantly more opposed to expropriation than their class counterparts elsewhere.

The variation in the views of small businessmen is interesting for yet another reason. Caracas excepted, manual workers were predictably constant nationalists: pluralities or majorities favor expropriation, though by different margins, across countries. Small businessmen, on the other hand, are far more variable. They favored expropriation in three countries but opposed it in two. Thus to understand how the climate of opinion on expropriation changes one should focus more on groups that are variable than on those that are constant.

2.5   Transnational and statist coalitions

Chile and Peru have witnessed some of the more dramatic confrontations over the state's takeover of foreign-owned property in recent years. The transnational coalition over natural resources broke down, and national business elites supported limited socialization. The transnational industrial coalition among large firms, however, did not break down. As the Peruvian and Chilean governments pushed state control over the industrial economy in the early 1970s, the transnational business community united in complaining loudly and effectively against such policies, as they had in the past.

Chile

Behavior

A transnational coalition between the foreign-owned copper companies and national business in Chile existed both at the end of World War II and during the 'Nuevo Trato' period in the 1950s, but it began to break down first in the early 1950s, and decisively so in the 1960s. A limited statist coalition, arguing first for regulation of the foreign-owned copper industry, and eventually for its socialization, came to include intellectuals, political leaders of the left and the right and government officials, and also the peak business organizations. The Chilean national business community remained unified, first as transnationalists and later as statists. These businessmen did not fear competition from the copper companies. They followed their leaders into limited statism primarily on political grounds, in response to the complex maneuvers necessary for the survival and influence of the conservative parties that eventually merged into the National party in the mid-1960s. Although some industrialists wanted to use the copper sector to generate foreign exchange earnings for industrialization, these arguments were secondary to the pre-eminent role played by politics in the support by Chilean business for limited statism. The socialization of the copper firms in 1971 was approved unanimously by the Chilean Congress. However, when the Chilean political climate changed again after the 1973 coup to favor private enterprises, Chilean business confederations, still united, began to advocate the transfer of ownership of the large copper mines from the state to themselves[19]. They thus remained nationalists but no longer statists, given this further change in the political environment. However, the military successfully insisted on continued state ownership of the large mines.

Attitudes

Chilean views on foreign property, polarized by class, responded mostly to the foreign firms in copper and non-manufacturing activities. The industrial component of US investment in Chile has been one of the two lowest (*Table 2.2*). In 1965, when the survey reported in *Tables 2.4* and *2.5* was taken, the ratio of manufacturing to non-manufacturing US private direct investment in Chile was 0.05, the lowest then of these seven Latin American countries. Because a number of Chilean entrepreneurs were foreign-born, and because the phrasing of the question might not have isolated the foreign-owned copper companies clearly from the investments in manufacturing (using first the word 'industries' and later 'large corporations'), the net Chilean upper-class support for expropriation may be understated. Even so, 35% supported such expropriations, as did a plurality of small businessmen.

In 1959–60, 94 managers from firms employing more than 100 persons were asked whether the effects of foreign investment were generally favorable for Chile. Of 66 managers responding, 35 thought them favorable without qualifications, and only 1 thought them unfavorable. The remaining 30 added qualifications often related to natural resources and utilities; 7 of these 30 were very worried about competition from foreign firms. This survey captures, then, a transition from the transnationalist to the limited statist coalition. All but one of the managers of these large firms thought well of foreign investment – a striking unanimity – but almost half of them expressed the kinds of reservations that would lead eventually to the socialization of the copper firms. Only a tenth were concerned about competition – the central ingredient of the national bourgeois coalition[20].

The swing of Chilean business toward the limited statist coalition over copper (while still adhering to the transnational coalition in manufacturing) had become more marked in 1964–65. Nearly all of the 138 industrialists employing more than 50 persons who were interviewed favored President Frei's proposed joint ownership of the copper mines by the Chilean government and the foreign firms instead of allowing them to remain as 100% foreign-owned subsidiaries. But these industrialists were still opposed to the full socialization of the copper mines. Chilean industrialists thus made a unified transition from the transnational to President Frei's limited statist coalition. There was still very little evidence of a national bourgeois coalition in Chile; Chilean industrialists welcomed direct private foreign investment in manufacturing with few, if any, reservations[21].

In 1975, when Chile was under military rule favorable toward foreign firms, 170 Chilean opinion leaders were asked about private foreign investment. Their perceptions of what firms did about reinvestment, taxes, exports, and employment of foreign personnel were much closer to what they felt should be done, and to what was being done, than were those of Venezuelan leaders (where a similar study was also made). Chileans believed in non-discrimination between national and foreign firms (all differences reported below were statistically insignificant). Asked about the economic and social impact of private investment, those saying that it was beneficial ranged to 85% for Chilean firms and to 74% for US firms. Asked about what profits should be as a percent of investments, 31% of Chilean leaders said that national firms should make more than 20% profit and 55% said more than 15% profit; the respective figures for profits of US-owned firms in Chile were 32% and 58%. However, Chilean businessmen were somewhat less likely than either Chilean government officials or university student leaders to say that investment by US firms in Chile was beneficial[22].

A smaller survey was conducted in 1976 among 55 manufacturing companies, majority-owned by Chileans in Santiago or Valparaíso, and employing over 200 persons. Virtually all agreed that foreign investment was 'necessary and beneficial' for Chile; 93% added that it was also needed for the healthy development of local firms; 80% backed a low tariff policy 'that would force their companies to become more competitive against international competition'. However, in a 1978 survey of 285 member firms of the National Association of Manufacturers, support for a low tariff policy had dropped substantially as its effects were felt: 39% expected a loss of their ability to compete, 44% expected no change, and only 11% expected to benefit from lower tariffs[23].

In general, the behavior of Chilean industrialists corresponded to these attitudes. The National Association of Manufacturers supported the government's policies, although it argued in 1977 for 'effective antidumping legislation to protect local producers from unfair competition'. When the new banking law in 1978 lifted restrictions on foreign investment in banks, local bankers hailed the measure, expecting to increase capital flows and to learn new banking techniques[24]. Chilean business resented undiluted foreign competition through trade the most. But its transnational ideology, and the still limited competition from foreign firms, allowed it to welcome a rise in direct private foreign investment.

In sum, Chilean businessmen in large firms shifted from a transnational to a limited statist coalition on the issue of the foreign-owned copper firms from the 1950s to the early 1970s with relatively few divisions within the national business community. They shifted again, still united, to support their national privatization in the late 1970s. Their reasons remained political throughout, although the political context changed and economic self-interest became more evident. They remained committed to the transnational coalition in manufacturing, viewing foreign investment as highly beneficial and adhering to non-discriminatory policies. Only a very few showed national bourgeois feelings, fearing competition, and few expressed wishes to restrain foreign-owned firms. These attitudes and behavior were consistent with the comparatively low levels of foreign investment in manufacturing (*Table 2.3*). The experience of the Allende socialization program further reduced the general foreign presence, thus lowering Chilean fears of the foreign industrialist. Transnational ideologies prevailed among large manufacturing firms facing only modest industrial competition. Small businessmen supported the socialization both of the copper firms and of manufacturing by 1965, this being well past national bourgeois views, closer to general statism, and sharply at odds with the transnationalist views of the larger Chilean firms[25]. But national policy under authoritarian rule after 1973 was firmly transnationalist, setting aside most objections to the international openness of the Chilean economy.

Peru

Attitudes

Public opinion in Lima of private direct foreign investment became far more selective during the 1960s. In 1961, 39% believed that foreign property should be expropriated by the government. In 1966, only 31.2% said that all foreign enterprises in Peru should be nationalized. While support for general expropriation declined, support for selective expropriation increased. In 1958, 36% said that US business investments should be either limited, reduced or eliminated. In 1966, 75% said that all or some foreign enterprises should be nationalized by the state. Therefore, while fewer favored state control over all foreign firms, twice as many favored a more selective approach. Two-thirds of the respondents to the 1966 survey still thought that foreign enterprises contributed to development. The International Petroleum Company (IPC) was a target for expropriation for 20.4% of the total sample in 1966 among the more selective respondents. Adding these to those who felt all foreign firms should be socialized indicates that a majority of Lima's citizens favored the takeover of IPC some two years before a military government did that[26]. Limeños thus showed a growing ability to discriminate among foreign firms and were willing to leave a number of large private foreign-owned firms beyond the grasp of the government.

Behavior

Foreign-owned firms in Peru relied on Peruvian interest groups to lobby for the general interests of the private sector, regardless of the nationality of the firm. US firms were dominant in the mining society, but dominated only some sectors of the National Association of Manufacturers[27]. National and foreign firms reacted similarly to many key events in Peru after 1968. The socialization of IPC was popular. The Lima business community accepted the government's claim that IPC was a special case, and found it politically prudent not to challenge the military government over an issue that the latter considered one of national security. But when President Juan Velasco Alvarado's government (1968–1975) issued the industrial code in 1970, the foreign and national business community opposed it jointly[28]. The relationship between foreign and national firms was not, however, a close alliance based on ideological affinities; rather it was a transnational coalition with specific purposes[29]. Peruvian business separated foreign-owned natural resource and utilities firms from their own interests by the late 1960s and early 1970s for political reasons[30], without substantial fear of foreign competition from these enclave-like firms.

The Peruvian private sector led the attack against the government's takeover of the national and foreign fishmeal sector in 1973, and the National Association of Manufacturers criticized the government's handling of the economy in 1978, blaming the crisis on the socialization of the economy 1968, and, also, on 'communist infiltration in the public sector'. Relief was demanded in credit, taxes, and more flexible labor legislation to benefit the entire private sector regardless of nationality. But Peruvian business had become more discriminating in its attitudes toward foreign firms in the 1970s. Local bankers, for example, complained loudly that the new banking legislation approved in 1977 'puts the clock back at least ten years, by granting to foreign capital privileges not available to Peruvian business'[31].

In sum, the Peruvian response to foreign investment was strongly shaped by the overwhelming presence of foreign firms in the natural resources and utilities sectors[32]. The industrial component of US investment in Peru was the third lowest of the seven Latin American countries in 1955 and the lowest in 1979. Peruvian business severed its ties with many of the expropriated foreign firms for political factors rather than reasons of industrial competition. Peruvian business thus adopted the limited statist position in natural resources and utilities while it remained within a transnational coalition in the manufacturing sector, as did Chilean business in both cases. However, the greater Peruvian discrimination against foreign firms may be understood from a comparison of Peru and Chile in *Table 2.1*. Foreign investment of all kinds declined in Chile in the first half of the 1970s, while it rose steeply in Peru, suggesting an incipient Peruvian national bourgeois behavior, which was present in Chile only among small business.

2.6   Toward national bourgeois coalitions

Venezuela, Colombia and Argentina exhibit the growth of a national bourgeois coalition in manufacturing where the ties with foreigners are weakened. In contrast to the political unity maintained in the shift from a transnational to a limited statist coalition in the cases of natural resources and utilities, national business tends to divide as private direct foreign investment in manufacturing rises. Nevertheless, a large portion of national business prefers a policy of discrimination, seeking special benefits from their own government for national industry. This is notable in Venezuela and, somewhat less so, in Colombia. Argentina has experienced more oscillation in recent decades between transnational and national bourgeois coalitions.

Venezuela

In the late 1950s, as competitive civilian politics took hold in Venezuela, there was a transnational coalition between the foreign-owned oil companies and the Venezuelan private sector, led by its peak association (Fedecámaras). It broke down in the aftermath of the 1966 tax reform crisis when national business felt ill-used by the oil firms. Venezuelan business also came to fear the political danger of a too-close identification with the oil firms[33]. Unlike the Chileans, Venezuelan business did not have parties to carry its political burdens and had to act as an independent interest group responding to government and party mobilization of opinion. But, concerning oil (as in Chile concerning copper), a relatively unified national business community gradually shifted from a transnational coalition with the oil companies to a limited statist coalition that came to support oil socialization for political reasons. There was not much concern with industrial competition between foreign and national firms, while the forward and backward linkages between the oil companies and the rest of the Venezuelan economy were modest[34].

The Venezuelan transnational coalition of the mid-1960s had broad support. Caracas respondents were the only ones to agree across social classes that foreign enterprises should not be expropriated (*Tables 2.4* and *2.5*). A study of Latin American business attitudes in the early 1960s showed that Venezuelan managers were most likely to oppose state intervention in the economy and to welcome foreign firms[35].

And yet Venezuelan attitudes toward private foreign investment already showed some complexity in the early 1960s, when a large survey asked respondents to identify the best and the worst foreign influences. Industrial and agricultural workers, slum dwellers and peasants were typically unable to answer this question. In general, except for university students and professors, all groups identified communism as the worst foreign influence. Most groups also indicated by small margins that capitalism was a good, not a bad, foreign influence (even lower-class respondents agreed), but several groups showed pluralities that believed that foreign capitalism did more harm than good, including university students and professors, high government officials, industrial executives and white-collar commercial employees. Although the question was rather general, an incipient national bourgeois coalition was appearing in the early 1960s including about a fifth of industrial executives and a third of small businessmen and government officials[36].

An elite-led national bourgeois coalition suspicious of the United States and of private foreign investment had arisen by the early 1970s. Asked whether 'the basic interests of our country' and the United States were in agreement, only 49% of the public in Caracas believed so, second from the bottom of 14 countries surveyed in 1972; the educated elite was a bit higher at 54%, but that was the lowest score of the 14 countries[37]. Asked 'whether or not you think [the United States] will be a serious threat – militarily, economically or otherwise' – to your country 'during the next ten years', Venezuelans were second only to Canadians in identifying an economic threat (28%) and third, behind Canada and Japan, in believing that a combined military and economic threat was likely (37%). The respective statistics for Venezuela's university educated elite were 35% and 54%, second to Canada's in both[38]. Asked in an open-ended question about US actions in international affairs, specific references to US policies toward Venezuela were more negative than positive by a 3 to 2 ratio among the general public, but by a 15 to 2 ratio among the university educated[39].

In the Fall of 1974, 95% of Venezuelans (N = 2191) responding to a national survey approved of the state's expected takeover of the petroleum sector (which occurred on 1 January 1976), although the university educated and higher income groups preferred a state–private joint venture to a pure state enterprise. On private foreign investment beyond oil, the public had been changing more quickly than the elite since the early 1960s. The public as a whole divided closely (41% *vs.* 39%) on whether foreign investment was good for Venezuela; a plurality (49%) would exclude foreign firms from operating in Venezuela. The educated and higher income groups supported private foreign investment; pluralities of those with primary education or less opposed it[40].

Changes had also been occurring within the elite. They, too, approved of the takeover of the oil companies. Unlike Chilean elites surveyed simultaneously in 1975, the perceptions of the Venezuelan elites of what foreign-owned firms did about reinvestment, taxes, exports, and employment of foreign personnel were much more different from what they felt should be done, and from what was being done, than in Chile. Venezuelan elites discriminated between firms by nationality of ownership more than did the Chileans: while 90% of the Venezuelan elites felt that national firms were beneficial for Venezuela, only 69% thought so about US-owned firms; while 51% of them thought that national firms should make over 20% profit, and 76% thought that they should make over 15% profit, the respective figures for US-owned multinational firms were only 32% and 59% (all three differences are statistically significant[41]). And by 3 to 1 margins, they wanted their sons to work in nationally owned firms[42].

Although Venezuelan businessmen were more favorably inclined toward multinational enterprises than government officials or university students, these businessmen nevertheless favored special conditions for national firms over foreign firms. They favored a lower rate of reinvestment for national than for foreign firms, in contrast both to other Venezuelan elites and to Chilean business. They believed that all firms were then paying the same average amount of taxes as a percent of gross income, but that national firms should pay less, in contrast to Venezuelan government officials who preferred to tax all firms more heavily but equally. Venezuelan businessmen also lobbied for preferences for Venezuelan firms in engineering; to compete with foreign-owned insurance firms, national insurance firms stressed that they provide more management jobs for nationals[43].

At the beginning of the 1980s, Venezuelan government policies were generally consistent with the evolution of national business views. The government of President Luís Herrera Campíns (1979–1984) slowed down, but did not stop, the takeover of foreign firms judged to have violated some national objective. Thus in 1979, for example, the Herrera government forced the Reynolds Metal Co. to sell its shares in the Alcasa Aluminum Co. to the Venezuelan government (on the grounds of mismanagement) and it moved to buy out Nestle's share in a powdered milk joint venture (on social grounds). On the other hand, the Venezuelan Development Corporation began in 1981 to divest itself of several dozen firms in the light industrial sector and in tourism. While foreign firms could bid, in principle, to purchase these state firms as they became private, the principle of discrimination in favor of nationals was upheld[44].

There was, however, no elite consensus in Venezuela about the disadvantages of foreign firms. Government officials and university students worried about dependency and the balance of payments. Businessmen were much less concerned about dependency, but a fifth of them feared competition and almost half mentioned alleged economic disadvantages of private foreign investment[45].

In conclusion, by the 1970s, Venezuelan business had broken its transnational coalition with foreign oil firms on political grounds, and had joined the limited statist coalition that led to their takeover. They also began to adopt national bourgeois views, favoring their own firms and discriminating against foreign-owned firms. Venezuelan elites, more than the general public, had also come to perceive the possibility of economic conflict with the United States. Criticism of foreign oil firms, and of some general practices of foreign firms, had spread from the early 1960s to the mid-1970s even to the elites, but more moderately so. Yet these findings also indicate the upper limits of business nationalism. Venezuelan elites in the 1970s were more favorable than the public as a whole toward some private foreign investment – in contrast to the early 1960s. The elite had maintained a basic commitment to a capitalist economic system requiring some openness to foreign capital, yet there was also a strong belief in discrimination according to nationality of firm ownership.

Venezuelan business had evolved toward a national bourgeois coalition, favoring public policies to help national but not foreign-owned firms, in response to political changes, to be sure, but also to rising competition from foreign firms. US direct investments in manufacturing in Venezuela increased far more rapidly than in other Latin American countries or in the world as a whole from 1955 to 1979, and the industrial component of US investments there increased 22 times (*Tables 2.1* and *2.2*). The change in objective conditions in Venezuela, therefore, changed business perceptions and behavior from transnationalist toward national bourgeois.

Colombia

Colombia has had a national bourgeoisie longer than Venezuela, but growing more slowly from the 1950s to the 1980s. Colombian industrialization resulted largely from domestic entrepreneurship, except in the extractive industries[46]. Even foreign oil firms never assumed the political centrality that copper firms did in Chile or oil firms in Venezuela, because coffee, and later manufacturing, which remained predominantly in Colombian-owned firms, were more important for the Colombian economy[47]. Colombian entrepreneurs, however, were already divided in the early 1960s over policies toward private foreign investment in manufacturing. Businessmen in Medellín (Antioquia) thought and behaved as national bourgeois while businessmen in Bogotá and Cali remained transnationalists[48].

Attitudes

Colombian national bourgeois attitudes in the early 1960s remained moderate. Managers rarely gave unqualified approval to private direct foreign investment, arguing that foreign investment should stay away from fields in which Colombian firms were already active. While highly concerned about foreign firm competition, only a few businessmen recommended any control or channeling of foreign investment by the government[49].

Bogotá businessmen remained firm transnationalists in the early 1960s. In 1962, 62% of 61 Bogotá members of the National Association of Manufacturers (ANDI) thought that the government's mildly protectionist foreign exchange policy was detrimental to industrial activity, opposing policies that sought to favor them. There were no significant differences in the propensity toward nationalism between native-born and foreign-born industrialists. The more inefficient producers (those with the highest proportion working below their capacity) supported government policy more; the slight propensity is akin to the hypothesis that small business, often less efficient, is more likely to be more nationalistic[50]. About 36% of a national survey (N = 273) of small businessmen in 1962 supported the expropriation of foreign industry, but a majority did not[51].

On balance, Colombian elite opinion was favorable toward private foreign investment. Out of a national sample (N = 990) in 1971, 76% thought that foreign investment was very important for the Colombian economy; 60% thought the country needed more foreign firms, while only 17% felt there were too many; 76% thought that the government should stimulate more foreign investment. Colombian businessmen were more favorable toward private foreign investments than other elites[52].

However, there was also evidence of national bourgeois attitudes. Among the major disadvantages of foreign investments, 14% (ranking third) cited competition with Colombian firms. They were also asked: 'As new companies are formed, using foreign capital, what percentage of such a company should be owned by Colombians?' Only 9% said that 49% or less should be owned by Colombians; another 24% said 50%; and 62% said that Colombians should own at least 51% of any new firms[53].

Behavior

The peak Colombian associations of industries and banks in Bogotá mounted the major private sector campaign against the Andean Pact statute on foreign capital in 1971. Their criticisms coincided closely with those of the foreign business community; the latter's ideas and interests were sponsored publicly by their Bogotá industrial and financial counterparts who believed that their own defense had to include a defense of the interests of the foreign investor. The objective basis for this close identity of transnational interests was the lack of significant competition between Bogotá and foreign business[54].

The situation throughout Colombian business was more complex, however. The federation representing the interests of small Colombian manufacturers (ACOPI) generally supported the government's position on the statute but took little public part in the debates. The larger national entrepreneurs from Antioquia, striving for survival in competition with multinational enterprises, broke with the Bogotá business elite. Antioquia industrialists in food and textiles felt competition from foreign firms most acutely, and they led the opposition to private foreign investment. The conflict between Bogotá transnationalists and Medellín national bourgeois was most visible when the presidency of ANDI shifted after Colombia moved to implement Decision 24 of the Andean Pact that regulated private foreign investment[55].

Bankers, on the whole, have remained transnationalists. The government's regulations on foreign banks issued in the spring of 1974, acting under loopholes allowed by Decision 24 of the Andean Pact statute on foreign investments, removed most restrictions on the operations of foreign banks. The president of the Colombian bankers' association hailed the regulations for maintaining 'the principles of reciprocity required by other countries toward Colombian banks wanting to establish themselves abroad' – 6 of the 35 foreign banks in Panama in 1974 were Colombian, and the Banco de Bogotá had set up a joint venture in Ecuador in 1973 and opened a subsidiary in New York in 1974. The Colombian bankers, however, were unable to prevent the passage of legislation in 1975, or to obtain its repeal subsequently, forcing foreign-owned banks to no more than a 49% equity position, notwithstanding loud complaints[56].

Other Colombian businessmen fit the national bourgeois mode more closely. The Colombian coal producers' association (Fedecarbon) opposed a Colombian government agreement to develop its coal reserves relying on Brazil's Siderbras so that Colombian coal entrepreneurs could develop their own programs. Colombia approved a 'buy Colombian' law for the public sector in 1972, which was toughened in 1978. Its tax relief law of 1976 was discriminatory: it could be used only by majority-owned Colombian firms. Government regulations issued in 1979 for the electronics sector sought to reserve the local electronics market, especially the manufacturing of color television sets, to existing Colombian manufacturers. And the Colombian development plan announced in 1980 protected the smaller national firms quite fully and committed the government to assist national firms in winning government contracts that would evolve from the implementation of the plan. Colombian firms would also have first priority in the fulfilment of the Colombian share of industrial sector allocations among Andean Pact countries[57].

In sum, there had been a division between transnationalists and national bourgeois in the Colombian business community, and within the elite at large, for a longer time than in Venezuela. The pace of change, however, was faster in Venezuela. US direct investments in manufacturing grew twice as fast from 1955 to 1979 in Venezuela than in Colombia (*Table 2.1*); even though the industrial component of US investments remained much greater in Colombia, change in this regard had also been more pronounced in Venezuela. Venezuelan elites had been far more transnationalist in the early 1960s than the Colombian elites, but they may have reversed roles by the 1970s. While Colombians called for more private foreign investment and even more foreign firms operating in the country, Venezuelans were sharply divided over foreign investment and preferred to cut back on foreign firms. Thus the division in Colombia between transnationalists, especially in Bogotá and in banking generally, and national bourgeois, especially in Medellín and among small manufacturers generally, appeared to continue, and it may have become sharper – as the intra-business battles over the implementation of the Andean Pact's statute on foreign investment and the strong elite preference for Colombian majorities in joint ventures would suggest. The growth of a national bourgeoisie proceeded at a more measured pace in Colombia than it did in Venezuela.

Argentina

Argentina was the first substantially industrialized Latin American country. In 1955, the manufacturing component of US direct investments was higher in Argentina than elsewhere in Latin America, and twice as high as the worldwide ratio for US investment overseas (*Table 2.2*). However, US manufacturing investments in Argentina grew much more slowly than was the norm for Latin America in the 1970s; Argentina fell to fourth place in terms of the predominance of industry in US investments by 1979 (*Tables 2.1 and 2.3*). Argentina has long had a substantial national bourgeois coalition, but it has not grown much. The Argentine government has even been able to open the country to transnational forces at times (especially in the late 1970s) over national business opposition. The changing relative

autonomy of the state from social and economic forces, and especially the
policy preferences of the armed forces, appear to explain best policy changes
toward international trade and investment.

Attitudes

Substantial majorities of upper- and middle-class Argentines in Buenos
Aires in 1965 were opposed to expropriating foreign firms; lower-class
respondents were closely divided (*Table 2.4*). However, differences between
small businessmen and manual workers toward foreign investment remained
statistically insignificant in four surveys from 1961 to 1972 (*Table 2.6*). The
observed variations from one survey to another are best explained by the
dimensions of the sample (class polarization was marginally more pronounced in metropolitan Buenos Aires) or by the change in the wording of
the 1972 question (ideally having less foreign investment need not commit a
respondent to expropriate, as in the question asked in earlier years). Thus
Argentine small businessmen and manual workers appeared to be about
equally divided over foreign investment over time.

Small business majorities opposed expropriation of foreign firms in the
1960s (*Table 2.6*). Pluralities of all Buenos Aires social classes favored the
promotion of foreign enterprise in Argentina in May 1966 (N = 850), the
proportions rising from 46% among those with no more than primary
education to 74% of those with university education. However, one-fifth of
the public was opposed to promoting foreign enterprises in Argentina; this
was a constant across social classes varying only between 20% and 23%.
Buenos Aires respondents had also endorsed an aspect of discrimination
central to a national bourgeois coalition: asked about the kinds of activities
from which foreign enterprise should be barred in Argentina, 9% said from
all but only 13% said from none. The predominant set (40%, with the
balance not knowing) would bar foreign enterprises from specific sectors,
with oil at the top of the list[58].

The same selectivity was evident in a 1965 survey: 71% of 2014
respondents favored the admission of private foreign capital, ranging from
64% for 'core' Peronists to 77% of supporters of the middle-class Radical
party then in office – a statistically significant difference. However, 77% of
the core Peronists and 79% of the Radicals also supported more control over
foreign corporations[59]. There was, of course, no contradiction: foreign
firms were welcome, but they had to be controlled even more. Selectivity in
foreign investment was the norm for Argentines across political party
preferences and social class. Even if Radicals were more supportive of
foreign investment, they were just as insistent as the Peronists that it be
controlled.

Foreign investment had become somewhat more salient by a June 1972
survey, when Argentines were asked about the major problems facing the
country. With multiple responses possible, 57% of lower-class Argentines

Table 2.6 Attitudes toward foreign investment in Argentina, 1961–72 (percentages)[a]

Attitudes	1961[b]		1962[b]		1965[c]		1972[d]	
	Small business	Manual workers	Small business	Manual workers	Small business	Manual workers	Small business	Manual workers
(N)	(178)	(124)	(246)	(114)	(55)	(46)	(290)	(140)
Negative	48	57	47	48	38	63	67	68
Positive	52	43	53	52	62	37	33	32
Chi-square	2.342		0.037		6.194		0.044	

[a] All chi-square tests are statistically insignificant at the .01 level for one degree of freedom. 'Don't know' and other responses excluded.
[b] 'Would you favor or oppose expropriation of foreign-owned industries, that is, having the government take over large corporations owned by foreigners?' Negative attitudes support expropriation. National sample.
[c] Same question. Negative attitudes support expropriation. Buenos Aires only (see *Table 2.5*).
[d] 'Surely you have heard that they are talking about the extent of participation of foreign capital in the economy of the country. What would be the ideal rate of participation of that foreign capital?' Negative responses include those who said little or none; positive responses are those who said much, considerable or medium. National sample.

Source: Secondary analysis of data deposited at the Roper Center, Yale University. For 1961, US Information Agency, 'International Relations' (USIA – LA 8); for 1962, USIA, 'Alliance for Progress' (USIA – LA 13); for 1965, USIA, 'International Relations' (USIA – WSIII); for 1972, 'Economics and Politics' (OP 039).

thought that inflation was the key problem; 58% identified unemployment; and 18% said 'domination by foreign enterprise'. In addition, 35% of the upper classes singled out the last point[60]. Thus concern about foreign enterprises was greater among the rich, who could afford the luxury to worry about it, who had the intellectual skills to think about the issue, and who owned the businesses that might suffer from their competition.

National bourgeois attitudes were already prevalent in the national business community by 1971. Although there was substantial support among 112 industrialists from the largest Argentine firms for foreign participation in industry (96.4%) and in the development of technology in Argentina (92.9%) as well as for major tenets of US foreign policy (Argentine industrialists did not break with international capitalist norms that required substantially open borders), on the critical question of the terms of entry for foreign firms, they adopted discriminatory national bourgeois positions. Only 37.5% of the industrial executives said that foreign capital should participate with few or no restrictions. In contrast, 29.5% favored mixed and equal participation with Argentine corporations, another 21.5% would require Argentine predominance in equity ownership, and 10.7% would limit foreign participation to loans, credits and licensing agreements. Argentine citizens who are executives in foreign firms are significantly more likely to argue for no control over profit remittances, but only 36.6% of them take this view. Most are willing to advocate some profit remittance control. There are, however, no significant differences between executives by nationality of firm on whether few or no conditions should be attached to the participation of foreign investments in the Argentine economy: consistent with a national bourgeois perspective, majorities of both kinds of executives reject that view[61].

The development of the national bourgeois views of Argentine business is illustrated in *Table 2.7*. Neither small nor big businessmen distinguished among firms by nationality or ownership in 1961. However, small business-men were divided in their attitudes toward all private firms, while big business was very favorable toward all private firms. Differences between small and big businessmen were significant in 1961: big businessmen remained transnationalists, while there was a large national bourgeois minority among small businessmen. By 1972, national bourgeois views predominated among small businessmen, who sharply distinguished among firms by nationality of ownership: they had very negative views of foreign firms, and very positive views of national firms. Big businessmen continued to avoid making distinctions among firms by nationality, but their own divisions had come to resemble those of small business a decade earlier. Differences toward foreign firms by size of Argentine firm became statisti-cally insignificant. Transnationalist views retreated, as national bourgeois views spread throughout the entire Argentine business sector regardless of firm size. However, because a majority of big businessmen still thought well

44

Table 2.7 *Argentine business attitudes toward firms by nationality of ownership, 1961 and 1972 (percentages)*

Attitudes	1961[a]						1972[b]					
	Small business attitudes		Big business attitudes		Attitudes toward foreign firms		Small business attitudes		Big business attitudes		Attitudes toward foreign firms	
					Business size						Business size	
	Foreign	National	Foreign	National	Small	Big	Foreign	National	Foreign	National	Small	Big
(N)	(178)	(180)	(20)	(20)	(178)	(20)	(290)	(300)	(17)	(17)	(290)	(17)
Negative	48	40	10	25	48	10	63	15	47	24	63	47
Positive	52	60	90	75	52	90	37	85	53	76	37	53
Chi-square	2.509		1.558		10.690		145.283		2.061		1.678	

[a] 'Would you favor or oppose expropriation of foreign-owned industries, that is, having the government take over large corporations owned by foreigners?' Same question repeated for privately owned Argentine industries. National sample. Negative attitudes support expropriation. The first two chi-squares are statistically insignificant, but the third is significant, at the .01 level for one degree of freedom. 'Don't know' and other responses excluded.

[b] 'As you know, in the country there are a number of private companies (that are not of the state) with Argentine capital and others with foreign capital. If you think about the companies with Argentine capital what would you say they are like for the development of the country? And private companies with foreign capital? What would you say they are like for the country?' National sample. Negative attitudes include those who said 'it depends'. The first chi-square is statistically significant at the .001 level; the other two are not significant at the .001 level, in all cases for one degree of freedom. 'Don't know' and other responses excluded.

Source: Secondary analysis of data stored at the Roper Center, Yale University. For 1961, US Information Agency, 'International Relations' (USIA – LA 8); for 1972, 'Economics and Politics' (OP 039).

of the effect of foreign firms on Argentina, the consolidation of a national bourgeois coalition lagged.

The change in attitudes of small business made it not only more nationalist but also more capitalist. In 1961, small businessmen were divided over whether all firms, regardless of nationality of ownership, should be expropriated. By 1972, small businessmen had an optimistic view of the impact of private national firms in Argentina. They had moved away from general statism to support national capitalism and oppose foreign firms. In 1972, 88% of 280 small businessmen thought that the actual participation of foreign capital in Argentina was much or considerable, and 83% of 290 thought that it would be ideal if foreign capital participation was reduced from its actual levels. Big businessmen did not make such distinctions yet (consistent with the views reported in *Table 2.7*)[62].

Behavior
Argentine business opposed most forms of socialization but supported national bourgeois policies favoring national over foreign firms. They opposed President Arturo Illia's (1963–1966) decision to cancel foreign petroleum company contracts and worried over his conflicts with the International Monetary Fund and the World Bank[63]. However, Argentine business used the concern over foreign domination of the Argentine economy to block some new investments during General Juan Onganía's presidency (1966–1970). Foreign minority-owned joint ventures began to behave as national firms, seeking state support against the new foreign firms. Petroquímica Argentina SA, whose equity was owned in part by five foreign firms, led the fight in 1968 along with three other 'Argentine' firms with minority foreign equity interests against a proposed $114 million investment by Dow Chemical in ethylene production. Similarly, Acindor's plan (minority-owned by US steel) for an integrated steel plant was blocked by a coalition of military officers concerned about national security and autonomy and local steel sheet producers fearful of fresh competition. The Onganía government – which hardly had a nationalist reputation – tightened the law against foreign firm acquisitions in 1968; it took over the foreign-owned overseas telecommunications firms in 1969; it reduced protective tariffs on autos and petro-chemicals, where foreign firms dominated; and it restricted the activities of foreign banks. The program of national firm rehabilitation prevented foreign takeovers, and discriminated against foreign firms by giving debt and tax relief assistance to national firms only. This government aid even included 33 large Argentine firms listed on the Buenos Aires Stock Exchange in 1970[64].

The Cámpora government (in power two months in 1973) increased wages and lowered taxes for the working class, and it protected local firms against foreign takeovers. It gave preferred treatment to locally owned firms, and controlled foreign remittances. Its investment promotion law

reserved incentives only for majority-owned Argentine firms. After the
overthrow of President Isabel Perón (1974–1976), the government of
President General Jorge Videla (1976–1981) reaffirmed the legislation giving
priority to majority-owned Argentine firms in receiving government investment incentives, but it made it possible for foreign-owned firms to receive
some incentives on a selective basis[65].

The post-1976 military government did not repudiate the national
bourgeois principle of discrimination, but it successfully sought to reverse
the process of foreign divestment that occurred in Argentina in the first half
of the 1970s (*Table 2.1*). One important feature of the Videla government's
economic policy was the sale of industrial state enterprises to the private
sector. In virtually all cases, these firms were purchased by Argentine
businessmen. Foreign investors needed prior government approval before
making a purchase, and, while there was no absolute veto against acquisitions by foreign firms, the procedures were clearly biased in favor of
national business. These sales subsidized national business in yet another
way: while payments on principal were indexed according to rises in the
wholesale price index, the rate of interest to be paid was well below
prevailing market prices[66].

The principal conflict between the Videla government and the business
sector did not, however, involve distinctions by nationality of firm. As the
1980s opened, the Argentine manufacturing sector, regardless of nationality
of the firm, was complaining loudly against the tariff and exchange-rate
policies that removed industrial protection, which had previously been very
high, and that sought to increase industrial efficiency and competition, and
to lower prices, by facilitating the imports of manufactured goods. Argentine manufacturers complained far more than Chilean manufacturers, even
though Chilean tariffs had been slashed far more vigorously than had
occurred or was even forecast in Argentina[67]. This is an example of the
tactical re-emergence of elements of a transnational coalition to defend the
entire business sector against policies that businessmen perceived as excessively 'laissez-faire'.

Argentina has had, in sum, a national bourgeois coalition that has drawn
broad support from the mass public, business, and the armed forces in and
out of office. The fact of foreign divestment in the early 1970s weakened the
weight of the national bourgeois views on government policy in the late
1970s, but the aggressive free trade policies of the Videla government had the
effect of bringing together most Argentine manufacturers regardless of the
nationality of the firm. It remains clear that a transnational coalition has
clearly broken down in Argentina; not even a majority of Argentine
industrial executives working for foreign-owned firms can be considered
transnationalists. National bourgeois norms, though somewhat weakened in
the late 1970s, remain important in Argentine private views, lobbying
behavior, and public policy.

2.7   The consolidation of national bourgeois coalitions

Mexico

A national bourgeois coalition has long reigned in Mexico. National business and government have developed a sustained partnership – often hidden by volleys of hostile rhetoric over specific issues – to build up the wealth of Mexican firms and the equity participation of Mexican business. Reliance on government support existed even in that most laissez-faire of Mexican presidencies, Miguel Alemán's administration (1946–1952), or in the more hostile environment of Luis Echeverría's administration (1970 –1976)[68].

Attitudes

The differences among Mexican business confederations, few before the end of World War II, accelerated thereafter. The National Confederation of Chambers of Commerce (CONCANACO) retained the more laissez-faire position within a transnational coalition with foreign firms in the late 1940s and early 1950s. The organization representing the interests of small industrialists (CNIT or CANACINTRA), however, came to advocate government intervention in the economy by the mid-1950s, and to criticize the unhindered entry of foreign firms into the Mexican economy. Mexico City small businessmen supported the 'expropriation of foreign-owned industries' by a 2 to 1 margin in 1965 – a stronger nationalist position than small businessmen in other countries or than manual workers in Mexico City, Caracas, urban Brazil or Buenos Aires (*Table 2.5*). The larger National Association of Industries (CONCAMIN) adopted an intermediate view, gradually shifting from the transnational to the national bourgeois views.

By the early 1960s, CONCAMIN and CNIT had come to agree in substance, though still disagreeing in tone, that private foreign investment could enter provided that it was supplementary to Mexican firms and that control of equity passed gradually into Mexican hands. They opposed competition from foreign firms where Mexican firms were already active. The rapid rise of foreign investment in Mexican manufacturing from 1955 to 1965 (*Table 2.1*) assisted this convergence of views. A 1980 survey of 94 industrialists from these two organizations registered no significant differences between them in attitudes toward foreign investment. Even CONCANACO shifted to oppose the rapidly rising foreign investment in commercial activities as early as 1955. Thus the differences among the major Mexican business confederations narrowed 20 years after they had become notable. All abandoned the transnational coalition to advocate government intervention that discriminated against, and selected among, foreign firms to the benefit of nationally owned firms[69].

The strength of the national bourgeois coalition depended not just on business attitudes but also on more general views within the Mexican political system. In 1963, only 28% of 740 Mexican white- and blue-collar workers in Mexico City and in some smaller towns agreed that 'foreign capital is necessary for the development of Mexico and Mexico ought to do everything so that foreign companies would come to the country'. On the other hand, only 26% were willing to prevent the entry of new foreign firms into Mexico or to take over existing foreign firms.

The predominant response (45%) agreed that 'foreign capital could contribute to the development of Mexico and Mexico ought, with some care, to act so that some selected foreign companies would come to the country'[70]. Workers thus endorsed the selectivity that business was seeking. However, twice as many Mexicans in the 1965 survey (*Tables 2.4* and *2.5*) supported expropriation of 'large corporations owned by foreigners' as would be expected from the 1963 survey. That discrepancy cannot be resolved, although one possible reason is the oscillation in the Mexican experience itself. And yet the larger point remains: at either level of support for expropriation, there was a consensus across class in Mexico. The key difference is between consensus on statist or on national bourgeois policies.

By the early 1970s, the Mexican elite – like the Venezuelan elite – had broken its transnational alliance with the United States. Asked in the spring of 1972 about what the United States had been saying and doing recently in international affairs, the Mexican elite was 71% unfavorable, by far the most of any of the elites of 14 countries surveyed simultaneously. A plurality of the Mexican public (49%), in contrast, was favorable to the US, but the trend in mass public opinion of the United States was decidedly negative: good opinion scores in the early 1970s were the lowest recorded since surveying began in the mid-1950s[71].

Mexican business attitudes followed suit. In the first half of 1969, 57% of 200 Mexican entrepreneurs called for controls over the entry of foreign capital, and an additional 13% wanted to prohibit its entry. The competition these Mexican firms had from other Mexican firms remained stable from the time of their foundation until the end of the 1960s. However, whereas 22% had no competition of any kind when they were founded, that was so of only 3% at the end of the 1960s; and while only 31% had competition from foreign firms at the time of foundation, 50% had it at the end of the 1960s. Foreign competition was particularly important in the more modern sectors of the economy, where it affected 54–63% of Mexican firms, in comparison with traditional sectors where only 36–39% of Mexican firms had foreign firm competition[72]. National bourgeois views did not simply seek abstract psychological or ideological satisfaction; they were grounded in each firm's own experience and need for survival.

A large survey (N = 1013) of Mexican elite views was carried out in late 1973 in Mexico City, Guadalajara and Monterrey. Consistent with the argument that elites remain faithful to a degree of openness toward international capitalism, 92% of the Mexican elite thought that foreign investment was important to the Mexican economy, 70% thought that it was beneficial on balance, and 58% thought its effect had been good[73].

The convergence of attitudes toward foreign investment within the Mexican business community had also been completed. There were no longer any statistically significant differences between the views of executives of large or medium Mexican companies on whether foreign investment was beneficial on balance, or whether its effect had been good, or on the encouragement of foreign investments or on the number of firms in Mexico. Only 25% of the executives of large Mexican companies, and 21% of those in smaller firms, thought there were too few foreign firms in Mexico. The modal response was that the number was about right (26% and 24% respectively thought there were too many). Mexican businessmen preferred not to socialize existing firms, but neither did they want more foreign firms to come in. While Mexican business was much less likely than other elite groups to think there were too many foreign firms – with the socializing implications of that statement and the possible need to break with international capitalist commitments – they were also slightly less likely than others to say there were too few: labor leaders, executives of US firms and media leaders were more likely than Mexican business leaders to think there were too few foreign firms[74].

The national bourgeois colors of Mexican business showed up also in their views of Mexicanization: about 82% of the executives of the smaller Mexican firms and 80% of the executives of the larger firms thought that, when a new company was established in Mexico through foreign investment, over 50% of the ownership should be in Mexican hands. Mexican business was more 'nationalist' on this point, so close to their self-interest, than Mexican professionals, labor leaders, secondary school teachers or university students. Moreover, 85% of the executives of large Mexican firms, and 81% of the executives in the smaller firms, thought favorably of Mexicanization. Mexican business, formerly transnationalist, had united regardless of firm size (none of these differences was statistically significant) even more impressively than in Argentina[75].

Another large Mexican elite survey (N = 800) was conducted in urban Mexico in November and December 1976, the closing weeks of the administration of President Luis Echeverría. Conflicts between the Mexican government and businessmen (both national and foreign) had at that time reached a high point in the modern history of Mexico[76]. And yet elite attitudes toward foreign business were *not* more polarized in 1976 than they were three years earlier. For example, the same question was asked of several elite groups in both surveys, namely, whether investment by foreign firms in Mexico was more beneficial or more harmful for the country. In 1973, 'more beneficial' answers ranged from 45% of university professors to 90% of

Mexican executives in US companies. In 1976, these answers ranged from 47% of university students (who had scored at 48% in 1973) to 91% of Mexican executives in US companies. Government officials scored at about the median: 67% said it was more beneficial in 1973 and 72% said so in 1976. All of these differences are statistically insignificant[77].

Given, therefore, that the basic attitudes among the country's elites had not changed, notwithstanding President Echeverría's own policies and views, it is less surprising that the relationship between politics and business in Mexico returned to a more typical pattern after José López Portillo's (1976–1982) assumption of the Mexican presidency.

The 1976 survey, however, also shows that national business in Mexico continued to adhere to national bourgeois views even when it might have been expected to have rallied to the support of business brethren from overseas. To be sure, national business in Mexico did support the essential ingredients of a capitalist economy: they thought overwhelmingly (90%) that foreign firm investment was more beneficial for Mexico; 57% thought there should be more foreign investment in Mexico; and 80% of them opposed that the Mexican government take over 'completely' large corporations owned by foreigners[78]. This is not very different from the Mexican past, or from business attitudes in other countries. However, business executives in Mexican companies also believed (53%) that the Mexican government should discourage foreign firms from buying into existing Mexican companies; 80% of them believed that it was a good idea to require that firms established in Mexico with foreign investment should be at least 51% Mexican. Only 3% of these Mexican businessmen thought that there should be less Mexican government control over foreign firms operating in Mexico, and 48% thought that there should be more control (with the balance thinking that the controls were about right). Consistent with the argument that Mexican businessmen in joint ventures with foreign firms may be veiled national bourgeois as well, only 5% of Mexican executives in US firms operating in Mexico called for less Mexican government control of US firms and 92% of them thought that it was a good idea to require that firms established in Mexico with foreign investment should be at least 51% Mexican[79].

While majorities of Mexican businessmen in Mexican firms believe that foreign firms facilitate access to foreign markets and contribute technology and managerial skills, the majorities of these same businessmen also believe that foreign firms exploit the country's natural resources without giving adequate compensation (54%); that they 'often' interfere in the internal affairs of Mexico (59%); that parent firms 'often' make decisions in business without regard to Mexican interests (67%); and that US companies are monopolistic and fix prices (66%)[80].

While it is certainly true that other Mexican elite groups tended to be even more critical of foreign firms, business criticism of foreign firms over a variety of issues was striking even at a time when the objective political conditions might have called for a unified business front against what was perceived as an anti-business administration. The common actions taken by businessmen were important but limited, and in no way signalled a retreat from basic national bourgeois policies and attitudes. As in Argentina in the late 1970s, there was a partial reappearance of aspects of a transnational business coalition for limited, tactical goals. In general, however, major Mexican business confederations criticized the Echeverría administration less because it was economically interventionist and more because it was interventionist in the 'wrong' direction. What businessmen advocated was not a passive state, but one that was supportive of them[81].

Behavior

The behavior of Mexican business matches its beliefs. Opposition to the foreign-owned electricity companies began with the small manufacturers early in the century, before the revolution, and it gradually spread through the social structure. Larger industrialists, and even commercial interests, began to support stricter regulation of the utilities. While CNIT led the struggle against the foreign-owned utilities in the 1950s, the rest of the private sector did not oppose their socialization in 1960. The critique of the sulphur companies was also launched in the 1950s by CNIT, which wanted sulphur resources to be used more for Mexican chemical industrial development (through forward linkages and vertical integration) than for exports – a view eventually adopted by the Mexican government. The campaign spread to the larger manufacturers, who enlisted the government and achieved Mexicanization to their own benefit[82]. The sulphur companies had become isolated from the rest of the Mexican business community by the 1960s. In 1967, Pan American Sulphur was compelled to sell to a consortium of the Mexican government and private Mexican business. In electricity as in sulphur, Mexican business joined a limited statist coalition, even though its more normal behavior was national bourgeois. There has been, however, an oscillation between these two views that may explain the apparently contradictory survey opinions reported earlier for the mass public.

National bourgeois behavior predominates throughout the business community. In 1966, erstwhile transnationalist CONCANACO asked the government to halt all foreign investment because it feared an invasion by J. C. Penney Co. The Chamber of the Graphic Arts Industry and the Chamber of the Publishing Industry complained of unfair foreign competition. The Coordinating Council of the Automobile Parts Manufacturing Industry asked the government in 1967 to ban the opening of new factories making auto parts already being made in Mexico. Mexican firms in the food industry demanded in 1968 that the government stop acquisitions by foreign firms. The principal national business and employer organizations published advertisements in the press in 1972 supporting the law on foreign investment (issued in 1973), having lobbied successfully to make it conform to their own interests. Although foreign business had hoped for a dramatic relaxation of controls over new investment projects as López Portillo replaced Echeverría in the presidency, the proportion of projects rejected by the Foreign Investment Commission decreased only from 15.3% in 1973–1976 to 10.6% in 1977. Of 1373 new foreign firm subsidiaries established in Mexico under the 1973 foreign investment law, only 44 were exempt from the requirement of Mexican 51% equity ownership (fewer in 1980 than in 1979)[83].

A presidential decree issued in January 1979, seeking to promote investments in the manufacture of capital goods, characteristically restricted access to the package of incentives to firms that used 60% of inputs from Mexico itself or that set up an approved program to increase the local content of its production. A firm also had to be majority-owned by Mexicans in order to qualify for the full range of these incentives. Later in 1979, the López Portillo government revamped procedures for public sector buying of machinery and equipment. Henceforth state enterprises were obliged to hold a special bidding for Mexican private firms, which had to be awarded the contract provided their bid price was no more than 15% higher than the prevailing international price (excluding freight)[84]. The Mexican government remained fully committed to pro-national bourgeois precisely because President López Portillo wished to improve the state's relations with Mexican business. Oligopoly and its defense in the national and in the firm's interest had become prevailing Mexican government and Mexican business policy.

In conclusion, a national bourgeois coalition had become consolidated in Mexico. The rise of foreign investment in manufacturing first split and later reunified Mexican business. While limited statism was at times supported, selectivity and discrimination were the predominant policies. Mexican business thought it had benefited from Mexicanization, and continued to support policies making it more difficult for new foreign firms to enter and compete in the Mexican market. National bourgeois beliefs and behavior were consistent with objective trends: US investments in Mexican manufacturing had outpaced world and Latin American norms from 1955 to 1975 so that the industrial component of US investments in 1975 was almost five times higher in Mexico than for the world as a whole (*Tables 2.1* and *2.2*).

Brazil

A national bourgeois coalition has also developed in Brazil over time, but Brazil and Mexico differ in the coalition's efficacy. Whereas national bourgeois policies have prevailed in Mexico through time, a transnationalist policy predominated in Brazil temporarily in the late 1960s and early 1970s. The Brazilian military and technocratic coalition in power at the time successfully resistent national bourgeois pressures in a highly authoritarian political setting that enhanced state autonomy. But Brazilian business nationalism found government allies again by the mid-1970s. Government policy was reoriented toward national bourgeois policies, consistent with the fact that Brazil had the largest amount of US investment in manufacturing, the fastest rate of increase of such investments in the early 1970s, and an industrial component of US investments that was three times larger than the worldwide norm (*Tables 2.1, 2.2 and 2.3*). The 'political opening' that reduced authoritarian controls in the late 1970s also reduced the relative independence of the state from its 'natural' allies in the national business community. In that specific political context, the efficacy of national bourgeois advocates grew.

Attitudes

A large national survey (N = 2168) in Brazil in 1961 found overwhelming support for Brazilian government encouragement of private foreign invest-ment (84%), but a division already on whether US companies operating in Brazil helped economic development: half answered no, or with qualifica-tions, and only 44% said yes[85]. A survey of 627 white- and blue-collar workers in Rio de Janeiro and in some small towns in 1960 showed that only 16% agreed that 'foreign capital is necessary for the development of Brazil and Brazil ought to do everything so that foreign companies would come to the country'; on the other hand, only 25% would not permit any new foreign firms to enter the country or would nationalize existing ones. The modal response (44%), in Brazil as in Mexico, was that 'foreign capital could contribute to the development of Brazil and Brazil ought, with some care, to act so that some selected foreign companies would come to the country'[86]. Thus the Brazilian mass public, too, endorsed selectivity toward foreign firms.

Business elites shared these views. In 1962, 136 executives from Brazilian-owned firms employing over 200 people in São Paulo, Guanabara and Minas Gerais were asked about Instruction 113, approved in 1955, allowing liberalized foreign exchange rules for the importation of machinery and equipment for transnational firms (it was impossible for a wholly Brazilian-owned firm to use it). Of 125 executives responding, 38% were unfavorable, 32% had mixed feelings, and only 30% were favorable to this key regulation that allowed the growth of direct foreign investment. The executives agreed (58%) that Instruction 113 was good for Brazil – it was just not good for their firms[87]. Opposition to Instruction 113 was greatest among the largest and most powerful Brazilian firms[88], whose large or larger multinational competitors benefited from the measure. Small businessmen were probably less likely to be able to use complex monetary procedures, nor were the new foreign firms necessarily competing with them. However, small business in urban Brazil was not by any means in favor of foreign firms: by a 2 to 1 margin they favored their expropriation in 1965 (*Table 2.5*). Thus, as in Mexico and Colombia, the growth of direct foreign investment in manufacturing divided the industrial sector at first.

Behavior

Brazilian industrialists also divided in their lobbying behavior. The campaign against Instruction 113 was led by the Federation of Industries of the State of São Paulo (FIESP), while the larger National Association of Manufacturers (CNI) remained quiet. Conflicts also arose between the state federations of industry in national bourgeois São Paulo and transnationalist Guanabara. When Brazilian industrialists acted together in the late 1950s and early 1960s, however, the national bourgeois tendencies prevailed. The CNI orchestrated a successful campaign against making Instruction 113 available to American Can Company, and it stopped Hilton Hotel investments[89]. The CNI appeared rather nationalist to the US embassy, which credited it with a leading, though unpublicized, role in the passage of a profits remittance bill in 1962 and with financing 'the campaigns of extreme, politically active groups, including the Communists, when their interests coincide'. The campaign against American Can Co. included student demonstrations too[90]. The sharpened conflict over foreign investment may have increased support for expropriation of large foreign firms well above the levels of earlier years. In 1962, 38.1% of 3238 urban Brazilians supported their expropriation. By 1965, however, there had been essentially no further increase of support: 41.2% of 1759 urban Brazilians supported expropriation of large foreign firms then[91]. The Brazilian governments that followed the 1964 military coup were more hospitable toward private foreign investment and may have put a cap on pro-expropriation attitudes. The Castelo Branco government modified the rules of the game in favor of foreign capital, despite the protests formulated by members of the national business community, especially those from the state of São Paulo.

National bourgeois policies were gradually reasserted. All financial institutions were required to allocate at least half of their credit operations to firms majority-owned by Brazilian nationals by the late 1960s[92].

The consolidation of the national bourgeois coalition occurred only in the second half of the 1970s as the 'political opening' provided new means for national business to assert itself. Under pressure from national industrialists, especially from the state of São Paulo, Brazil's National Economic Development Bank (BNDE) slashed interest rates on loans to majority-owned Brazilian firms to buy Brazilian-made machinery and equipment. 'Buy Brazilian' regulations for state agencies were tightened. Brazilian industrialists pressed for easier credit facilities, tax relief, and selective relief from price controls. In response to pressures from local manufacturers, especially in the capital goods sector, to protect their oligopoly position, the Industrial

Development Council (CDI) began to use its fiscal incentives more selectively. By early 1977, BNDE and CDI had tightened up policies on importing machinery and equipment, denied incentives to new foreign investments in capital goods and eased credits for the sale or purchase of industrial equipment made in Brazil, denying them both to foreign-owned firms manufacturing capital goods or to firms seeking to buy such goods from new foreign-owned firms in Brazil. The president of the Brazilian Capital Goods Manufacturing Association (ABDIB) hailed these measures as 'making the entrance of foreign capital difficult'[93].

Specific cases illustrate the consolidation of national bourgeois policies. The Ministry of Industry and Commerce blocked the sale of 100% of equity of Consul SA, a locally owned refrigerator maker, to Philips of Holland in 1975. The project that was approved ensured a Brazilian equity majority in association with Whirlpool. The Metal Structure Manufacturers' Association urged the ministry to block a new plant by Kawasaki Heavy Industries at Curitiba because local firms were already manufacturing those goods. West Germany's Demag obtained CDI incentives for a project in Minas Gerais but was denied access to cheap credit by BNDE's subsidiary FINAME because of the opposition by São Paulo equipment producers to a new competitor[94]. The machinery industry syndicate of the state of São Paulo and the Brazilian Machinery Industry Association began work on a code in 1978 to ban foreign investment in certain fields 'adequately attended' by local firms so as 'not to pulverize the market' – i.e. to preserve local oligopolies.

CDI turned down a request by Elliott, a subsidiary of the US Carrier Corp., for tax incentives to manufacture steam turbines for oil prospecting. Elliott was supported in its bid by its eventual customer, the Brazilian petroleum state enterprise Petrobras, because the turbines produced by existing Brazilian firms did not comply with American Petroleum Industry standards. Zanini and Dedini, both Brazilian capital goods manufacturers, enlisted the support of another state enterprise, Embramec, a holding company of the BNDE, which believed that the nascent capital goods sector had to be protected and that Brazil did not need a third manufacturer of turbines. The president of ABDIB argued that multinational subsidiaries 'do damage to the economy taking up room that could be filled by a Brazilian company that was really developing its technology'. ABDIB said that they were 'not against foreign capital, but we are totally opposed to the absurdity of allowing or, what is worse, encouraging, the entry of foreign companies into areas that are already well served by national companies'. The case pitted state enterprises against each other, and also revealed that some nationalist claims of Brazilian firms are more grounded in competitive self-interest than in diffuse nationalism. Zanini produced turbines through a subsidiary, AEG Turbinas, a joint venture 30% owned by the German AEG–Kanis Turbinenfabrik; and Dedini entered into negotiations with

Elliott in 1978 to establish a joint venture (Dedini itself was 25% owned by Kawasaki and C. Itoh). Similarly, the Brazilian northeast development agency (SUDENE) vetoed a proposal by Hughes Tool do Brasil, a wholly foreign-owned subsidiary, to manufacture extra long life hard rock oil drill bits. CDI also denied it fiscal incentives. Both responded to ABDIB claims that these were already manufactured by a Brazilian producer. And yet, in this case, Hughes went ahead anyway, assured by Petrobras of a ready market for its product[95].

The Brazilian government agency regulating the electronic data-processing industry (CAPRE) set down criteria in 1977 to select three firms to participate in a tight oligopoly for the manufacture of minicomputers; one of the three would be the Brazilian state enterprise COBRA, which used technology from the UK's Ferranti (which owns 25% of COBRA's equity) and from US Sycor. The criteria included local equity participation, high local content, and unrestricted use of technology. At that time, over four-fifths of the Brazilian minicomputer market was supplied by three foreign firms. Data General Corp. complained to the US government that Brazil was setting up an oligopoly to halt the export of minicomputers to Brazil and to discriminate against 100% foreign-owned subsidiaries. US officials brought up the subject in trade talks with Brazil, and put the matter on the GATT negotiating agenda, complaining about the abrupt cutting off of US minicomputer exports to Brazil. Fearing stiffer competition, COBRA lobbied strongly against choosing any multinational enterprise subsidiary; Brazilian firms also lobbied strongly to the same end. The Brazilian government agreed; it decided to restrict the minicomputer market entirely to Brazilian firms. In addition to COBRA, three other firms were selected that used Japanese, French and German technology, and were in no case more than 25% foreign owned. As a part of this policy, IBM was subsequently denied a request to import 300 minicomputers into Brazil. As a consequence of this policy, COBRA had captured about 90% of the minicomputer market by mid-1979. The Brazilian government has also been looking for ways to extend national bourgeois policies to the manufacturing of medium-sized computers and of peripheral equipment, but its policies in 1979–80 were still somewhat contradictory in these areas. At least in minicomputers, Brazil appeared willing to forgo the possibility of obtaining the best technology, especially because COBRA only assembled imported computer components (lacking its own research and development capability), for the sake of bolstering local state and private firms associated with less well-known international firms. This policy also contributed to inflation, since COBRA's computers cost much more than prevailing international prices[96].

National bourgeois advocacy is strongly linked to the self-interest of the firm. Brazil's Ministry of Transportation awarded a contract to supply locomotives to the national railway system to two Brazilian firms,

Equipamentos Villares SA and Engenharia e Maquinas SA, that had never manufactured locomotives in the past. The loser was a subsidiary of General Electric, one of the oldest operating in Brazil, which had long been the sole manufacturer of locomotives in the country. Carlos Villares, the president of one of the two successful firms, had been the head of ABDIB during its campaign for discrimination in favor of local firms and against subsidiaries of foreign firms. Similarly, in mid-1978 the Brazilian government awarded the entire huge contract for the Itaipú hydroelectric project to a consortium of European, Brazilian and Paraguayan firms. The winning Consorcio Industrial Electromecanica (CIEM) was led by Mecanica Pesada, a subsidiary of the French Schneider group, in association with French, German and Swiss firms along with Bardella SA, a leading Brazilian capital goods firm, and a consortium of small Paraguayan firms. Neither US bid included locally owned Brazilian firms, only subsidiaries of US and Japanese based enterprises. The CIEM bid had the highest local content component of all the bids. The inclusion of the small Paraguayan firms served well Brazil's policy of linking Paraguay to Brazil through the Itaipú project. And the president of the key firm, Bardella, was Claudio Bardella, then head of ABDIB[97].

The government of President General João Figueiredo (1979–1985) sought to reduce some of the more overt state subsidies to the Brazilian economy in order to increase its efficiency and competitiveness, although national bourgeois policies remained at the center of the new economic design. For example, a large package of policy changes announced in December 1979 reduced many government subsidies to all types of firms operating in Brazil. Among others, the law that prevented tax or duty reductions on imported products similar to those already produced in Brazil would be phased out. However, the local capital goods sector would still be exempted from much of the impact of the law's repeal. Earlier in 1979 the Figueiredo government announced the sale of a number of state industrial firms to the private sector. However, only firms whose 'incontestable' control was in Brazilian hands could bid for such purchases, and the BNDE exercised its veto right against the resale of former state firms by a Brazilian firm to a foreign firm. The National Monetary Council also changed its policies early in 1979, requiring banks to reserve half of their funds for private Brazilian-controlled firms; before then, the reserved half included national private firms and state firms. The change freed national private firms from competition from both state and multinational firms. Thus even the Figueiredo government policies that reduced state subsidies or that sold off state firms maintained faith with the evolving national bourgeois policy milieu[98].

In sum, the spread of foreign investments in manufacturing divided the Brazilian business community, but national bourgeois views and behavior eventually came to prevail. Although in the late 1960s and early 1970s transnationalist government policies were more evident in Brazil than in Mexico, Brazilian business, led by capital goods producers, worked to turn Brazilian government policy around in the second half of the 1970s by taking advantage of the more open political climate. The national bourgeois behavior of the leading Brazilian firms was intimately tied to their own self-interest. The strategy of nationalism was rational for the firm: the protection of its own local oligopoly, even recognizing that the interests of the country and those of the firm were not always identical. Brazilian businessmen criticized the spread of both multinational enterprises and state enterprises. They argued eloquently, albeit self-interestedly, about the role of the Brazilian private sector in the country's future. And they sought to enlist core government agencies to assist them in their struggle against these two competing firm types[99]. They thus sought simultaneously to expand the state to regulate the foreigner and to curtail it otherwise at home. That was the mark of national capitalism[100].

2.8   Implications and conclusions

The attitudes and behavior of national business in Latin America have shifted during the past three decades. The open transnational embrace of the 1940s had become a far cooler handshake in the late 1970s. The ties between transnational and national business have not been broken and, short of an unlikely repeat of the Cuban experience, are not likely to be. Business nationalism ordinarily stops well short of general advocacy of the socialization of foreign-owned manufacturing firms or the closure of borders to foreign investment. National business thus keeps the essential elements of the faith of international capitalism. But, just below that standard, views have changed dramatically.

Primarily for political reasons, national business in Chile, Peru and Venezuela, as earlier in Mexico, supported the socialization of existing foreign-owned firms in natural resources and in utilities. It usually remained united in a policy shift from an early transnational coalition to a limited statist coalition that sealed the fate of these foreign firms. In a changed political climate, Chilean business came to prefer nationalization to socialization – but it continued to exclude the transnationalization of existing copper firms.

Changes in industrial structure also led to changes in business attitudes. That, in turn, altered business political activity, eventually helping to reshape government policy. National bourgeois attitudes and behavior in the manufacturing sector have led to the advocacy and implementation of selective and discriminatory national government policies to favor national firms at the expense of foreign-owned firms. The preference for laissez-faire and for the avoidance of government intervention in the economy is focused only on state enterprises; it takes a back-seat to national business use of political resources to redress the perceived imbalance in the marketplace that favors foreign firms. The creation or defense of local oligopolies becomes the preferred policy of large locally owned firms. Nationalization policies, through joint ventures or other means, come to receive widespread national business support.

Business nationalism is thus neither diffuse nor irrational from the point of view of the firm, nor merely serving some psychological need. Nor is it necessarily for the good of the whole country, the increase of national welfare, or the public interest. A far more plausible explanation is that it serves the firm's needs for a secure and predictable environment better than any alternative: it reduces competition, protects profits, and generates a protected market in government contracts. It maximizes the material income of national firms as well as the 'psychic income' of their owners[101]. The early strategy of national firms led to the erection of tariffs for protection against competition through foreign trade. The more recent strategy leads to the erection of new barriers against the entry of new foreign firms, and to making nationally owned firms the predominant supplier of the national government and its enterprises. The barriers are not absolute; they do not close the border. Instead, they typically rely on discriminatory policies of taxation, credit access and government purchases.

Business nationalism in manufacturing ordinarily begins in small local firms and then spreads throughout the business structure to those firms that find competition rather than complementarity from multinationals. Investment in manufacturing thus first divides national business, and only much later may reunite it. Whenever such manufacturing investments are still quite limited, as in Chile or Peru, large national industrial business firms may remain in a transnational coalition. Whenever such investments increase rapidly, the shift from transnational to national bourgeois behavior may be especially abrupt, as in Venezuela. The national bourgeoisie may not always succeed. There may be setbacks, as in the decade following the 1964 military coup in Brazil or in the years since the 1976 coup in Argentina. There are occasional, tactical re-enactments of a transnational business coalition, for limited purposes, against government policies (as in Mexico in the mid-1970s and in Argentina in 1980–81). But the long-term trend across countries suggests a strong and persistent shift away from transnationalism and toward national bourgeois attitudes and behavior.

In the long run, the two groups whose attitudes concerning policies toward foreign investment have changed the most have been the armed forces and national business. The poor had been consistently unconcerned with it; intellectuals, in the aggregate, had been consistently and predictably hostile. The concerns of the armed forces are now typically focused on natural resources and other 'basic' endeavors for national security, while national business may be more significant for other sectors of the economy.

As in Brazil, national business may be able to mobilize military support for its own benefit by extending the national security mantle to the benefit of nationally owned firms in the capital goods sector.

As the private sector divides between nationally and foreign-owned firms, new possibilities of political alliances in Latin American countries, which may nudge national bourgeois business in fresh directions, are opened up but thus far little exploited[102]. National bourgeois attitudes would make it more difficult, though not impossible, for governments to persist in pursuing indefinitely a relatively unqualified open borders policy, as Brazil did in the late 1960s or Argentina in the late 1970s. They would also highlight a conflict between the development of a nationally owned, deepened industrial structure, on the one hand, and access to the newest technology, lower prices, and more efficient penetration of foreign markets, on the other hand[103]. A deeper industrial structure, with strong roots in the national economy, was once possible through the imposition of local content and related requirements on the subsidiaries of multinational firms – a strategy quite compatible with export promotion and access to new technology. But the rise of a more vibrant national business community raises the issue of local control along with even higher local content challenging the package of presumed benefits that multinational enterprises could provide. National governments may now have a strategic choice in achieving further and deeper industrial development. One relies on multinational enterprises with benefits in export markets, lower inflation, and top technology but at the cost of less local content and control; the other relies on national business where the costs and benefits are reversed.

The implications for foreign-owned firms, and for their parent multinational enterprises, are already evident to many of them. A survey of 100 US firms affiliated with the Council of the Americas, conducted between August and December of 1970, showed that a third of the 15 firms in extractive sectors, but only 15% of the 48 manufacturing firms, feared expropriation. On the other hand, 60% of the firms in extractive sectors and 50% of those in manufacturing feared restrictive economic policies; in their responses to an open-ended question, 9 of the 100 firms explained the rise of economic nationalism in Latin America by referring specifically to the hostility against foreign investment found among Latin American businessmen[104]. Some national bourgeois policies already have international implications, as in Andean Pact regulations on foreign investment, and in the effort led by Mexican business members of the Association of Latin American Industrialists of the Latin American Free Trade Association (changed in 1980 to the Latin American Integration Association) to reduce foreign firm competition with existing Latin American enterprises by channeling foreign direct investment only into new sectors not covered by national firms, and by avoiding an 'incentives race' among governments to attract foreign investment[105].

Conflicts arising out of government selectivity and discrimination in policies toward foreign-owned firms to benefit nationally owned firms may become more frequent. Regardless of the future of expropriation policies, the growth of the mix of industrial and political problems of discrimination is evident. The responses of foreign firms may also become more complex. Some will become more 'national', retaining only 49% foreign-firm ownership in order to receive beneficial national firm treatment. The 'enemy' of the multinational enterprises also shifts away from historical, predictable nationalists on the political left to a part of national business. 'Allies' may include parts of national governments and some state enterprises along with portions of the national business community. Multinational enterprises will divide: those that become 'national' may seek to discriminate against newer multinational entrants into national markets, while others seek to retain longer their more distinct multinationality.

The United States government may discover new problems, too. One theme of US policies toward Latin America has been to enable these countries to become masters of their affairs, and to promote the growth of an internal social base of support against communism and toward free enterprise through strong, confident and capable national governments and business. Latin American business is certainly anti-communist, and it has a strong preference to limit government control over its own affairs. It has flourished vigorously in the recent past, yet its emergence, far from leading to a harmony of interest with the United States, has created new problems. Born behind national government protection, Latin American business continues to rely on new forms of governmental protection to squeeze US-based firms, in response in part to the alleged crowding out effects felt from the growth of multinational enterprises. Support for some aspects of a relatively classic 'liberal' economic order at home has not expanded into support for a classic 'liberal' international economic order without important qualifications. The early qualifications included impediments to free trade; the newer qualifications include impediments on multinational firm investments and operations. Discrimination in trade has spilled over to discrimination in access to local credit, government purchases of goods and services, fiscal and other incentives, as well as the reservation of sectors of economic activity for national firms alone. New oligopolies are a part of national policy, shutting off some US exports and preventing some US direct investments.

US government policy is complicated by additional factors. Expropriation cases focus the attention of government agencies and of the presidency more easily. Discrimination cases are less likely to warrant sustained presidential or high official attention. Their lower level of importance may also make it more difficult to build a transorganizational consensus within the US government about appropriate policies, which may lead to disarray within the US government, abetted by an even greater disarray within US-owned firms. Banks that are lending to the governments and national firms engaging in and benefiting from limited discriminatory policies against foreign firms may not wish to see any US government retaliation. Some US firms in minority equity positions in some Latin American countries may be national enough to benefit from the discrimination against another US-based firm. Cross-pressures within the US private sector are likely to be far stronger than in the simpler expropriation cases. The 'enemy' will be blurred, too. It will include some US-based firms as well as the subsidiaries of multinational firms based in countries that are US allies. The purely internal enemy may include a Latin American business community that supports US policy on many issues that do not touch on the survival of their own firms. US government and firm allies may include parts of the host government as well as other national firms. The rise of national bourgeois attitudes and behavior in Latin America, in sum, may signal the successful end of past US policies and preferences intended to achieve the emergence of competent national Latin American public and private elites. The US government now faces the hell of success.

Acknowledgements

I am grateful to my co-authors, and also to Susan Kaufman Purcell, Philippe Schmitter, Francisco Sercovich, Lawrence Whitehead, Van R. Whiting, Jr. and Raymond Vernon for comments on earlier drafts. Of course, I am responsible for having paid insufficient heed to some of their perceptive criticism. I am also grateful to Dr Leo P. Crespi, of the Office of Research of the US Information Agency and later of the US International Communication Agency, for making available to me a number of publications by these agencies that are cited in the notes.

Notes

1 Ronald H. Chilcote and Joel C. Edelstein, 'Alternative Perspectives of Development and Underdevelopment in Latin America'. In their *Latin America: The Struggle with Dependency and Beyond*. Wiley, New York, 1974, pp. 51, 53, 56.

2 James Petras and Thomas Cook, 'Dependency and the Industrial Bourgeoisie: Attitudes of Argentine Executives toward Foreign Economic Investment and US Policy'. In James Petras (ed.) *Latin America: From Dependence to Revolution*. Wiley, New York, 1973, p. 163.

3 Oswaldo Sunkel, 'Capitalismo transnacional y desintegración nacional'. *Estudios internacionales*, 4 (16), January–March 1971.

4 Gustavo Esteva, 'El comercio exterior de México en el proceso de planeación'. *Foro internacional*, 6 (22–23), October 1965–March 1966, p. 352.

5 Frank Brandenburg, *The Development of Latin American Private Enterprise*. Planning Pamphlet no. 121, National Planning Association, Washington, 1964, p. 46.

6 So argued the 'Linowitz Commission'. See Commission on United States–Latin American Relations, *The Americas in a Changing World*. Quadrangle Books, New York, 1975, p. 36.

7 Nelson A. Rockefeller, *The Rockefeller Report on the Americas*. Quadrangle Books, New York, 1969, p. 89.

8 See Abraham F. Lowenthal, ' "Liberal," "Radical," and Bureaucratic" Perspectives on US–Latin American Policy: The Alliance for Progress in Retrospect', and Christopher Mitchell, 'Dominance and Fragmentation in US–Latin American Policy'. In Julio Cotler and Richard Fagen (eds), *Latin America and the United States: The Changing Political Realities*. Stanford University Press, Stanford, Calif., 1974; and Arthur Schlesinger, Jr., 'The Alliance for Progress: A Retrospective'. In Ronald Hellman and H. Jon Rosenbaum (eds), *Latin America: The Search for a New International Role*. Sage Publications, New York, 1975.

9 Unless otherwise identified, all computations are based on data concerning US investments from US Department of Commerce, Office of Business Economics, *Survey of Current Business*, 36 (8), August 1956, p. 19; 41 (8), August 1961, p. 22; 46 (9), September 1966, p. 34; 52 (11), November 1972, pp. 28–9; 56 (8), August 1976, p. 49; and 60 (8), August 1980, p. 27.

10 Computed from Herbert K. May and José Antonio Fernández Arena, *Impact of Foreign Investment in Mexico*. National Chamber Federation, Washington, DC, no date, p. 19.

11 Computed from Bernardo Sepúlveda Amor, 'Política industrial y empresas transnacionales'. In Bernardo Sepúlveda Amor, Olga Pellicer de Brody and Lorenzo Meyer (eds), *Las empresas transnacionales en México*. El Colegio de México, Mexico, 1974, pp. 51, 158–61; *Business Latin America*, 10 June 1981, pp. 182–3.

12 Computed from Stefan H. Robock, *Brazil: A Study in Development Progress*. Lexington Books, Lexington, Mass., 1975, p. 67.

13 Business International Corp., *Operating Successfully in a Changing Brazil*, New York, 1975, p. 49; and James Schlagheck, *The Political, Economic and Labor Climate in Brazil*. Wharton School, Philadelphia, 1977, p. 17.

14 Computed from Gilberto Arango Londoño, *Estructura económica colombiana*. Banco de Comercio, Bogotá, 1972, pp. 244–5.

15 Laura Randall, *An Economic History of Argentina in the Twentieth Century*. Columbia University Press, New York, 1978, p. 236.

16 Computed from José Antonio Mayobre, *Las inversiones extranjeras en Venezuela*. Monte Avila, eds, Caracas, 1970, p. 32.

17 For general arguments, see Raymond Vernon, *Sovereignty at Bay: The Multinational Spread of US Enterprises*. Basic Books, New York, 1971, Ch. 2; and Raymond F. Mikesell, 'Conflict in Foreign Investor–Host Country Relations: A Preliminary Analysis'. In R. F. Mikesell (ed.), *Foreign Investment in the Petroleum and Mineral Industries*. The Johns Hopkins Press, Baltimore, 1971, Ch. 2. Some of the best case studies with broader theoretical implications, done with Latin American material, are cited subsequently.

18 Secondary analysis of the US Information Agency's 1965 World Survey III. Data stored at the Roper Center, Yale University.

19 Theodore H. Moran, *Multinational Corporations and the Politics of Dependence: Copper in Chile*. Princeton University Press, Princeton, 1974, pp. 172–215; *Business Latin America*, 4 October 1978, p. 320.

20 Albert Lauterbach, *Managerial Attitudes in Chile*. Instituto de Economía, University of Chile, Santiago, 1961, pp. 3–6, 55–6.

21 Dale L. Johnson, 'The National and Progressive Bourgeoisie in Chile'. *Studies in Comparative International Development*, 4 (4), 1968–1969, pp. 64, 70–1.

22 Nancy S. Truitt and David H. Blake, *Opinion Leaders and Private Investment*. Fund for Multinational Management Education, New York, 1976, pp. 6–9, 12, 64, 82–3, 107. Chi-square tests reported in the text, computed on the original data, were never significant at the .01 level for one degree of freedom.

23 *Business Latin America*, 12 January 1977, p. 16; 13 September 1978, p. 296.

24 ibid., 14 December 1977, p. 395; and 19 April 1978, p. 123.

25 James Petras suggests this hypothesis in *Politics and Social Forces in Chilean*

Development. University of California Press, Berkeley, 1970, p. 48.

26 Charles T. Goodsell, *American Corporations and Peruvian Politics*. Harvard University Press, Cambridge, Mass., 1974, pp. 113–15. Goodsell argues, however, that there was a general increase of support for expropriation, whereas the case for selectivity seems to me to be stronger.

27 ibid., pp. 88–90.

28 George M. Ingram, *Expropriation of US Property in South America*. Praeger, New York, 1974, pp. 69, 75–6.

29 Goodsell (note 26), p. 217.

30 'Declaration Made by the Representatives of the Peruvian Private Sector'. In Daniel Sharp (ed), *US Foreign Policy and Peru*. University of Texas Press, Austin, 1972, pp. 287–8.

31 *Business Latin America*, 17 May 1973, p. 160; 25 January 1978, p. 32; *Latin America Economic Report*, 5 (36), 16 September 1977, p. 143.

32 For a superb discussion of the relationship between the Peruvian state and foreign capital, see Alfred Stepan, *The State and Society: Peru in Comparative Perspective*. Princeton University Press, Princeton, 1978, Ch. 7.

33 Franklin Tugwell, *The Politics of Oil in Venezuela*. Stanford University Press, Stanford, Calif., 1975, pp. 79–81, 88–91, 95, 114–15, 120, 160–2.

34 William G. Harris, 'The Impact of the Petroleum Export Industry on the Pattern of Venezuelan Economic Development'. In Mikesell (note 17), pp. 141–2.

35 Albert Lauterbach, *Enterprise in Latin America: Business Attitudes in a Developing Economy*. Cornell University Press, Ithaca, 1966, pp. 102, 117–22.

36 José A. Silva Michelena, *The Illusion of Democracy in Dependent Nations*. The MIT Press, Cambridge, Mass., 1971, p. 197. There is also a discrepancy between two US Information Agency (USIA) surveys. A secondary analysis of its 1962 national survey, 'The Alliance for Progress' (USIA – LA 13), shows pluralities of small business and of manual workers favoring expropriation of foreign firms, in response to the same question reported in *Table 2.5* only for Caracas respondents in 1965. It is unclear whether three years made the difference, or whether it is a difference between metropolitan Caracas and a national sample. The 1962 and the 1965 surveys are consistent, however, in that in neither are there any statistically significant differences between small business and manual workers toward expropriation. Consensus prevailed at both times, but its content was rather different. Because surveys outside Caracas were less reliable and because the other evidence suggests that these 1962 results may be anomalous, they are not emphasized in the analysis. Data stored at the Roper Center, Yale University.

37 US Information Agency, Office of Research and Assessment, 'US Standing in Foreign Public Opinion Following the President's Visit to China', R-27-72, 16 May 1972, pp. 8, 28.

38 ibid., 'Foreign Images of External Threat and Expectations of US Defense Assistance'. R-51-72, 25 October 1972, pp. 3, 21.

39 Computed from ibid., 'US Standing in Caracas, Venezuela, Following the President's Visit to China'. R-35-72, 25 August 1972, p. 3.

40 ibid., 'Venezuelan Opinion on Nationalization of Oil and Attitudes toward Foreign Investment'. N-1-75, 8 September 1975, pp. 2, 4, 8, 10.

41 Computed chi-squares were 26.090, 15.029 and 35.167 respectively, all significant at the .001 level for one degree of freedom.

42 Data from Truitt and Blake (note 22), pp. 12, 86–7.

43 ibid., pp. 31, 117; David E. Blank, *Politics in Venezuela*. Little Brown, Boston, 1973, p. 223; Lawrence G. Franko, 'Joint International Business Ventures in Developing Countries: Mystique and Realities'. In Robert B. Williamson, William P. Glade, and Karl M. Schmitt (eds), *Latin American–US Economic Interactions*. American Enterprise Institute, Washington DC, 1974, pp. 238–9.

44 *Business Latin America*, 19 September 1979, p. 297; 7 January 1981, pp. 2–3.

45 Truitt and Blake (note 22), p. 110. Computations of chi-square statistics, however, did not show statistically significant differences at the .01 level for one degree of freedom either on the issue of competition or on the general economic issues between business, government or student leaders.

46 Seymour W. Wurfel, *Foreign Enterprise in Colombia*. University of North Carolina Press, Chapel Hill, 1965, p. 78.

47 William P. McGreevey, *An Economic History of Colombia*. Cambridge University Press, Cambridge, 1971.

48 Brandenburg (note 5), p. 46.

49 Lauterbach (note 20), pp. 193–4.

50 Aaron Lipman, *The Colombian Entrepreneur in Bogotá*. University of Miami Press, Coral Gables, 1969, pp. 23, 38, 107–8. The reported chi-square test was not statistically significant at the .01 level for one degree of freedom.

51 Secondary analysis of the US Information Agency's 'The Alliance for Progress' (USIA – LA 13) 1962 survey for Colombia. Data stored at the Roper Center, Yale University. As was the case for other countries in 1965 (see *Table 2.5*), there were no statistically significant differences on this question between small business and manual labor (chi-square was 1.066 for one degree of freedom).

52 US Information Agency, Office of Research, 'Opinions Regarding Foreign Investment in Colombia'. R-34-71, 17 December 1971, pp. b, 1, 2, 4.

53 ibid, pp. 27, 29.

54 Gail Richardson Sherman, 'Colombian Political Bases of the Andean Pact Statute on Foreign Capital', *Journal of Inter-American Studies and World Affairs*, 15 (1), February 1973, pp. 111–14, 119–20.

55 John Carlsen, 'Colombia's Policies on Private Foreign Investment and Foreign Technology'. In John Carlsen and Peter Neers, *Peru's and Colombia's Policies on Private Foreign Investment and Foreign Technology*. Institute for Development Research, Copenhagen, Danish Private Business, D74.1, May 1974, pp. 51, 56, 65; and Constantine V. Vaitsos, 'The Changing Policies of Latin American Governments toward Economic Development and Direct Foreign Investment'. In Williamson, Glade and Schmitt (eds) (note 43), p. 100.

56 *Latin America Economic Report*, 2 (16), 26 April 1974; 2 (49), 13 December 1974, pp. 193–4; *Business Latin America*, 23 January 1974, p. 31; 8 October 1975, p. 322; 17 March 1976, p. 82.

57 *Latin America Economic Report*, 2 (13), 29 March 1974, p. 49; 2(47), 29 November 1974, p. 185; *Business Latin America*, 4 January 1973, p. 6; 21 January 1976, p. 18; 25 January 1978, p. 30; 20 May 1979, p. 175; 23 July 1980, p. 234.

58 *Polls*, 2 (3) Spring 1967, p. 30.

59 Jeane Kirkpatrick, *Leader and Vanguard in Mass Society: A Study of Peronist Argentina*. The MIT Press, Cambridge, Mass., 1971, pp. 193–4. The computed chi-square reported in the text was 16.883, significant at the .001 level for one degree of freedom.

60 *Hanson's Latin American Letter*, no. 1463, 31 March 1973, p. 2.

61 Petras and Cook (note 2), pp. 148–58, 166. The two chi-square statistics computed were 8.395, significant at the .01 level for one degree of freedom, and 1.383, which was not so. Petras and Cook reached different conclusions in their analysis of the same data. They were more impressed with the overall support for US policy and capitalism, and by the willingness of Argentine industrialists to work with foreign firms. This is, of course, the upper limit of business nationalism. However, the preference for selectivity and discrimination is more significant for the daily life of the firm and for the conduct of national affairs than the other more cosmic issues, short of the choice made in Latin America only by Cuba.

62 Secondary analysis of 'Economics and Politics' (OP 039). Data deposited at the Roper Center, Yale University. Differences in small businessmen's views about actual and ideal foreign capital participation were statistically significant at the .001 level, chi-square equal to 292.995; differences among big businessmen were insignificant at the .01 level, chi-square equal to 0.279 (both for one degree of freedom).

63 Richard D. Mallon with Juan V. Sourrouille, *Economic Policymaking in a Conflict Society: The Argentine Case*. Harvard University Press, Cambridge, Mass., 1975, p. 28.

64 Randall (note 15), p. 167; *Business Latin America*, 18 July 1968, p. 226; 22 August 1968, p. 267; 2 April 1970, pp. 105–6.

65 *Business Latin America*, 31 May 1973, p. 169; 28 November 1973, p. 381; 28 July 1976, p. 238; 10 August 1977, p. 255.

66 Argentina, Ministry of Economy, Coordination and Economic Planning Secretariat, *Economic Information on Argentina* no. 101, November 1979, pp. 44–5; *Business Latin America*, 14 March 1979, p. 84.

67 *Business Latin America*, 7 February 1979, p. 48; 4 April 1979, p. 112; 20 June 1979, p. 196; and 15 October 1980, p. 334.

68 Raymond Vernon, *The Dilemma of Mexico's Development*. Harvard Uni-

versity Press, Cambridge, Mass., 1963, pp. 161–2.

69 ibid., pp. 163–75; Olga Pellicer de Brody, 'El llamado a las inversiones extranjeras, 1953–1958'. In Sepúlveda, Pellicer de Brody and Meyer (note 11), pp. 93–101; Alexander Bohrisch and Wolfgang Konig, 'La política mexicana sobre inversiones extranjeras'. *Jornadas*, **62**, 1968, pp. 48–9; and Robert J. Shafer, *Mexican Business Organizations*. Syracuse University Press, Syracuse, NY, 1973, pp. 105, 118; Dale Story, 'Industrialists, the State and Public Policy in Mexico'. Paper presented at the National Convention of the Latin American Studies Association, Bloomington, Ind., 1980, pp. 19–20.

70 Joseph A. Kahl, *The Measurement of Modernism*. University of Texas Press, Austin, 1968, pp. 25–6, 104.

71 US Information Agency, Office of Research and Assessment, 'Foreign Evaluation of US Policies Following the President's Visit to China', R-39-72, 1 September 1972, pp. 3, 38; and 'US Standing in Mexico City between the President's China and USSR Visits'. R-47-72, 3 October 1972, p. 13.

72 Flavia Derossi, *The Mexican Entrepreneur*. Development Centre of the Organization for Economic Cooperation and Development, Paris, 1971, pp. 11, 73, 77–80, 208–9, 226.

73 US Information Agency, Office of Research, 'Mexican Elite Attitudes toward Foreign Investment'. R-7-74, 16 May 1974, pp. 1–2.

74 ibid., pp. 4–6. No chi-square test was statistically significant at the .01 level for one degree of freedom.

75 ibid., pp. 12–13. No chi-square test was statistically significant at the .01 level for one degree of freedom.

76 Soledad Loaeza, 'La política del rumor: México, noviembre–diciembre de 1976', *Foro internacional*. In Centro de Estudios Internacionales, *Las crisis en el sistema político mexicano (1928–1977)*. El Colegio de México, Mexico, 1977, pp. 119–50.

77 ibid., p. 4; and US International Communication Agency, Office of Research and Evaluation, 'US Investment in Mexico: Attitudes of Key Mexican Elite Groups', R-29-78, 18 October 1978, p. 1 and Table 9. No chi-square test was statistically significant at the .01 level for one degree of freedom.

78 'US Investment in Mexico', Tables 7, 9 and 14.

79 ibid., Tables 12, 13, 16.

80 ibid., Tables 20–23.

81 See Carlos Arriola, 'Los grupos empresariales frente al Estado (1973–1975)'. *Foro internacional*, **16** (4), April–June 1976, pp. 449–86.

82 Miguel S. Wionczek, *El nacionalismo mexicano y la inversión extranjera*. Siglo XXI, Mexico, 1967, pp. 44, 46, 59, 70, 85, 95, 100, 130, 133, 148–52, 223–9, 256–9, 266–7, 291, 301–4. For a somewhat different emphasis, see Marco Antonio Alcázar, 'Las agrupaciones patronales en Mexico'. *Jornadas*, **66**, 1970, pp. 84–90.

83 Shafer (note 69), p. 324; *Business Latin America*, 3 October 1968, p. 317; 4 January 1973, p. 2; 16 November 1977, pp. 361–2; 10 June 1981, pp. 182–3.

84 *Business Latin America*, 21 February 1979, p. 64; 23 May 1979, p. 161.

85 Lloyd A. Free, *Some International Implications of the Political Psychology of Brazilians*. Institute for International Social Research, Princeton, 1961, pp. 26–7, 34.

86 Kahl (note 70), p. 104.

87 Raimar Richers *et al.*, *Impacto da ação do govêrno sôbre as emprêsas brasileiras*. Fundação Getúlio Vargas, Rio de Janeiro, 1963, pp. 5, 16–17, 19–20, 118–20.

88 Nathaniel H. Leff, *Economic Policy-Making and Development in Brazil, 1947–1964*. Wiley, New York, 1968, p. 64.

89 ibid., p. 65; and Philippe C. Schmitter, *Interest Conflict and Political Change in Brazil*. Stanford University Press, Stanford, Calif., 1971, pp. 350–1. See also Brandenburg (note 5), p. 46. For a Marxist history of Brazil's national bourgeoisie, see Nelson Werneck Sodré, *História da burguesia brasileira* (3rd edition). Civilização Brasileira, Rio de Janeiro, 1976, especially pp. 354–66 on the post-World War II period. Although the approach is different, its findings are quite consistent with those of this chapter: 'The bourgeoisie of developing countries clashes with the interests of imperialism' (p. 355).

90 Philip Raine, *Brazil: Awakening Giant*. Public Affairs Press, Washington, DC, 1974, p. 140. Raine was Political Counselor of the US embassy at the time. See also Leff (note 88), p. 65.

91 Secondary analyses of US Information Agency's 'The Alliance for Progress'

(USIA – LA 13) in 1962 and 'Brazil: Alliance for Progress Study' in 1965. Data stored at the Roper Center, Yale University.

92 Carlos Estevam Martins, 'Brazil and the United States from the 1960s to the 1970s'. In Julio Cotler and Richard Fagen (eds), *Latin America and the United States*. Stanford University Press, Stanford, Calif., 1974, p. 277; and *Business Latin America*, 25 May 1967, p. 165.

93 *Business Latin America*, 9 April 1975, pp. 113–14; 9 June 1976, p. 180; 6 April 1977, pp. 108–9.

94 ibid., 18 August 1976, p. 261; 4 May 1977, p. 144; 10 August 1977, pp. 251, 254–5; 22 February 1978, pp. 57–60.

95 *Latin America Economic Report*, 5 (37), 23 September 1977, p. 148; 6 (22), 9 June 1978, p. 174; *Business Latin America*, 9 August 1978, pp. 250–4.

96 *Latin America Economic Report*, 5 (41), 21 October 1977, p. 179; 6 (1), 6 January 1978, p. 7; *Business Latin America*, 22 June 1977, p. 193; 28 September 1977, p. 307; 8 March 1978, p. 75; 12 July 1978, p. 218; 6 June 1979, pp. 178–9.

97 *Business Latin America*, 8 March 1978, p. 75; 12 July 1978, pp. 217–18.

98 ibid., 21 March 1979, p. 91; 9 May 1979, p. 146; 5 September 1979, p. 287; 12 December 1979, pp. 393–5.

99 For example, Henry Maksoud, *Idéias para a nação progredir com liberdade e empreendimento*. Editora Visão, São Paulo, 1978, pp. 113, 115, 124–8; *Visão*, 48 (8), 19 April 1976, whole issue, but especially pp. 25–8; and 'A empresa privada nacional e o desenvolvimento industrial brasileiro'. *Cadernos economicos*, no. 24, 1975.

100 For a thoughtful and detailed analysis of the links among these three key actors, see Peter Evans, *Dependent Development: The Alliance of Multinational, State and Local Capital in Brazil*. Princeton University Press, Princeton, 1979, especially Ch. 3. Evans' principal interest is to sketch the nature of the relations among the three strands of capital and their partial integration into a 'triple alliance'. Evans is careful, however, to analyze not only collaboration but also competition among these 'allies', underscoring especially the 'surprising' strength that he found among the Brazilian bourgeoisie. Moreover, Evans notes 'the exclusion of the majority of the Brazilian bourgeoisie from participation in the triple alliance' – a fact that 'weakens the political foundations of dependent development in Brazil' (p. 283). Consequently, although the main determinants of success for the Brazilian development strategy (according to Evans) lie within the international economic system, the main threats to that strategy (also according to Evans) come from what I have called the national bourgeois coalition: a 'nationalist' alliance of local business, the military, other branches of the state apparatus and other nationalists outside the state (pp. 288–9). Also consistent with this chapter is Evans' discussion of joint ventures as compromises where local partners contribute their political (and at times economic) resources and where both foreigners and nationals have important strengths. Moreover, conflicts continue within joint ventures as between firms (although in different forms). While Evans does emphasize collaboration in a 'triple alliance' more than does this chapter, there is coincidence in stressing the continuing importance and strength of local capital, the splits that have occurred within it and also the conflicts between national and multinational firms in Brazil under conditions when most of the former are not members of Evans' 'triple alliance', as both he and this chapter suggest, that lead national business to seek support from the state to redress the perceived imbalance in the marketplace in favor of multinational firms.

101 For a discussion of the maximization of 'psychic income' at the expense of material income, see Harry G. Johnson, 'A Theoretical Model of Economic Nationalism in New and Developing States'. In Harry G. Johnson (ed), *Economic Nationalism in Old and New States*. University of Chicago Press, Chicago, 1967, pp. 1–16.

102 For a discussion of other aspects of industrialist attitudes, suggesting that a classical national bourgeois ideology had not crystallized in Brazil on other issues, see Fernando Henrique Cardoso, *Ideologías de la burguesía industrial en sociedades dependientes*. Siglo XXI, Mexico, 1971, pp. 152–233. See also Peter Evans, 'Shoes, OPIC and the Unquestioning Persuasion: A Look at Multinational Corporations'. Paper presented at

a conference on 'The United States, US Foreign Policy and Latin American and Caribbean Regimes', Washington, DC, March 1978.

103 For a discussion of deepening industrial structures, see Guillermo O'Donnell, 'Reflections on the Patterns of Change in the Bureaucratic–Authoritarian State'. *Latin American Research Review*, **13** (1), 1978, pp. 3–31.

104 Robert H. Swansbrough, *The Embattled Colossus: Economic Nationalism and US Investors in Latin America*. University of Florida Press, Gainesville, pp. 185, 195, 200.

105 *Business Latin America*, 21 March 1968, pp. 95–6.

Public policy, foreign investment, and implementation style in Mexico

Merilee S. Grindle*

Much of the politics of modern economic relations between the United States and Latin American countries involves government-to-government negotiation and diplomacy, with affected parties appealing to their national governments for protection or representation. Important issues and controversies of this kind are analyzed in the chapters by John Odell and Robert Paarlberg in this volume (chs 5 and 7). But government-to-government relationships do not exhaust the range of international economic issues whose creation, management, or resolution are found in the political arena. The regulation of direct foreign investment, for example, draws the governments of Latin American countries into political relationships with private companies and corporations, both domestic and foreign. Accordingly, attempts by Latin American states to monitor and regulate foreign direct investment deserve a prominent position in any discussion of the politics of economic relations between the United States and its southern neighbors, even when the US government is not a direct party to political interaction. Similarly, as suggested by Jorge Domínguez in the preceding chapter, domestic political alliances and processes frequently have international ramifications, even when foreign actors are not directly involved.

Historically, foreign investment has had a critical impact on the economies of Latin American states. Only in recent decades, however, have governments in the region begun to formulate legislation that would limit the sectors in which foreigners might invest, restrict the extent to which foreigners might control economic enterprises, control the influx of new technology, and determine the location of new ventures and the employment of national managerial talent. The conditions that have encouraged these states to challenge the economic power of foreign investors and the constraints on their capacity to carry out such policies are therefore an important focus of study. The case of Mexico is instructive and its political and economic experiences can be useful in evaluating similar trends and conditions in other Latin American contexts. Moreover, the overriding importance of US capital among its foreign investors places Mexican efforts to regulate that investment on the agenda of US–Mexican economic relations. In the following pages, the factors that have influenced policy-

* Department of Political Science, Brown University.

making related to foreign investment in Mexico and that have conditioned the response of potential or actual investors are analyzed.

The regulation of foreign investment in Mexico, as elsewhere, is characterized by ongoing bargaining and negotiation between various agencies of the state and the investors, a process in which each attempts to use its power to achieve policies favorable to its interests. But this chapter indicates that important determinants of outcomes underlie the bargaining process. To begin with, there are important constraints on the choice of policies available to the Mexican state in its attempts to regulate foreign investment in the country. In addition, presidential administrations have a notable impact on policy-making toward foreign capital, a characteristic explored in section 3.2. At the same time, the bargaining positions of foreign investors are limited by both global and Mexican environments, a topic explored in the next section. Finally, the extent to which accommodation during implementation influences the relationship of foreign investors to the state is analyzed. Here it will be argued that among a variety of factors that account for Mexico remaining an attractive destination for US investment has been the government's use of policy instruments that allow foreign firms some leeway for resolving problems on a case by case basis. This has often kept foreign investor–government conflicts from escalating into government-to-government confrontations. Thus, it will be suggested that together with an understanding of the content of the policies the government has formulated must go an appreciation of its style of implementation. In conclusion, the chapter addresses the question of the predictability of future policies toward foreign investment in Mexico and the impact of the country's new oil wealth on them.

3.1   Foreign investment and the power of the state in Mexico

Mexico is a major Latin American recipient of direct private investment from the United States. While most countries in the region, even such large ones as Argentina and Venezuela, have experienced declines (albeit for different reasons) in the proportion of total US investments directed to them in recent years, Mexico's share of the total amount has grown consistently since the early 1960s (see *Figure 3.1*). The country is also an exception to the general pattern of declining US investment in the Third World in favor of more industrialized regions[1]. Among Latin American countries, only Brazil accommodates more private investment from the 'Colossus of the North' (see *Table 3.1*). Moreover, US investment accounts for an overwhelming proportion of all foreign capital in Mexico, figuring as the source of 79% of the total in 1970[2]. In addition, an ever-increasing portion of this money is concentrated in manufacturing ventures, making the country one of the

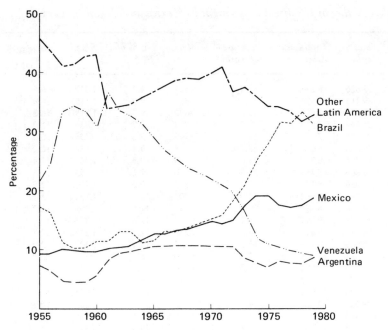

Figure 3.1 *Value of US direct investment in Latin American countries (percentage of total US investment in Latin America in US $m.)*

Source: US Department of Commerce, *Survey of Current Business*, various
volumes.

favorite sites for US investment in that sector (see *Table 3.2*)[3]. Thus, not
only has US private investment in Mexico grown, it has also found its way
into the most modern and dynamic sectors of the country's economy.

A closer look at the structure of US investment in Mexico reveals that its
importance to the economy is greater than even these aggregate figures
would suggest. While it accounts for a relatively minor portion of total
private and public investment in Mexico, it is highly concentrated in a few
key industrial enterprises, such as chemicals, machinery, food processing,
and transportation[4]. Moreover, US-based transnational firms rank among
the largest enterprises in all industrial sectors (see *Table 3.3*) and account for
a major portion of the manufactured goods exported by Mexico. Furthermore,
US companies often reap more profits and grow more rapidly than national
firms within the same industries. Where these foreign firms have used their
economic strength to squeeze out or acquire competing national firms, a
progressive denationalization of key manufacturing industries has resulted[5].
It is not surprising, then, that the Mexican government has become more
assertive in its attempts to guide and influence the impact of this foreign
investment on the economic, social, and political structures of the country.
In doing so, it has responded to growing international awareness of the

Table 3.1 *Value of US direct investment in Mexico and Brazil (US$m.)*

Year	Total world	Total Latin American	L.A. as % of world	Mexico	As % of L.A.	Brazil	As % of L.A.
1954	17 626	6 244	35.4	524	8.4	1 049	16.8
1955	19 313	6 608	34.2	607	9.2	1 115	16.9
1956	22 177	7 459	33.6	690	9.2	1 218	16.3
1957	25 394	7 434	29.2	739	9.9	835	11.2
1958	27 255	7 751	28.4	745	9.6	795	10.3
1959	29 805	8 098	27.2	758	9.4	828	10.2
1960	32 778	8 387	25.6	795	9.5	953	11.4
1961	34 664	8 255	23.8	826	10.0	953	11.5
1962	37 226	8 424	22.6	867	10.3	1 084	12.9
1963	40 686	8 662	21.3	907	10.5	1 132	13.1
1964	44 386	8 894	20.0	1 034	11.6	997	11.2
1965	49 328	9 391	19.0	1 182	12.6	1 074	11.4
1966	54 711	9 826	18.0	1 248	12.7	1 247	12.7
1967	59 486	10 265	17.3	1 343	13.1	1 327	12.9
1968	64 983	11 033	17.0	1 466	13.3	1 484	13.4
1969	71 016	11 694	16.5	1 640	14.0	1 636	14.0
1970	78 178	12 252	15.7	1 786	14.6	1 807	15.1
1971	86 198	12 982	15.1	1 838	14.2	2 045	15.8
1972	94 337	13 667	14.5	2 025	14.8	2 505	18.3
1973	103 675	13 527	13.0	2 379	17.6	2 885	21.3
1974	118 613	14 704	12.4	2 825	19.2	3 658	24.9
1975	124 212	16 394	13.2	3 200	19.5	4 579	27.9
1976	136 396	17 125	12.6	2 976	17.4	5 416	31.6
1977	149 848	18 882	12.6	3 230	17.1	5 930	31.4
1978	168 081	21 336	12.7	3 712	17.4	7 170	33.6
1979	192 648	24 368	12.6	4 575	18.8	7 514	30.8

Source: US Department of Commerce, *Survey of Current Business*, various volumes.

Table 3.2 *Top ten countries for US investment in manufacturing 1974–1979 (US$m.)*

Country	1974	1975	1976	1977	1978	1979
Canada	13 450	14 691	15 965	16 696	17 625	19 237
UK	7 371	7 555	7 734	8 849	10 070	12 026
W. Germany	4 814	5 328	6 706	7 031	8 324	8 344
France	3 478	3 844	3 997	4 139	4 629	5 229
Brazil	2 578	3 106	3 673	3 937	4 684	4 914
Australia	2 256	2 352	2 495	2 597	2 881	3 143
Mexico	2 173	2 422	2 218	2 391	2 752	3 419
Belgium-Lux.	1 829	2 021	2 218	2 607	2 812	3 186
Italy	1 688	1 716	1 879	1 983	2 389	2 845
Netherlands	1 580	1 655	1 783	2 046	2 523	3 000

Source: US Department of Commerce, *Survey of Current Business*, various volumes.

Table 3.3 *Ownership of 300 largest manufacturers in Mexico (1972)*

	Foreign			Mexico		
Size	US	Foreign	Total	Private	State	Total
Top 100	39	22	61	27	12	39
101–200	31	15	46	43	11	54
201–300	27	16	43	54	3	57
Total	97	53	150	124	26	150
Percentage	32	18	50	41	9	50

Source: Richard S. Newfarmer and Willard F. Mueller, *Multinational Corporations in Brazil and Mexico: Structural Sources of Economic and Noneconomic Power*, Report to the Subcommittee on Multinational Corporations of the Committee on Foreign Relations, United States Senate, August 1975, p. 54.

harmful effects of foreign private investment as well as to its specific relationship with investors from the US and elsewhere.

Throughout the world, and 1960s and 1970s were marked by the growth of governmental, academic, and popular concern about the impact of foreign private capital on domestic political and economic conditions. In most of the Third World in the early post-war years, foreign investment was regarded as a necessary and integral part of achieving economic development, and both national entrepreneurs and governments welcomed the influx of such capital. In the past 15 years, however, increasing criticism has been leveled against the deleterious effects of foreign investment. Attention has focused particularly on the amount of economic and political power transnational corporations are capable of wielding in underdeveloped regions of the world, and a variety of specific consequences of their activities are widely described. In addition, foreign investment is criticized as a primary means of perpetuating extreme economic dependence and economic, social, and political underdevelopment[6].

Mexican officials, as well as the country's most important economic and political analysts, have shared in the 'consciousness raising' about the potentially damaging effects of foreign investment. Their concern, of course, has deeper historical roots in Mexican foreign policy[7]. Increasingly since the late 1960s, however, concerned Mexicans have spoken and written of Mexico's growing economic dependence on the United States even as the country has become more industrialized, of the incursion of US private investment into sensitive sectors of the national economy, and of the influence that large US corporations seem to wield with the government[8]. For most of them, Mexico is a weak and exploited victim of the combined political and economic power of the United States. Mexico's vast population of peasants, workers, and unemployed are seen to be those most adversely affected by the relations that have developed with investors from abroad. Even the new sources of hydrocarbon wealth discovered in the 1970s threaten to increase the country's dependence on the US[9].

While the tone of the criticism of Mexico's economic relationship with the US has been harsh and insistent, as officials have become more sensitive to the impact of foreign investment, their response has been to channel, regulate, and monitor it rather than to stifle the influx of capital into the country. This response of the Mexican state can be explained by a number of general conditions that act as constraints on the range of policy responses available to it and thus on its capacity to control foreign investment in the country.

Constraints and policy options

To begin with, underlying all policy initiatives is the influence exerted by the state capitalist model of economic development that Mexico has chosen to pursue since the 1940s[10]. This model has explicitly relied upon an active state, intervening widely in the economy to create the conditions for rapid industrialization[11]. Equally, its political role has been to establish conditions of domestic peace, to gain control over worker and peasant organizations, and to ameliorate tensions that would impede economic growth. The purpose of state intervention has been to stimulate and support a domestic elite of industrial, commercial, and financial entrepreneurs, the national bourgeoisie described by Domínguez in the previous chapter. As a consequence, the Mexican economy has been typified by private and public sectors that are both active and mutually dependent. Although carping, complaining, and tensions are in evidence in this relationship, it is undeniable that those elites and the state itself have been the principal beneficiaries of Mexico's development and that each is maintained and strengthened by the activities of the other. Centrally important to both is foreign capital.

Until the late 1960s, the state sought to encourage industrialization through a policy of import substitution. More recently, problems widely acknowledged to result from an overzealous and uncritical acceptance of import substitution have led administrations since 1970 to adopt a policy favoring more export-oriented growth[12]. In both cases, however, foreign investment has been considered a critical ingredient in the success of the overall strategy of capitalist development. For policy-makers since the 1940s, neither the government nor the national private sector has seemed strong enough to spearhead the rapid industrialization they desired. Foreign capital has therefore been sought out as an aid to economic development, and both public and private sectors have courted alliances with foreign investors. In policy-making and private sector circles, therefore, there is a built-in bias in favor of the existence of foreign investment in the country as well as in favor of a capitalist model of economic development[13]. In dealing with foreign investors, the state is thus wary of taking measures that would drastically limit the possibilities for capitalist accumulation.

Closely related to this constraint on its power to regulate foreign investment is the close intertwining of the US and the Mexican economies[14]. The United States is the destination of nearly 70% of all of Mexico's exports; currently, much of this export activity is carried out between subsidiaries of US firms in Mexico and their parent companies, a situation that constrains the country's trade policies. In addition, the majority of goods imported into Mexico come from the United States. US banks hold a large proportion of all loans and credits to Mexico. Tourism in Mexico and sources of employment in the US further increase the dependence of the country on the neighboring economy. Given these and other linkages between the two countries, and the heavy concentration of foreign investment from the US, Mexican policy-makers are well aware of the economic consequences that could ensue if the government should attempt to exclude US private capital from the country or to drive out US-based transnational corporations. The possibilities for retaliation and economic stagnation in terms of massive outflows of capital, more restrictive trade policies from the US, specific restrictions on imports from border industries (*maquiladores*), and a closed border to Mexican migration are generally sufficient to keep most policy-makers from contemplating a major change in overall strategy. Indeed, two presidents in the post-war period have taken unusually assertive stands against foreign corporations in Mexico and have been chastized by a flight of domestic and foreign capital from the country. These lessons have not been lost on subsequent administrations, and policy toward foreign investment is made with an implicit appreciation of the complex economic and political linkages between the two countries.

But there are other factors that influence decision-makers in attempts to regulate, guide, and control foreign investment. Particularly important in the economic sphere, for instance, has been the influence of Mexico's own highly diversified private sector. Individuals in this sector have developed close ties to US private capital through activities such as joint ventures, investments, management and directorship positions within US subsidiaries in Mexico, and through personal contacts. Added to this is the frequent use of illegal *prestanombres*, whereby Mexican nationals lend their names to joint ventures to obscure the extent of foreign capital associated with them. In addition, national entrepreneurs often have interests in common with foreign investors such as maintaining low tax rates and ensuring political and economic stability. On the other hand, Mexican private sector interests have also acted as a national bourgeois coalition to bring pressure on the government to restrict the activities of foreign investors when these have threatened their interests, a situation explored in detail in chapter 2. Thus, for instance, national businessmen were important in encouraging the Adolfo López Mateos administration (1958–1964) to formulate policies restricting the range and form of activities open to foreign investors[15]. Frequently, however, the government acts to protect or encourage its national entrepreneurs without their direct involvement in decision-making[16].

A fourth factor that acts as a constraint on the process of foreign investment policy-making is the simple but crucial matter of the bureaucratic and technical capacity of the state[17]. In explaining changes and continuities in policies, for instance, it is important to consider whether there exists sufficient knowledge of economic interactions to identify problem areas and their effects on the national economy, the expertise to develop policy responses to these problems, and the bureaucratic infrastructure necessary to carry out the policies formulated. In Mexico, as new bureaucratic entities have been created to assemble and analyze economic data, the government has been more able to introduce complex policy instruments. Prior to the 1940s, much of the state's repertoire of activities was limited to controlling foreign investment through nationalization and expropriation[18]. In the early 1950s, it initiated attempts at economic planning and gradually developed the expertise and personnel to engage more seriously in economic regulation[19]. Late in the same decade, the Ministry of the Economy was revamped and staffed with economists whose expertise and advice was used by the López Mateos administration to establish policies for increasing Mexican involvement in foreign-owned enterprises and to channel investment to sectors considered appropriate for the country's development[20]. As the state has developed new capabilities to influence the behavior of foreign investors and has developed experience in utilizing various policy instruments, it has assumed a larger role in the economy of the country and is now regarded as the chief source of alternative power to the transnational foreign investor[21].

All of these factors – a capitalist model of economic growth that envisions a role for foreign capital, the implications of US involvement in the Mexican economy, the influence of domestic economic forces, and the bureaucratic and technical skills available to the state – act together to limit the effective range of alternatives available to regulate foreign private investment. They are the source of both continuity and change in policies. Continuities are largely a result of the hold of the strategy for economic development favored by the government since the 1940s and economic and political dependence on the United States. Changes in policy content, on the other hand, result from the sensitivity of the government to internal economic pressures, and from the gradual accumulation of technical and bureaucratic expertise. In addition, the impact of individual presidents on the style and content of state policy is important for understanding trends in the government's approach to foreign investors. This in turn is important for appreciating the process through which foreign investors and the Mexican government resolve their differences.

3.2   The *sexenio* and the content of public policy

During the *sexenio*, the six-year term of office of each president, the individual chosen to lead the country has great power to determine the goals the government will pursue. He assumes office with considerable discretion to select subordinate officials, down to the middle ranks of the administrative corps. By Mexican practice, the initiation of each *sexenio* is accompanied by a massive turnover of personnel in elective, party, and bureaucratic positions. All posts ultimately depend upon appointment, and public and party personnel tend to be highly responsive to the policy and stylistic cues of the president[22]. In addition, of course, those selected by a president and his advisors are likely to share the general ideological preferences of those to whom they owe their jobs. Under this arrangement, many ministries, departments, or bureaus develop as closely knit organizations personally committed for the duration of the *sexenio* to pursuing the policies of the president. This influence over the bureaucratic apparatus is echoed among much of the party structure also. The capacity to mobilize the commitment of bureaucratic and party personnel, the weakness of the legislative branch, and the mantle of legitimacy and charisma enjoyed by the incumbent president for six years give him a central position in determining the policies to be pursued by 'his' *sexenio*.

But the individual leading the *sexenio* is not the 'near dictator' he has been called in some analyses[23]. He, too, is a creature of the system and must conform to the rules of the game of Mexican politics, including those surrounding foreign investment. In addition, he must repect the ideology of the Revolution of 1910, conform to a variety of traditions established by previous presidents – not the least of which is the constitutional requirement that he step down from power after six years – and remain responsive to powerful domestic interests, especially those of the national bourgeoisie. He is, therefore, limited in practice by a number of environmental constraints such as those outlined in section 3.1. Nevertheless, the important position of the president has meant that there are identifiable differences among administrations with regard to policies pursued in the regulation of foreign investment.

There has been a long-term trend to apply more restrictive policies to foreign investors, but some administrations have been more energetic than others in following this path. It has been possible, in fact, for students of domestic Mexican policies to identify a pendulum pattern in regulating foreign investment that corresponds to presidential administrations. As will be seen below, a rhetorically liberal or populist *sexenio* tends to be followed by a more conservative and business-oriented administration; it, in turn, tends to be followed by a *sexenio* that returns to a more nationalist approach. Thus, the long-term trend toward increasing the regulatory power of the state has been punctuated by variations in individual *sexenios*, beginning with the administration of Manuel Avila Camacho (1940–1946), when Mexico began to pursue rapid industrialization.

Import substitution and foreign capital: the 1940s and 1950s

During World War II, the pace of industrialization accelerated as entrepreneurs responded to scarcities of imported goods by beginning to manufacture products for the internal market[24]. Import substitution began as an informal process, but became explicit government policy for achieving rapid industrial growth during the administrations of Avila Camacho and of Miguel Alemán (1946–1952). Near the end of the war, government policy-makers became more sensitive to the need to protect nascent industries from foreign domination and, in response, Avila Camacho announced a general policy to require Mexican majority ownership (51%) in certain key industries. A government decree of 1944 gave official blessing to this policy of Mexicanization that has endured to the present time as a central goal of Mexico's relationship with foreign investors. In contrast to the aggressively nationalist policies of the administration of Lázaro Cárdenas, by the 1940s expropriation and nationalization had become unattractive policy instruments because the rapid growth, import-substituting development model explicitly accepted the importance of foreign investment and sought to create favorable conditions for attracting more such capital[25].

While Avila Camacho supported the policy of Mexicanization, his successor, Miguel Alemán, was more motivated by the forthright desire to attract foreign capital to industrialize the country as rapidly as possible. Because of his perspective, the 1944 decree remained in effect but was rarely implemented. Instead, his administration began experimenting with import permits in 1948 to limit the amount and kind of manufactured goods brought into the country, particularly consumer goods. These permits, allocated to individuals or firms on a case by case basis, together with generous policies toward investment in the country, encouraged foreign companies to begin producing or assembling in the country what they had formerly imported. In the case of automobile manufacturing under Alemán, for instance, a few parts manufactured in Mexico were required to be integrated into vehicles assembled in the country and import quotas were introduced for assembled vehicles. These measures were added to prior legislation that offered lower tariffs for importing unassembled automobiles than for completed ones[26]. Thereafter, integration requirements became a standard instrument of government policy. During this period, as under the previous administration, a marked shift of foreign investment away from mining and infrastructure development to the manufacturing sector continued (see *Table 3.4*).

Alemán's successor, Adolfo Ruíz Cortines (1952–1958), energetically continued the policy of import substitution and sought to encourage foreign investment in the country. By this time, however, policy-makers had sufficient experience with the effects of such investment on the domestic economy to advocate other measures for guiding foreign capital in directions thought to be more beneficial to Mexico. Thus, the most important policy innovation of the Ruíz Cortines government was the 1955 Law for the Development of New and Necessary Industries, which provided a variety of incentives in the form of reduced taxes for companies producing goods new to the Mexican market or for which local production was insufficient[27]. Import permits remained an important means of protecting investment in domestic manufacturing and of attracting foreign capital, and the number of goods requiring permits expanded. During most of this period also, the domestic business sector was supportive of the government's drive to stimulate the influx of capital and to channel it into certain sectors of the industrial economy.

Table 3.4 *Value of foreign investment by activities 1940–1970*

Year	Value (US$m.)	Mining (%)	Industry (%)	Electricity (%)	Commerce (%)	Transportation and Communication (%)
1940	449	24	7	31	4	32
1945	569	24	18	24	5	26
1950	566	20	26	24	12	13
1955	953	18	35	20	15	6
1960	1081	16	56	1	18	3
1965	1745	7	69	0.7	16	0.5
1970	2822	6	74	0.1	16	0.3

Source: Richard S. Weinert, 'The State and Foreign Capital'. In José Luís Reyna and Richard S. Weinert (eds), *Authoritarianism in Mexico*. ISHI Publications, Philadelphia, Pa., 1977, p. 114.

However, by the late 1950s, pressure had begun to mount from this quarter, as foreign capital became an increasingly important factor in the national economy[28]. As Jorge Domínguez indicates in chapter 2, domestic entrepreneurs began to be more threatened economically by the foreign firms active in the country and they sought protection from the state. In addition, policy-makers were growing more apprehensive about the relationship between industrialization and the country's balance of payments. The cost of importing goods to manufacture or assemble products locally was a major reason for sharp deficit increases in 1956, 1957, and 1958 in the balance of payments. Nevertheless, Ruíz Cortines did not depart radically from the general policies of the Alemán period; his administration was committed to import substitution and wished both to attract and guide foreign investment through incentives, rather than to control or regulate it through restrictions.

Mexicanization: the 1960s

It remained for López Mateos (1958–1964) to initiate more restrictive policies. At the outset of his administration, foreign investment was restricted from activities in telecommunications; in 1959, the government bought out foreign interests in the electric power and light and steel industries. As a consequence, the president earned his credentials as an economic nationalist and was instrumental in expanding the role of the state in the economy. Mexicanization assumed a more prominent role and instruments that affected majority foreign-owned enterprises, such as discriminatory taxation, were increasingly introduced and domestic industry was protected through higher tariff barriers. Government contracts and purchases were also awarded on a discriminatory basis and the selective use of permits and licenses was introduced. In addition, laws to establish conditions in specific industries, such as automobiles, telecommunications, and mining, were promulgated. The government continued to expand the variety of bureaucratic procedures for dealing with foreign firms – permits, applications for tax exemptions, approval of proposals for new investments, tariff exemptions. These mechanisms were to encourage firms to assume a minority position in favor of Mexican capital, to stimulate local manufactures, and to penalize firms that demonstrated reluctance to toe the government's line. However, so energetic were the administration's efforts, in addition to what domestic and foreign entrepreneurs considered to be 'destabilizing' rhetoric from López Mateos, that the country experienced a significant outflow of capital from domestic and foreign sources in 1960 and 1961[29]. The president and his advisors were soon forced to be more conciliatory toward the private sector in general and foreign investment in particular. Ultimately, the pendulum swing under the *sexenio* of López Mateos was constrained by the need to maintain and attract foreign investment and to deal with the retaliatory activities of the domestic private sector. Thus, when the state demonstrated hostility to private capital in general, the transnational coalition discussed by Jorge Domínguez was temporarily strengthened.

The policy of encouraging Mexicanization through the use of selective enforcement of various instruments continued during the more conservative Gustavo Díaz Ordaz administration (1964–1970). Foreign investment, especially from the US, began to accelerate considerably and the government was noted for its courtship of both the domestic and foreign private sectors. At the same time, while business supported the administration's friendly attitude toward private capital in general, it also argued for a more restrictive stance toward foreign investment, especially when its own prosperity was threatened by foreign competition. Increasingly, domestic entrepreneurs argued for more restrictions on foreign capital, using their peak organizations to pressure the government. Concurrently, the sophistication of government ministries strengthened the capacity of the state to monitor the effects of foreign investment. In part because of the data and analysis produced by various government departments, criticism of foreign investment began to mount during this period, and by the time Luis Echeverría became president (1970–1976) a series of studies and critiques was available that helped influence him to take a more aggressive stance toward the foreign firms.

Conflict and accommodation: the 1970s

Interestingly, when asked by the American ambassador in 1972 if the government's policies toward foreign investment had altered, the Minister of Industry and Commerce replied forcefully, 'Yes, we are changing the rules of the game'[30]. And indeed, the policies of the Echeverría administration marked a much more concerted effort to regulate the activities of foreign direct investors, in response both to growing international criticism of foreign investment and to specific experience. By 1970, government officials and others had become highly sensitive and critical toward the harmful effects of foreign capital on balance of payments, technological dependence, inflation, unemployment, and denationalization. National business organizations were also increasingly outspoken critics of foreign direct investment. The government remained committed to rapid industrial growth, but the accumulated experience with import substitution and the damaging effects of its headlong pursuit encouraged a change of policy toward more export-oriented industrialization[31]. This required that Mexican industry become less protected, more efficient, and more competitive internationally. It also required that the state assume a stronger stance toward foreign firms in order to force them to conform more consistently to Mexican national interests.

Initially, the Echeverría administration acted to restrict more economic activities to the exclusive control of the state – petrochemicals, electrical utilities, and mining rights, for instance – and others were reserved for private sector ventures that were 51%, 60%, 67%, or 100% owned by Mexican nationals – as was the case with steel, fertilizer, cement, auto parts, petrochemical processing, urban transportation, fishing, and some food processing, among the others. Then two key pieces of legislation directed toward foreign investors were introduced, the Law to Promote Mexican Investment and Regulate Foreign Investment of February 1973 and the Transfer of Technology Law passed in late 1972.

The law to regulate foreign investment empowered the government to approve or disapprove all plans for new investment by multinational firms and required certain percentages of Mexican capital to be involved in all such ventures. It set up a national registry to monitor investment of foreign capital. The law established a variety of measures that would be taken into consideration in evaluating a firm's proposal[32]. It also introduced provisions restricting foreign companies in the acquisition of existing Mexican firms and established stricter legal penalties on Mexican nationals who served as *prestanombres*. A National Commission on Foreign Investment was established to implement the regulations on a case by case basis. The legislation, vague and general in many respects, permitted the commission to overlook some of the stipulated criteria in individual cases if this was thought to be 'in the national interest', the definition of which was left to the discretion of the commission. Much of the law has been explained as a codification of previously existing policy, but it is clear that the new commission was an attempt to provide greater central direction and control over foreign investment, while at the same time allowing the government flexible instruments to apply in individual cases.

The second major legal innovation of the Echeverría *sexenio* was the law on the transfer of technology. Mexico, along with other Latin American states, developed a greater sensitivity to the increased economic dependence that can result from control over sophisticated technology by foreign firms, a process that is detailed by Debra Miller in chapter 6. The new law set up a registry where all license and royalty agreements with foreign firms had to be evaluated, approved, or rejected by government officials. A series of criteria to guide the decision-making process was established, but here again the registry was given discretion to decide when technology transfer was in the national interest and when it was not[33]. Once again, also, the law was to be applied on a case by case basis. The law and the functioning of the registry received the support of much of the domestic private sector; henceforth, domestic entrepreneurs would be in a stronger position, backed by legal and procedural requirements, to bargain with foreign firms[34]. A patent and trademark law regulating the use of industrial property was a much more forceful piece of legislation passed in 1976. It was a product of the last and most tense period of the Echeverría *sexenio*, however, and was not implemented by the José López Portillo administration (1976–1982).

Thus, the Echeverría *sexenio* departed from the more modest attempts of previous administrations to regulate the behavior of foreign direct investors. Nevertheless, while the policies themselves were more assertively Mexicanist, they were formulated to include broad possibilities for flexible administration by officials. This tended to soften the impact of the laws and allowed the more conservative administration of José López Portillo to live with the legislation and with the apparatus set up to implement it. At the same time, the enforcement of the laws became notably more sympathetic to foreign investors.

As under López Mateos, Echeverría's policies and highly critical rhetoric concerning multinational firms and foreign investment created a crisis of confidence in the Mexican regime by the end of his *sexenio*. The devaluation of the peso in late 1976 led to a serious flight of capital from the country.

Thus, when López Portillo took over, the economy was in serious trouble and the business community seriously attacked the legitimacy of the regime. Foreign and domestic capitalists joined once again in resisting the activities of a government thought to be inimical to private capital. In response, López Portillo was strongly pressured to encourage investment in Mexico, from both foreign and domestic sources, by a more accommodating and less critical approach to the private sector in general[35]. Under his guidance a rapprochement with domestic private interests was energetically pursued. But his government also favored stimulating the production of goods for export that was initiated under Echeverría. In pursuit of this strategy, multinational corporations and their international market linkages were viewed as organizations whose presence in Mexico needed to be encouraged and channeled into areas considered most beneficial to Mexico. In the automotive industry, for example, manufacturers were charged with reducing the trade deficit associated with their activities at the same time that price controls on vehicles for private use were lowered. In addition to applying Echeverría's laws less stringently, López Portillo's administration also instituted programs to refund export taxes when manufactures were involved and applied these on a discriminatory basis depending upon the degree of Mexican capital involved as well as other criteria[36].

3.3   Attitudes of foreign investors in Mexico

The changes and continuities of various administrations in regulating foreign investment are summarized in *Table 3.5*. As indicated, each administration followed a general policy for encouraging industrialization, tended to exhibit a generalized attitude toward foreign investment, and promulgated specific legislation to encourage, guide, control, or influence it. It is interesting to note that the growth of foreign investment was not greatly affected by change of *sexenio* (column E). Since 1965, in fact, in spite of a long-term trend toward increasing regulation of foreign investment, foreign investment has grown by at least 6% a year and frequently by more than 19%, except for one year, 1976 (see *Table 3.6*).

If it is true that the government of Mexico has become more assertive with regard to the activities of foreign direct investors, why have these chosen to invest in the country and even to increase their activities? What, in fact, does Mexico have to offer foreign firms with capital to invest? Of course, to begin to understand the attitudes of foreign companies toward investment in Mexico, it is important to emphasize that it is not alone in developing more restrictive policies. Indeed, although the Law to Promote Mexican Investment and Regulate Foreign Investment and the Transfer of Technology Law of the Echeverría administration go far in defining the conditions under which foreign capital will be welcomed in the country, there are few

Table 3.5 *Presidential administrations and foreign investment in Mexico*

A Sexenio	B General development policy	C General attitude toward foreign investment	D Specific legislation and policies toward foreign investment	E Value of US direct investment in Mexico ($m.)
Manuel Avila Camacho 1940–1946	Rapid industrialization; initial phase of import substitution; consumer goods	Favorable; some nationalist concern	Mexicanization of key industries	—
Miguel Alemán 1946–1952	Rapid industrialization; import substitution; consumer goods	Highly favorable; uncritical; use of incentives	Restrictions on imported manufactures; tax incentives to invest	414[a]
Adolfo Ruiz Cortines 1952–1958	Rapid industrialization; import substitution; consumer goods	Favorable; some nationalist concern; desire to channel investment	Law for Development of New and Necessary Industries (tax incentives)	661[b]
Adolfo López Mateos 1958–1964	Rapid industrialization; import substitution; consumer, intermediate, and capital goods	Favorable, but critical of private sector in general; use of both incentives and restrictions	Mexicanization; integration; discriminatory use of policy instruments as sanctions against foreign investment when need for compliance; enforcement of previous legislation; laws for specific industries	864.5[c]

Gustavo Díaz Ordaz 1964–1970	Rapid industrialization; import substitution; intermediate and capital goods	Favorable; use of both incentives and restrictions	Mexicanization; integration	1444.2[d]
Luís Echeverría 1970–1976	Rapid industrialization; export-oriented, balanced growth; primary, intermediate, and manufactured goods exported where appropriate	Favorable only if on Mexico's terms; nationalist criticism of multinationals and private sector in general	Mexicanization; integration; Law to Promote Mexican Investment and Regulate Foreign Investment; Law on Transfer of Technology; laws for specific industries; patent and trademark law; incentives/penalties for balance of payments impact	2540.5[e]
José López Portillo 1976–1982	Rapid industrialization; export-oriented, balanced growth; primary, intermediate, and manufactured goods exported where appropriate	Favorable, but concern for national interests	Mexicanization; integration; registration; monitoring; incentives for balance of payments impact	3839.0[f]

[a] 1950; [b] average, 1954–1958; [c] average, 1959–1964; [d] average, 1965–1970; [e] average, 1971–1976; [f] average, 1977–1979.

Source: Column E, US Department of Commerce, *Survey of Current Business*, various volumes.

Table 3.6 *Growth in direct foreign investment in Mexico, 1940–79*

Year	Total foreign investment ($m.)	Percentage increase over previous year (%)	US foreign investment ($m.)	Percentage increase over previous year (%)
1940	449	—	—	—
1945	569	—	—	—
1950	566	—	414	—
1955	953	—	607	—
1960	1081	—	795	—
1961	1130	4.5	—	—
1965	1745	—	1182	—
1966	1938	11.1	1248	5.6
1967	2096	8.2	1343	7.6
1968	2316	10.5	1466	9.2
1969	2516	11.2	1640	11.9
1970	2822	9.5	1786	8.9
1971	3018	6.9	1840	3.0
1972	3208	6.3	2025	10.1
1973	3495	8.9	2249	11.1
1974	3857	10.4	2854	26.9
1975	4219	9.4	3177	11.3
1976	—	—	2976	6.3
1977	—	—	3230	8.5
1978	—	—	3712	14.9
1979	—	—	4575	23.2

Sources: 1940–75 – Richard J. Weinert, 'The State and Foreign Capital'. In José Luís Reyna and Richard S. Weinert (eds), *Authoritarianism in Mexico*. ISHI Publications, Philadelphia, Pa., 1977, pp. 112, 114; James Wilkie (ed), *Statistical Abstract for Latin America*. Latin American Center, University of California, Los Angeles, 1977, p. 427; 1976–79 – US Department of Commerce, *Survey of Current Business*, various volumes.

provisions in the laws themselves that were not incorporated in similar legislation of the Andean Common Market. Taking a broad international perspective, then, foreign investors often face an increasingly restrictive environment and Mexico's policies can be interpreted as one manifestation of this general phenomenon. In addition, a firm's competitive position relative to others often encourages it to invest abroad. But there are other, more specific reasons why Mexico has remained an attractive target for foreign investment, particularly from the United States (see *Table 3.7*).

One clear advantage, of course, is the large size of the market offered by the country itself. Currently, the population of Mexico is over 67 million and it boasts a relatively large, consumption-oriented middle class by Latin American standards. More recently, companies have looked favorably on Mexico as a staging area for greater penetration of markets in other Latin American countries, especially those in Central America and the Caribbean[37]. Another asset Mexico has is its closeness to the United States

Table 3.7 *Reasons for investing in Mexico (responses from 346 US firms active in Mexico)*

Reason for investment	Number of mentions	Percentage of total responses
Penetration into a growing market	196	27.5
Economic stability	151	21.2
Anticipation of relatively higher profits	86	12.1
To develop new industry in the country	72	10.1
To maintain sales in the face of tariff barriers	69	9.7
Lower labor costs	47	6.6
To match or forestall a competitor's move	36	5.1
Export base for neighboring markets	23	3.2
Investment incentives	17	2.4
Offshore manufacture for export to the foreign investor	11	1.5
Availability of Mexican capital	4	0.6

Source: Harry J. Robinson and Timothy A. Smith, *The Impact of Foreign Private Investment on the Mexican Economy*. Stanford Research Institute, Menlo Park, California, SRI Project 4110, 1976, p. 137.

and its large markets. Without greatly increasing transportation or marketing costs, companies can take advantage of lower labor costs in Mexico to produce goods for the US[38]. Important too are factors such as the relatively advanced infrastructure development of Mexico and an overall high rate of return on investments in the protected market offered by the government. American investors have spoken not only of the lower wage scale of Mexican labor, but also of its relatively high educational level and adaptability to the discipline of industrial settings[39]. Previous investments have also given many foreign firms an interest in continuing their activities in the country, reaping the benefits available and attempting to settle their differences with the government rather than pulling up stakes and moving elsewhere.

Underlying all these advantages, however, is the reputation Mexico has developed for remarkable political and economic stability. Although this reputation was tarnished by the peso devaluation and political tensions of the last months of the Echeverría administration, the political system remains notable for the peaceful transfer of power from one administration to the next and the resolution of individual and group conflict without frequent resort to major uses of violence. This outward appearance of stability and continuity, rare in Latin America, clearly enhances its appeal for foreign investors, as revealed in *Table 3.7*. Only recently have foreign investors become apprehensive about the extreme inequities in the society that are a result of its path toward economic development; only recently have massive poverty, unemployment, and underemployment raised fears of future political instability.

In spite of the attractive qualities that Mexico has to offer the foreign investor, attitudes toward the investment climate are not uncritical. A 1975 survey of US firms with operations in Mexico indicated that the companies were hostile to government intervention in the economy in general and more specifically to its role in regulating the activities of foreign investors. The firms were outspoken in their desire to eliminate bureaucratic intervention and red tape in their operations and singled out the foreign investment law of the Echeverría administration as indicative of the hostile environment they perceived[40]. At the same time, the investigators reported that:

> It is believed by the respondents that the investment climate in Mexico should continue to attract foreign private investment, based in particular upon an expanding market and political stability. The questionnaires and interviews indicated a general satisfaction with the investments, and a recognition that foreign investment is basic to Mexico's planned economic growth[41].

Among foreign investors there is a general perception that doing business in Mexico can be rewarding to the investor because of the 'pragmatism' and 'flexibility' of the government. They acknowledge that the government's overall strategy for economic development includes a significant role for foreign capital and technology and that it is willing to negotiate 'pragmatically' with foreign interests to acquire these benefits[42]. Indeed, the extensive provisions for acquiring permits, licenses, and approvals from the government bring the companies and the government into frequent contact where they can discuss their differences. Many firms, even when not required to do so, report choosing high-level officials of the government to participate on their boards of directors. Accordingly, the investigators report that:

> This arrangement allows a two-way exchange of views and serves to educate both sides on the realities of government policies and operations as they relate to the needs of the business community. One respondent commented: 'We have found that this relationship has been much to our advantage, especially in an understanding of the problems and obtaining permits for action ... In all cases so far 99.9% of those individuals have acted as businessmen and not as pressures of the government'[43].

Thus, while on the one hand foreign investors are resentful of the harsh public criticism of their activities that comes from both government and non-government sources in Mexico, they consciously seek to develop close working relations with government officials on an individual basis and are confident that when problems arise they will be able to find a sympathetic, receptive, or at least 'pragmatic' ear within the government. This remained true even under the assertive Echeverría administration. Correspondingly, there have been few reports of difficulties in actually meeting the terms of the foreign investment law or the transfer of technology law, however critical the firms may be of the legislation in general[44].

A related perception about doing business in Mexico is that the government pursues 'flexibility' in implementing its policies toward foreign investment. Coupled with a pragmatic approach, investors perceive that the government's intent is to apply policies after evaluating the specific case before it. This has encouraged a bargaining relationship among individual firms and the government in which the companies are likely to make commitments to Mexican goals of industrial decentralization, job creation, or export promotion in return for favorable rulings about new or expanded investments, import necessities, or technology utilization[45]. Even when the government refuses to permit a certain activity, or fails to approve a contract, recent experience has been that it will entertain the applications of the investor a second or even third time and listen to new or revised arguments for why the activity should be permitted[46]. Thus, 'firms with adroitness, flexibility, and patience have been able to negotiate reasonable agreements with the government'[47]. No doubt, emphasis on 'pragmatism' and 'flexibility', in addition to frequent direct contacts between business and government personnel, encourage the foreign investors or their representatives to establish clientelistic relations with members of the public sector who are in a position to aid them. Certainly clientele linkages between public officials and Mexican citizens are a widely accepted means of acquiring favorable action from the government and it is to be expected that the same type of particularistic relationships would prove useful to individual foreign firms[48]. This may be particularly true when an investor seeks to acquire benefits from the government in order to place the firm in an advantageous position relative to its competitors.

Finally, foreign investors in Mexico are well aware of the *sexenio* pattern of presidential change and leadership. If a particular administration is more critical than usual of foreign investments – the López Mateos and Echeverría *sexenios* are cases in point – investors may be willing to stick it out until a new administration is initiated and pressure from dissatisfied interests under the previous *sexenio* helps to move the incumbents to greater accommodation, pragmatism, and flexibility. The *sexenio* change offers clearly defined and predictable opportunities for change in government attitudes toward foreign investment and provides investors with a rationale for believing in a brighter future. It also offers an opportunity for cultivating more sympathetic personal contacts and relationships with the cadre of officials who accompany the new president into office. Thus, even while foreign investors can see that the long-term trend is toward greater regulation and insistence on Mexico's definition of the national interest, they also perceive differences in how vigorously such goals are pursued from one administration to the next[49].

3.4   The Mexican style of implementation and accommodation

It is clear, then, that Mexico, like other countries, exhibits a set of more or less enduring constraints that characteristically condition its policy-making toward foreign investment. Presidents rarely stray too far from accepted principles, and, if they do, the succeeding administration is likely to re-establish traditional boundaries. For the foreign investors, there is also a set of constraints that serves as a framework within which interaction with the state takes place. Primary among these, of course, is the range of options available to the foreign investor on a global basis. These alternatives are structured by the type of activity the firm is engaged in and by factors such as the availability of markets, quality of infrastructure needed, and opportunities for expansion. But activities are also affected by the policies of the countries in which the firms seek to invest.

These general constraints set the conditions for the interaction of foreign investors and the state in Mexico and clearly influence the range of policies and behavioral responses available to each. But to explain this relationship in Mexico, as well as to understand its day-to-day functioning, it is important to consider what has been referred to here as a style of policy implementation. In Mexico, policy-makers have consistently chosen to formulate policies that can be implemented flexibly, often on a case by case basis. The policies and laws that have emerged dealing with Mexicanization, integration, imports, exports, and technology transfer have all accorded a high degree of discretion to the government in determining the application of the law, procedure, or policy. Import permits, discriminatory taxes, investment approvals, export requirements, and royalty agreements are methods of dealing with individual firms on a highly disaggregated basis. This style has been identified with the management of domestic issues in the Mexican political system and seems to have become operative also for foreign economic policy-making[50]. In terms of the investor–government relationship that develops under this kind of situation, there are a number of consequences.

First of all, the Mexican style of implementation enhances the central role of the bureaucracy in the regulatory process. Almost all interaction between the government and foreign investors is achieved through a process of application, review, and decision-making on an individual basis. Foreign enterprises in Mexico, then, are encouraged to consult directly, specifically, and frequently with the bureaucratic officials who have discretion to apply general, frequently vague legislation to the specific case[51]. The clientelism encouraged by the way policies are administered may mean, of course, that broad government goals are not easily achieved. While this also enhances the power of the individual bureaucrat and introduces significant opportunities for corrupt or evasive behavior, it nevertheless provides the government with the chance to oversee closely the activities of foreign firms and to apply subtle pressure on an individual basis if it should choose to do so. A second result of this style of policy is that it allows the government to decide how vigorously to pursue a general policy. Encouragement may or may not be given by a presidential administration to the promotion of either the letter or the spirit of the law, as was true in several cases reviewed earlier.

A third consequence is that the problems or dissatisfactions of foreign firms with general policy may be dealt with in disaggregated fashion; as a result, the firms are discouraged from organizing broadly to oppose the government. Indeed, the piecemeal, personalist, and disaggregated methods of conflict resolution in Mexico have frequently been cited as a source of the country's relative domestic tranquility and it appears that the same mechanisms help manage the relationship between foreign investors and the government[52]. Here again, the hand of the state is strengthened while foreign companies themselves are encouraged to believe, often with good reason, that they have the capacity to reach various accommodations with the bureaucracy. Clientelistic relations with government officials may even enhance competition among foreign investors and hinder their capacity to present a united front to the government. While this style undoubtedly opens up the possibility for the exertion of illegal or semi-legal influence and may be the cause of much corporate grumbling about lack of guidelines, absence of clear rules of the game, or unpredictable government actions, it nevertheless serves as a tool for achieving mutual accommodation between the government and the foreign investors[53]. Because of this, even periods noted for their critical attitude toward foreign investment, in particular the Echeverría *sexenio*, do not automatically result in retaliatory or confrontational behavior from the investors.

In general, then, both the operating constraints on policy-makers and investors and the overall style of Mexican policy have led to a situation of long-term predictability in the relations between the state and foreign investors. While a multitude of factors can be cited that have continued to make Mexico attractive to foreign investors when other countries in the region have become less interesting, the style set for the interaction of the companies and the government has been vital in their relationship. The implementation process has increased the possibility that a highly political economic issue, the regulation of foreign investment, will not often lead to bitter confrontations. A brief example of the relationship of the Mexican state to powerful transnational automobile firms provides evidence of the importance of mutual accommodation, as well as indicating the framework within which bargaining between them occurs.

3.5   A case in point: the automobile industry

In its efforts to initiate, stimulate, and control the activities of the large transnational firms that dominate the automotive industry within the country, the government of Mexico has been facing a situation that is increasingly common in modern economic relationships on an international level. On the one hand, there is a highly complex, technologically sophisticated industrial activity dominated internationally by a few extremely large firms that enjoy extensive advantages over smaller firms in terms of international market linkages, production at advantageous economies of scale, materials and parts procurement capabilities, and trademark recognition. On the other hand, there is a state apparatus that has gradually developed an awareness of the positive and negative impact the operations of these firms have on the country's economy and that has experimented with a variety of policy instruments to encourage their positive contributions – the stimulation of local industry, for example – and to ameliorate those considered most harmful to the country – the negative impact on a country's balance of payments, for instance.

The automobile industry in Mexico developed in its early years as a highly protected one, largely as a result of favorable government policies supporting import substitution. By late in the 1950s, however, the industry was costing the country considerable amounts of foreign exchange; by 1959, it accounted for 12% of the value of all imports[54]. The automobile industry therefore became identified by Mexican policy-makers as a source of trouble for Mexico's balance of payments. Under the administration of López Mateos, firms were first given a 'basic quota' of the number of vehicles they were permitted to produce each year. Then, in August of 1962, a decree was announced prohibiting imports of finished vehicles and requiring that components of those manufactured in the country total 60% of the production cost of the vehicle. The decree also established that specific parts had to be produced in Mexico. These restrictions were enforced through the preferential issuance of import licenses to companies that filed plans about meeting the goals of the decree.

In spite of this government initiative, however, growth in the demand for automobiles led to increased production and this in turn required greater volumes of imported parts and components, even though these were limited to 40% of the value of the finished vehicle. As a result, by the late 1960s, parts and components for automobiles accounted for about 20% of Mexico's import bill[55]. Therefore, in response to the long-standing awareness that automotive manufacturing was a problem industry and to the initial stirrings of interest in an export-oriented growth strategy, the government issued a new law in 1969 requiring that the automotive manufacturers begin a program of compensating exports for imports[56]. By 1970, manufacturers were to compensate for at least 5% of the value of their imports by exporting their products manufactured in Mexico, the percentage to increase each year until 1980 when they would be required to export as much as they imported. In return for meeting these requirements, the firms would be allowed to produce more vehicles in the country and thus expand the 'basic quota' of units allotted to them each year. Even this, however, did not relieve the deleterious impact the industry had on Mexico's balance of payments and even as exports grew, the trade deficit that could be traced to the industry increased markedly, from $240 to $550 million between 1970 and 1975[57]. Under Echeverría, the industry was the target for a decree that sought to limit the number of models produced by each company and therefore increase the efficiency of the industry and encourage the production of low-priced, 'popular' cars that would be internationally competitive and have greater export potential. In this *sexenio*, the president's more hostile attitude toward the multinationals was apparent. Early in the administration, for instance, the industry was warned that import permits would be difficult to acquire by firms that had not matched exports with imports by 1977 and the government indicated that Mexicanization requirements might be extended to the automotive industry[58].

In 1977, under the López Portillo administration, the government again sought to reduce the trade deficit associated with the industry and lower the price of automobiles produced in the country. In June of that year, the manufacturers were given two options: they could balance imports with exports or they could achieve greater integration by incorporating more Mexican-produced components into their vehicles[59]. The targets for the latter goals varied between 75% and 90%, depending upon the type of vehicle produced, and were calculated to appeal to the domestic business sector that had been disaffected under Echeverría. At the same time, the decree lowered price controls on vehicles for private use in an effort to sweeten the more rigorous requirements of the policy. As a result, the major US manufacturers raised their prices approximately 13.5% shortly after the decree was issued. This reversal of a traditional policy of maintaining price controls was widely regarded as a major innovation in public policy and as an indication of López Portillo's more favorable attitude toward foreign investment[60].

The policies directed toward the automotive industry were congruent with the strategy of industrial growth that was pursued by Mexico after 1940. Thus, in the 1940s and 1950s, the broad and uncritical acceptance of import substitution led to a general encouragement of automotive assembly plants in the country, in ignorance of the impact of these on balance of payments deficits or the efficiency of the industry as a whole. When these problems became evident by the late 1950s and early 1960s, an effort was made to ameliorate the most difficult consequences of import substitution for automobiles by requiring the integration of domestically produced parts. The late 1960s and early 1970s brought greater criticism of the strategy of import substitution and exports were increasingly seen to be an integral part of Mexico's development strategy. Correspondingly, policies for the automotive industry were initiated to help achieve this goal. In terms of the policies selected, policy-makers were also sensitive to the desires and demands of domestic manufacturers; as a result, Mexico has developed an extensive supplier industry that is largely controlled by Mexican nationals (under Echeverría, each company producing auto parts was required to be at least 60% owned by Mexican capital). The impact of accumulating expertise was also evident in the development of policy instruments to influence the automotive industry. Additionally, policies responded to differences in presidential preferences. The best example of such a change is the distinction between the Echeverría administration and that of his successor. Both were persuaded of the importance of the export-oriented growth strategy for the country. The measures by which each sought to achieve this, however, differed – Echeverría being more fond of the stick and López Portillo of the carrot in eliciting responses from transnational investors.

Since the 1940s, then, the Mexican government has followed a trend in policies for the automotive industry that encouraged the utilization of Mexican-produced parts in vehicles assembled in Mexico and that more recently attempted to stimulate exports of complete motor vehicles or component parts. The intent of these policies was to save on the foreign exchange used to import automobiles or components, to develop a broadly owned local supplier industry, and to control the prices of locally manufactured vehicles. The instruments used to achieve these goals were import quotas, regulations stipulating which components were to be locally produced, production quotas, price controls, import permits, and discriminatory tariffs. These instruments have been adjusted a variety of times since the 1950s to influence the development of the industry, but they have all remained as fairly constant features of policy.

It is interesting to note that while the government has been experimenting with various and more restrictive policies, the automobile industry has grown considerably in Mexico. Between 1965 and 1975, the average annual rate of growth was over 13%[61]. In 1972 and 1973, it grew by over 23%, in spite of Echeverría's more aggressive stance toward foreign investment. In terms of levels of production, value of production, and investments, growth was consistent despite government regulations and attitudes about foreign capital. In 1975, 1976, and 1977, growth slowed considerably, but this seems to have been as much in response to a worldwide recession in the industry as it was to Echeverría, his policies, or labor difficulties[62].

The general pattern of growth is somewhat surprising because investment in complex industries like motor vehicles in Third World countries is not necessarily of global benefit to a large transnational firm[63]. For instance, participation in a local market, as in Mexico, frequently means that a firm is required by government policies and controls to invest in manufacturing activities in the country. Automotive companies have chosen to do this in countries such as India, Brazil, Mexico, and Argentina because of the potential size of the domestic market, favorable government incentives, limited investment possibilities elsewhere, and positive evaluations of potential profits. When they do initiate manufacturing activities, however, their facilities are generally small scale, producing at perhaps one-tenth of international levels, and unit costs of production tend to be high. Moreover, in meeting requirements that a certain portion of the components of each vehicle be locally produced, costs are raised further for a terminal producer. Given the large number of components and the need for these to be produced to fairly exact specifications, manufacturers are likely to experience a variety of technical difficulties with local producers. Thus, the total cost of producing a vehicle in a developing country may be much greater than its cost in the home country. The industry has often survived because of highly protective government policies aimed at encouraging import substitution, but this has also inhibited the development of export capabilities because vehicles can be produced more cheaply elsewhere.

Of course, transnational automobile firms base their initial decision-making about investing in Mexico and entering into specific bargains with the government on the basis of global-level profit and loss calculations. In this regard, investments in Mexico are weighed against opportunities in other countries. Mexico is therefore able to formulate more restrictive policies in part because many other countries are also doing so. Furthermore, since the major firms have relatively large operations in Mexico, and large amounts of capital invested, they have a vested interest in continuing operations in the country as long as government policy does not seem to them to be excessively punitive. In addition, there may be real cost advantages to producing goods in Mexico and exporting them to the parent firms in the US or overseas[64]. This is most frequently the case with automotive parts that are not technologically complex, and whose production does not necessarily involve large volumes to achieve economies of scale. In such cases, the companies can benefit from the lower wage scales in Mexico and from opportunities for transfer pricing when exporting to the parent company.

Policies for the automobile industry in Mexico also make the country more attractive to the transnational firms. Thus, policies whose specific target is the automotive industry have allowed firms to trade off some of the possibly damaging effects of other, more general legislation. Thus, while Mexicanization has been a major goal of foreign investment regulation in Mexico, the automotive transnationals have strongly resisted this policy. Instead, they have agreed to policies more directly related to the special problems caused by the industry for Mexico, particularly those involved in balance of payments problems. Thus, integration that would encourage a domestic supplier industry and export goals were accepted as alternatives. Moreover, general quotas and broad guidelines have frequently allowed extensive bargaining and alternatives to the manufacturers in reaching government-imposed goals. As was the case with the general policies that Mexico has developed to deal with foreign investment, those specifically applied to the automotive industry are implemented through a variety of permits, quotas, approvals, controls, and discriminatory taxes and tariffs that permit and even encourage individual application and close consultation with government officials. Thus, one way to explain the expansion of the automotive industry in Mexico, in spite of increasing regulatory activities, is the realization that the government has remained open to dialogue, negotiation, and bargaining with the companies on a case-specific basis. But is this a realistic expectation for Mexico's actions in the future in regard to foreign investment in general?

3.6   Foreign investment and Mexico's future

In the mid-1970s, Mexico became a major source of an extremely valuable resource – oil. Current estimates are that proved Mexican reserves are over 60 billion barrels, and potential reserves over 250 billion barrels. In addition, in 1978 the government announced reserves of 70 trillion cubic feet of natural gas. These resource discoveries represent a source of vast new wealth for Mexico and the potential to resolve some of the mounting economic problems the country has faced in recent years – inflation, external debt, unemployment, constriction of the domestic market, and redistributive demands. But what does it mean for the future of foreign investment in Mexico? Is this new wealth likely to change the constraints on Mexican policy-making that have been outlined in this chapter? Is the style of implementation discussed on previous pages likely to change as a result?

Mexico's new wealth has already made the country an inviting site for new foreign investment and the country is in a stronger position to exact favorable terms as a condition of entry. There has been increasing competition among foreign financial institutions to make loans to the country, and the environment for indirect investment will be echoed in that for direct investment. This may alter the impact of the constraints that have operated on the policies selected by the government. It is virtually certain, however, that the strategy for industrialization and economic development will continue to preserve a legitimate role for foreign investment. There is little to indicate a radical revision of Mexican ideology toward capitalist development models. Moreover, for practical reasons, the country will continue to need to import advanced technologies if it is to develop its oil resources and to compete internationally with its manufactured goods[65]. Estimates are that $20 billion will be needed to develop the oil and gas industries between 1977 and 1980; half of this amount will probably come from external sources. In addition, with the desire to pursue an export-oriented growth strategy, investment from transnational firms is one way the country can make use of existing international marketing systems and produce goods that are attractive and known to foreign buyers. For their part, the foreign investors will continue to urge the Mexican government to adopt favorable policies and to modify legislation regarding foreign investment and the transfer of technology. The desire of the government to accommodate this source of investment was signaled in September of 1978 when the López Portillo administration announced its intent to be 'flexible' in administering its Mexicanization requirements[66]. Although the country has new economic potential because of its oil wealth, its economic worries are by no means over. There are serious problems in the agricultural sector, in the manufacturing sector, in the control of inflation, and in the management of oil resources that will cause Mexico to look beyond its own borders for capital, technology, and managerial skill.

Proximity to the United States and Mexico's economic dependence on its northern neighbor will continue to influence policy-making. The agenda of US–Mexican relations is a full one, involving complex issues of trade, fishing rights, migration, and energy. Certainly the government is interested in diversifying the source of its imports and the destination of its exports, as a number of foreign trips during the López Portillo administration suggest. Expanded trade with Japan, Canada, and Western and Eastern Europe is seen as one way of reducing the country's dependence on the United States. Certainly it is also interested in attracting investment capital from other countries. But the common border with the US, the ready accessibility of imports from that country, the market it provides for Mexican agricultural and industrial products, as well as renewed interest in investment possibilities in Mexico, will make any rapid altering of the existing economic relationship unlikely. In fact, since the mid 1970s, the economic linkages between the two countries have deepened: over 80% of Mexico's oil exports are destined for the US; and at least in the foreseeable future, until the Mexican economy can absorb more of its own labor force, employment opportunities in the United States will continue to be significant as a 'safety valve' for the regime. Currently, there are at least 5.5 million people unemployed in the country and estimates of unemployment and under-employment range from 30% to 50% of the labor force. Thus, increased dependency means that economic ties with the United States will remain critically important to Mexico, and will continue to constrain the alternatives considered by the government for controlling foreign investment[67].

The domestic private sector has increased considerably in political importance and power under López Portillo. As the economy becomes more diversified and complex, this sector will continue to play an extremely important role in generating pressure on the government to adopt policies to monitor better the behavior of foreign investors. Particularly where foreign capital is seen as competing with domestic investment, the private sector will encourage the government to adopt discriminatory policies. However, it must be remembered that at times in the past the government has been considered by this sector to have been overly aggressive toward foreign investment and to have endangered the economic environment for private capital in general. Issues such as increased taxation, controls on exports and imports, and monitoring of business activity may be resisted as strongly by domestic entrepreneurs as by foreign investors. When such issues have arisen in the past, the business elites have acted to moderate government policies regarding foreign investment. This influence will also continue to constrain the range of policy options available to each administration.

Finally, future policies will be affected by the growth in the technical capacity of the country's bureaucratic agencies that has been noticeable under the administrations of Echeverría and López Portillo. The cadre of economists and managers who people the important ministries and state enterprises has benefited from international discussion of the effects of foreign investment on domestic economies and has become sensitive to problems experienced in other countries. As in the past, as Mexico develops greater expertise and experience with foreign investment, it is likely that the government will move to experiment with new regulatory measures. The attempt of the López Portillo administration to begin to move away from licensing toward tariffs to regulate imports is one experiment indicative of this trend[68]. With regard to oil, Mexican policy-makers have attempted to monitor its exploitation carefully and to plan for the expenditure of the money it produces. This is not an easy task. Management problems in the state oil company are severe and sophisticated technology is needed for exploiting the 'black gold'. The planning apparatus will need to be astute to avoid increasing the technological dependence and development bottlenecks that have plagued other oil-rich countries. The president himself is likely to remain at the center of the decision-making process and to exert his impressive influence on how new oil revenues will be expended, and what impact they will have on policies toward foreign investment. Nevertheless, the increased complexity of Mexico's economic linkages with the US, as well as the growing strength of the domestic business sector, may further limit the policy alternatives considered feasible by the president and his advisors.

In the future, then, government policies toward foreign investment are likely to change as they have changed in the past – gradually and within the context of what is viewed by policy-makers as being economically prudent and politically feasible. Gradual development and experimentation have been the means by which the government has sought to exert control over foreign investment in the past 40 years. As indicated, there are economic, bureaucratic, and political reasons that are crucial in accounting for this kind of development and there is little reason to believe that such constraints will cease to be important in the future. However, it is essential to emphasize the observation stressed in this chapter that analysts must look beyond the content of policies designed to regulate foreign investment and even beyond the rhetoric of various presidential administrations and the regime itself in order to appreciate fully what government policy is. Actual policy is often determined by its implementation. As we have seen, the disaggregated case by case approach favored by the Mexicans means that the impact of policies may vary from administration to administration and from case to case. Moreover, the rhetorical statements of political leaders need not necessarily be accepted at face value, as was frequently the case during the Echeverría administration when the president's apparent radicalness was often belied by the policies actually pursued. In fact, the methods selected to implement policies regarding foreign investment in Mexico create a multitude of bargaining possibilities that allow for accommodation of differing interests.

Even in an age of increasing economic nationalism among Third World nations and the capacity of some of them actually to enforce more stringent foreign investment regulations, Mexico is interesting as a case of a country that has minimized open confrontations with foreign investors. Of course, other countries in the region are also noted for their tendency to separate the formulation of general policy from the more specific and flexible application of it in individual circumstances; such a style is not unique to Mexico. But officials in this country seem inordinately consistent in utilizing such methods for strengthening the government's bargaining position when dealing with international actors.

Related to this, of course, is the significant possibility that the style of implementation favored by Mexican policy-makers can easily result in the absence of policy. That is, extensive possibilities for exceptions, rule stretching, personal and political understandings, and accommodation make it difficult to implement policy consistently and much foreign investment can go unregulated as a result. Some international firms, for instance, are in a position to establish clientele and personal relations with implementors that enable them to pursue their economic goals relatively independently of government policy. They also use these ties to gain advantages over their competitors. The style of policy implementation is a potential tool available to the Mexican government to regulate investment, but it requires commitment and coordination if overall goals are not to be lost as a result of a series of disaggregated and particularistic bargaining relationships. A style that seems 'pragmatic' and 'flexible' may therefore mask a lack of direction and an inability to achieve goals that have been set. New oil wealth may present Mexico with new capabilities to regulate foreign investment, but the old mechanisms of implementation present the possibility that success in doing so may be limited.

From the perspective of the United States, Mexico's policies toward foreign investment, while important and worthy of sustained interest, are not among the most pressing international issues between the two countries, for many of the reasons explored in this chapter. In the future, policy-makers in the US will need to become more sensitive to deep social, political, and economic problems faced by Mexico that may well have international implications. There is, for example, continuing debate and skepticism in Mexico about the government's commitment and ability to deal with the extensive problems of unemployment and underemployment in the country. The economy must be able to create at least 800 000 jobs annually just to satisfy new entrants into the job market. In itself, this requires a major effort and yet it does not cut into the already existing massive unemployment level. Inflation, which increased officially from 20% in 1979 to 28% in 1980, is another critical problem for the country. To date, Mexico's oil wealth has not led to greater equity in the distribution of wealth in the country or to the alleviation of the grinding poverty of its rural areas. Agricultural and population policies are other critical areas that need to be monitored closely for the impact they have on domestic stability and economic development. The manner in which these difficult problems are addressed by the government will have significant international implications and will affect the issues of trade, energy, fishing rights, and migration that already loom large on the agenda of US–Mexican relations. Thus, the issues discussed in this chapter are only one aspect of an increasingly complex, interdependent, and ambiguous politico-economic relationship between the two countries.

Acknowledgements

I am grateful for the helpful comments of Jorge Domínguez, Janet Kelly, and Robert Paarlberg on an earlier draft of this chapter. I would also like to thank Richard Vilella for his research assistance. The author alone is responsible for opinions, findings, and conclusions.

Notes

1 *Latin American Economic Report*, 5 (50), 23 December 1977, p. 252. This source reports an increase from 68% to 74% between 1966 and 1976 in the proportion of US investment to the industrialized countries, and a drop from 26% to 19% in developing areas. Latin America in general, however, has been receiving a greater share of the funds destined for the Third World.

2 Richard S. Newfarmer and Willard F. Mueller, *Multinational Corporations in Brazil and Mexico: Structural Sources of Economic and Noneconomic Power*. Report to the Subcommittee on Multinational Corporations of the Committee on Foreign Relations, United States Senate, August 1975, p. 50. Mexico differs in this regard from Brazil, which received a large

portion of its investments from five different countries.

3 In 1960, for example, just under 50% of the direct investment from the US was destined for Mexican manufacturing; by 1974, the proportion had risen to.76%. See Newfarmer and Mueller (note 2), p. 37. For further analysis of the source and structure of foreign investment in Mexico, see Flavia Derossi, *The Mexican Entrepreneur*. Development Centre of the Organization for Economic Cooperation and Development, Paris, 1971; Jorge I. Domínguez, chapter 2 in this volume; Harry J. Robinson and Timothy G. Smith, *The Impact of Foreign Private Investment on the Mexican Economy*. Stanford Research Institute, Menlo Park, Calif., SRI Project 4110, 1976; Richard S.

Weinert, 'The State and Foreign Capital'. In José Luís Reyna and Richard S. Weinert (eds), *Authoritarianism in Mexico*. ISHI Publications, Philadelphia, Pa., 1977.

4 Newfarmer and Mueller (note 2), p. 52. Chemicals received 28% of the investment in manufacturing; machinery, 16%; food processing, 13%; and transportation, 9%.

5 ibid., pp. 67, 72, 89.

6 In the expanding critical literature on multinationals, for example, the corporations are frequently indicted for the effects they have on the social structures of Third World countries, creating enclave economies, increasing the maldistribution of wealth, encouraging inappropriate tastes or styles of dress, consumption, and manners, and alienating native entrepreneurs from the pursuit of national interests. It has become evident that multinationals may cost a government money in terms of the social and political infrastructure they require, such as educating a workforce and building or maintaining roads, port facilities, and energy sources. They are criticized because they may be responsible for remitting more money in profits to corporate headquarters than they bring into a country in investments, and they may encourage the adoption of inappropriate and expensive technologies and managerial or decision-making skills. Balance of payments problems are increasingly cited as resulting from these activities. Most importantly, perhaps, multinationals have been attacked because they concentrate enormous economic power that may reverberate in political influence within a host country. See, for example, the critical views expressed in Richard J. Barnet and Ronald E. Mueller, *Global Reach: The Power of the Multinational Corporations*. Simon and Schuster, New York, 1974. For another discussion of the effects of multinationals on development, see Paul Streeten, 'Costs and Benefits of Multinational Enterprises in Less Developed Countries'. In John Dunning (ed.), *The Multinational Enterprise*. Praeger, New York, 1971, pp. 240–58. See also, Charles T. Goodsell, *American Corporations and Peruvian Politics*. Harvard University Press, Cambridge, Mass., 1974; Luciano Martins, 'The Politics of US Multinational Corporations in Latin America'. In Julio Cotler and Richard Fagen (eds), *Latin America and the United States: The Changing Political Realities*. Stanford University Press, Stanford, Calif., 1974, pp. 368–402; Edith Penrose, 'The State and Multinational Enterprises in Less Developed Countries'. In Dunning, pp. 221 –39; Weinert (note 3); and Miguel Wionczek, 'Problemática política y económica de las transnacionales in el contexto latinoamericano'. *Comercio Exterior*, **25** (4), April 1975, pp. 444–50. See also the essays in Richard Fagen (ed.), *Capitalism and the State in US–Latin American Relations*. Stanford University Press, Stanford, Calif., 1979.

7 See Edith B. Couturier, 'Mexico'. In Harold Eugene Davis, Larman C. Wilson, and others, *Latin American Foreign Policies: An Analysis*. Johns Hopkins University Press, Baltimore, Md., 1975, pp. 117–35. One of the problems frequently cited for the downfall of the Porfirio Diaz administration and the outbreak of the Revolution of 1910 was the stranglehold that foreign investment from Britain and the US had achieved over the Mexican economy. Economic nationalism and sensitivity to the potential power of external economic actors has been an enduring legacy of the Revolution. The expropriation of the oil industry under President Lázaro Cárdenas in 1938 continues to symbolize to Mexicans the government's ideological commitment to economic independence.

8 See, for example, Fernando Fajnzylber, 'Las empresas transnacionales y el sistema industrial de méxico'. *El trimestre económico*, **42** (168), October–December 1975, pp. 903–31; Lorenzo Meyer, 'Cambio político y dependencia: México en el siglo XX'. *Foro internacional*, **13** (2), October –December 1972, pp. 101–38. For the relationship of Mexican foreign policy to domestic political concerns, see Jorge Domínguez, 'The Implications of Mexico's Internal Affairs for its International Relations'. Center for International Affairs, Harvard University, Cambridge, Mass., April 1980; and Wolf Grabendorff, 'Review Essay: Mexico's Foreign Policy – Indeed a Foreign Policy?' *Journal of Inter-American Studies and World Affairs*, **20** (1), February 1978, pp. 85–92; Marcia A. Grant, 'Domestic Determinants of Mexican Foreign Policy: The Case of Echeverría's "New Foreign Policy"'. Paper presented to the 1977 meeting of the American Political Science Association,

Washington, DC, 1–4 September 1977;
William H. Hamilton, 'Mexico's "New"
Foreign Policy: A Reexamination'. *Inter-
American Economic Affairs*, 29 (3), Winter
1975, pp. 51–8; Guy E. Poitras, 'Mexico's
"New" Foreign Policy'. *Inter-American
Economic Affairs*, 28 (3), Winter 1974, pp.
59–77; Yoram Shapira, 'Mexico's Foreign
Policy under Echeverría: A Retrospect'.
Inter-American Economic Affairs, 51 (4),
Spring 1978.

9 See Domínguez (note 8). See also Mario
Ojeda, 'México ante Los Estados Unidos
en la coyuntura actual'. In Centro de
Estudios Internacionales (ed.), *Con-
tinuidad y cambio en la política exterior de
México: 1977*. El Colegio de México,
Mexico, 1977.

10 Most analysts currently agree that the conditions facilitating the pursuit of Mexico's
development strategy were an outcome of
the Revolution of 1910. While the policy
was in evidence before the 1940s, it took
until that time to consolidate the power of
the government and its supporting economic and political structures and thus permit the full development of the growth
model.

11 For overviews and analyses of the Mexican
economy, see Roger D. Hansen, *The Poli-
tics of Mexican Development*. Johns Hop-
kins University Press, Baltimore, Md.,
1971; John F. H. Purcell and Susan Kauf-
man Purcell, 'Mexican Business and Public
Policy'. In James M. Malloy (ed.), *Au-
thoritarianism and Corporatism in Latin
America*. University of Pittsburgh Press,
Pittsburgh, Pa., 1977, pp. 199–226; Clark
W. Reynolds, *The Mexican Economy:
Twentieth Century Structure and Growth*.
Yale University Press, New Haven,
Conn., 1970; John B. Ross, *The Economic
System of Mexico*. California Institute of
International Studies, Stanford, Calif.,
1971; Raymond Vernon, *The Dilemma of
Mexico's Development*. Harvard Universi-
ty Press, Cambridge, Mass., 1963. Hansen,
pp. 43–55, reviews the role of the public
sector in Mexican development.

12 For a discussion of the positive and negative aspects of import substitution, see
Werner Baer, 'Import Substitution and
Industrialization in Latin America: Experiences and Interpretations'. *Latin
American Research Review*, 7 (1), Spring
1972, pp. 95–122. For import substitution
in Mexico, see René Villarreal, 'The Policy
of Import Substituting Industrialization,

1929–1975'. In Reyna and Weinert (note
3), pp. 67–107. For changes in Mexican
policy, see Ross (note 11); Leopoldo Solís,
'The External Sector of the Mexican
Economy'. In Joseph Grunwald (ed.),
*Latin America and the World Economy: A
Changing International Order*. Sage Publications, Beverly Hills, Calif., 1978, pp.
133–46.

13 See David Barkin, 'Mexico's Albatross:
The United States Economy'. *Latin American Perspectives*, 2 (2), Summer 1975, p.
76; Derossi (note 3), p. 73; Hansen (note
11); Purcell and Purcell (note 11).

14 For a more detailed description of these
conditions, see Richard R. Fagen, 'The
Realities of US–Mexican Relations'.
Foreign Affairs, 55 (4), July 1977, pp.
685–700; Newfarmer and Mueller (note
2).

15 See Vernon (note 11), pp. 171–2. See also
Douglas Bennett, Morris J. Blachman,
and Kenneth Sharpe, 'Mexico and Multinational Corporations: An Explanation of
State Action'. In Grunwald (note 12), p.
271. A detailed description of private sector attitudes toward foreign investment is
found in Derossi (note 3), pp. 73–86; and
in Jorge I. Domínguez in chapter 2 of this
volume.

16 There is some disagreement among students of Mexican politics about the degree
of independence of the state from the
powerful capitalist class in the country.
Certainly the economic history of the private sector reveals a consistently supportive and encouraging attitude on the part
of the state, leading some to posit that the
government functions as a creature of
these interests. However, recent case studies and interpretations of the relationship
between the state and the private sector
strongly support a view of a powerful
government with 'state interests' of its
own to pursue that interacts with a business community having its own set of
interests and methods of influencing the
government. For a description and analysis of the major business associations in
Mexico, see Robert J. Shafer, *Mexican
Business Organizations: History and
Analysis*. Syracuse University, Syracuse,
NY, 1973. A case study of the role of
business and its representative associations
in negotiating with the government is
found in Susan K. Purcell, *The Mexican
Profit Sharing Decision: Politics in an Authoritarian Regime*. University of Califor-

nia Press, Berkeley, Calif., 1975. While the terms 'the private sector' and 'the business community' are used throughout this chapter, it is recognized that such labels misrepresent the extent of homogeneity and similarity of interests within this diversified and large segment of the population. The terms are used for simplicity only. See chapter 2 by Domínguez in this volume for a discussion of divisions and coalitions within the private sector.

17 This is a point made by Moise Naim, 'Ideology, Dependencia, and the Control of MNC's'. Working paper, Sloan School of Management, MIT, 1977. See also Bennett, Blachman, and Sharpe (note 15), for a discussion of this point related to governmental activity in Mexico. On the influence of economists in policy-making, see Roderick Ai Camp, *The Role of Economists in Policy Making*. University of Arizona Press, Tucson, Ariz., 1977. On the role of developing bureaucratic expertise and changing relationships with multinational companies, see Theodore Moran, *Multinational Corporations and the Politics of Dependence: Copper in Chile*. Princeton University Press, Princeton, NJ, 1974.

18 Bennett, Blachman, and Sharpe (note 15), p. 277.

19 Vernon (note 11), pp. 115–16, reports that in the Ruíz Cortines administration, 'The government's surveillance and regulation of the activities of the private sector became more and more systematic and professional. Its industrial activities became more technical; its familiarity with the details of the private sector's operations broadened; and its economic controls over the private sector became more particularistic. Accordingly, one began to see even more selective methods of credit control than in earlier administrations; more discriminating applications of the tax-exemption provisions for "new and necessary industries"; more detailed demands on enterprises to adhere to price ceilings; more explicit limitations on the size and nature of foreign ownership in individual investment projects.'

20 Bennett, Blachman, and Sharpe (note 15), p. 272.

21 See Newfarmer and Mueller (note 2), p. 124; Ross (note 11), pp. 40–1; Weinert (note 3), p. 124.

22 See Merilee S. Grindle, *Bureaucrats,* *Politicians, and Peasants in Mexico: A Case Study in Public Policy*. University of California Press, Berkeley, Calif., 1977, chapter 3; Merilee S. Grindle, 'Policy Change in an Authoritarian Regime: Mexico Under Echeverría'. *Journal of Inter-American Studies and World Affairs*, **19** (4), November 1977, pp. 523–55.

23 The role of the president in Mexico is discussed in Grindle, *Bureaucrats, Politicians, and Peasants in Mexico* (note 22); Carolyn Needleman and Martin Needleman, 'Who Rules Mexico? A Critique of Some Current Views on the Mexican Political Process'. *Journal of Politics*, **31** (4) November 1969; Purcell (note 16); and Reyna and Weinert (note 3). See also Susan Purcell and John Purcell, 'State and Society in Mexico: Must a Stable Polity be Institutionalized?' *World Politics*, **22** (2), January 1978, pp. 194–227.

24 See Barkin (note 13), p. 70; Rafael Izquierdo, 'Protectionism in Mexico'. In Raymond Vernon (ed.), *Public Policy and Private Enterprise in Mexico*. Harvard University Press, Cambridge, Mass., 1964, pp. 261–4.

25 See Bennett, Blachman, and Sharpe (note 15), p. 277.

26 For analysis of the automobile industry in Mexico see Bennett, Blachman, and Sharpe (note 15); Douglas Bennett and Kenneth Sharpe, 'Agenda Setting and Bargaining Power: The Mexican State vs. Transnational Automobile Corporations'. Paper prepared for the Social Science Research Council Working Group on the Transnational Automobile Industry in Latin America, 8–10 December 1978; Douglas Bennett and Kenneth Sharpe, 'Transnational Corporations and the Political Economy of Export Promotion: The Case of the Mexican Automobile Industry'. *International Organization*, **30** (1), Winter 1976; Rhys Owen Jenkins, *Dependent Industrialization in Latin America: The Automotive Industry in Argentina, Chile, and Mexico*. Praeger, New York, 1977.

27 See Ross (note 11), p. 38; Solís (note 12), p. 135.

28 Vernon (note 11), pp. 114–15. See also Domínguez in this volume.

29 Vernon (note 11), p. 122; Bennett and Sharpe, 1978 (note 26), p. 30.

30 José Sainz Campillo, 'Si, se cambian las reglas del juego'. *Comercio Exterior*, **22** (10), October 1972, p. 943.

31 See Solís (note 12).
32 Thus, it made clear that investment would not be welcomed where it was composed of less than 51% domestic capital, where it would result in dominating the market in a particular activity, if it was expected to have deleterious effects on balance of payments, or if its effects on employment were not considered helpful. On the other hand, investment plans directed toward underdeveloped areas of the country, which promised to produce exportable goods, and which included programs for training local managerial and technical personnel, were to be considered favorably. See the discussion and detailed description of the law in Robert S. Tancer, 'Regulating Foreign Investment in the Seventies: The Mexican Approach'. In Lawrence E. Koslow (ed.), *The Future of Mexico*. Center for Latin American Studies, Arizona State University, Tempe, Ariz., 1977, pp. 196–206; Weinert (note 3).
33 Among the prohibitions on registering contracts are any that involve
   a. transferring knowledge already in the public domain;
   b. returning royalties that are too high;
   c. giving managerial control to the licensor;
   d. requiring return of improvements or investigations by the licensee;
   e. limiting R and D efforts by the licensee;
   f. containing requirements that the licensee purchase equipment, materials, or parts exclusively from a specified supplier;
   g. limiting exports in a manner contrary to the national interest;
   h. prohibiting use of other technologies;
   i. requiring that the licensee sell exclusively to the licensor;
   j. specifying personnel that must be employed;
   k. setting the price of production or prices of sale or resale;
   l. requiring the signing of exclusive distribution contracts, with the licensor for the national market;
   m. including excessive periods of duration of the contracts...;
   n. stipulating the jurisdiction of foreign courts – Mexican law shall prevail.
   See Jack N. Behrman, *The Role of International Companies in Latin American Integration: Autos and Petrochemicals*.

Lexington Books, Lexington, Mass., 1972, pp. 83–4. See also the description of the transfer of technology law in Tancer (note 32), pp. 206–9.
34 See Weinert (note 3), p. 122.
35 Business International Corporation, *Mexico: A New Look at a Maturing Market*. The Corporation, New York, 1978, pp. 43–4, 82–3; *Business Latin America*, 16 November 1977; *Latin America Economic Report*, 6 (39), 6 October 1978, p. 311.
36 *Latin America Economic Report*, 5 (40), 14 October 1977, p. 175.
37 *Latin America Economic Report*, 5 (49), 16 December 1977, p. 245; Robinson and Smith (note 3), pp. 9, 136.
38 Robinson and Smith (note 3), p. 146; see also Olga Pellicer de Brody, 'Mexico in the 1970s and Its Relations with the United States'. In Cotler and Fagen (note 6), p. 330.
39 *Latin America Economic Report*, 3 (19), 16 May 1975, p. 76. Labor costs in Mexico, while not low compared to other Third World countries, continue to be attractive to foreign investors because of the country's proximity to the US, which diminishes transportation and marketing costs.
40 Robinson and Smith (note 3). The majority of respondents held the opinion that the law was hampering foreign investment activities in Mexico.

Opinions about the 1973 foreign investment law (responses from 346 firms active in Mexico)

The law:	Yes %	No %	No answer %
Encourages new foreign investment	19.2	73.4	7.5
Gives adequate scope to expand operations	33.2	57.0	9.8
Is satisfactorily administered	38.3	38.3	23.4
Has reduced the inflow of direct investment into Mexico	75.2	16.4	8.4

N= 214

Opinions on the transfer of technology law were less critical, the majority of respondents saying that the law had no adverse effect on their operations.

Opinions about the tranfer of technology law

The law:	Yes %	No %	No answer %
Restricts the use of foreign technology in Mexico	48.6	47.1	4.3
Encourages the use of foreign technology in Mexico	8.7	76.4	14.9
Affects the operations adversely	18.8	72.1	9.1

N= 208

Robinson and Smith, pp. 24–25, 141, 143, 146. This survey was conducted in 1975 in Mexico. Questionnaires were sent to 600 firms belonging to the American Chamber of Commerce of Mexico; 239 responses were returned, representing 346 firms. In addition, interviews were conducted with a sample of 168 firms. See also *Business Latin America*, 15 March 1973, p. 85.

41 Robinson and Smith (note 3), p. 148. These responses were collected before the peso devaluation of 1976, which had detrimental effects on the profits of Mexican subsidiaries of multinational firms and which reverberated in increased criticism of government policies. The more accommodative stance of the López Portillo administration has done much to allay these apprehensions, however. See *Business Latin America*, 7 December 1977, p. 385, for a discussion of business reaction to the devaluation. Business International Corporation (note 35), chapter 8, provides an overview evaluation of doing business in Mexico from the perspective of US investors. For a further analysis of US business in Mexico, see Angela M. Delli Sante, 'The Private Sector, Business Organizations, and International Influence: A Case Study of Mexico'. In Fagen, 1979 (note 6).

42 Business International Corporation (note 35), pp. 43–4.

43 Robinson and Smith (note 3), pp. 104–5. See also Izquierdo (note 24), p. 259.

44 Business International Corporation (note 35), p. 92.

45 See, for example, *Business Latin America*, 1 March 1978, pp. 67–8.

46 Business International Corporation (note 35), pp. 92–6.

47 Robinson and Smith (note 3), pp. 13–14.

48 On clientelism in Mexico, see Grindle, *Bureaucrats, Politicians, and Peasants in Mexico* (note 22); and Izquierdo (note 24).

49 See *Business Latin America*, 12 August 1971; Robinson and Smith (note 3), pp. 13–14.

50 See Purcell and Purcell (note 11).

51 Frequently, the specific dealings of the foreign firms with Mexican government officials are mediated by large and influential law firms with offices in Mexico City.

52 Purcell and Purcell (note 11), pp. 203–8; Grindle, *Bureaucrats, Politicians and Peasants* (note 22), chapters 5 and 6.

53 Purcell and Purcell (note 11), p. 205. In comparison with Brazil, Mexico is noted among foreign investors for the general uncertainty of the rules of the game, according to one analyst. This can be both a positive and negative feature of dealing with the government from the perspective of the foreign investor. See Behrman (note 33), p. 74. Business organizations, such as the American Chamber of Commerce of Mexico, do attempt to exert pressure on the government. For an interesting analysis, see Delli Sante (note 41).

54 See Guillermo Edelberg, 'The Procurement Practices of the Mexican Affiliates of Selected United States Automobile Firms'. Ph.D. dissertation, Graduate School of Business Administration, Harvard University, 1963, p. 12; Bennett, Blachman, and Sharpe (note 15), p. 274.

55 Bartolomé Contreras Z., 'El futuro de la industria de automores en México'. *Comercio Exterior*, **20** (1), January 1970, p. 52; *Business Latin America*, 12 November 1970, p. 362.

56 See 'Compensación de importaciones de partes automovilísticas'. *Comercio Exterior*, **19** (11), November 1969, p. 864; Contreras (note 55), p. 52; Behrman (note 33), Appendix.

57 *Latin America Economic Report*, **5** (22), 10 June 1977, p. 88; *Business Latin America*, 4 August 1976, p. 247.

58 Pellicer de Brody (note 38), p. 330.

59 'La industria de automotores en una carrera de resistencia'. *Comercio Exterior*, **27** (7), July 1977, pp. 771–5.

60 Business International Corporation (note 35), pp. 68–9.

61 *Latin America Economic Report*, 5 (22), 10 June 1977, p. 88.

62 *Latin America Economic Report*, 5 (49), 16 December 1977, pp. 244–5; Business International Corporation (note 35), pp. 80–1; General Motors Annual Report, 1976.

63 For a general discussion of these problems, see Jack Baranson, *Automotive Industries in Developing Countries*. Johns Hopkins University Press, Baltimore, Maryland, 1969; and Baranson, *International Transfer of Automotive Technology to Developing Countries*. United Nations Institute for Training and Research, UNITAR Research Report No. 8, New York, 1971.

64 Baranson, 1971 (note 63), p. 76; *Business Latin America*, 12 November 1970, p. 363.

65 In negotiations with Japan in the Fall of 1978, for instance, the sale of oil was discussed in terms of an exchange for technology and finance capital. *Latin America Economic Report*, 6 (42), 27 October 1978, p. 329.

66 *Latin America Economic Report*, 6 (39), 6 October 1978, p. 311.

67 For a useful discussion of energy and the future of US–Mexican relations, see Kevin Middlebrook, 'Energy Security in US–Mexican Relations'. In David Deese and Joseph Nye (eds), *Energy and Security*. Ballinger, Cambridge, Mass., 1980.

68 Business International Corporation (note 35), p. 102.

Venezuelan foreign economic policy and the United States

Janet Kelly Escobar*

Anyone who has stood at the end of a railroad platform waiting for a friend will recall what queer people he mistook for him. The shape of a hat, a slightly characteristic gait, evoked the vivid picture in his mind's eye. In sleep a tinkle may sound like the pealing of a great bell; the distant stroke of a hammer like a thunderclap .... Certainly for the most part, the way we see things is a combination of what is there and of what we expected to find. [Walter Lippmann, *Public Opinion*]

4.1   Introduction: The United States and economic nationalism in Venezuela

The most outstanding trend in US–Venezuelan relations is the steady growth of economic nationalism in Venezuela. This trend is not limited to the case of Venezuela, of course; it has marked the development of relations between the United States and many Latin American countries, as well as much of the developing world. Economic nationalism in this context is the use of state policies to alter the 'natural' workings of a liberal or free economic system in favor of the country concerned. It has also been referred to as mercantilism, or neo-mercantilism. Such words tend to create reactions in the United States of disapproval, foreboding and opposition, sometimes with a blind eye to the broader spectrum of international relations. As Lippmann pointed out above, such expectations or preconceived notions have a way of dominating our perception of events, even to the point of distorting rather obvious truths. But forewarned is forearmed: in this chapter I shall attempt to get down to things as they are, avoiding if possible the resort to Lippmann's stereotypes.

In the days of Cordell Hull, in the course of World War II, the United States dedicated itself to the maintenance of liberal principles in world economic relations. Persistent opposition to many of these principles in the Third World has slowly acted to break down some American preconceptions. There has been a grudging realization on the part of many policy-makers that economic nationalism is here to stay as long as inequalities exist

* Universidad Simón Bolívar, Caracas.

among nations and as long as a liberal international economic system continues to grant the bulk of its favors to the developed world. The tricky question from the American point of view is how to make intelligent distinctions among foreign manifestations of economic nationalism. Which acts are legitimate and which are not? Which will benefit longer-run relations with the United States and which will be harmful? In which cases do political considerations outweigh economic considerations? In other words, at what point does economic nationalism in Venezuela and in similar countries pose a significant threat to the overall American interest?

The thesis of this chapter is that in very few cases can it be argued that the growth of economic nationalism seriously threatens American interests. Just as the 'Munich analogy' has given an excessively bad name to any act of appeasement, so the 'analogy of the 1930s' has condemned without trial all acts of economic self-protection, from domestic subsidies to exporters (probably a universally practiced ploy) to cartel creation and maintenance (less universally practiced, but perhaps universally envied). In fact, one must distinguish carefully between the effects of economic nationalism writ large, as in the case of Schachtian policies in Hitler's Germany, and economic nationalism in today's developing countries, where neither the purpose nor the effect is to create closed blocs, autarky, or damage to the smooth functioning of the international economic system. Venezuela is typical of a large group of Latin and developing countries in its attempts to use nationalistic policies to bring about economic development, domestically and internationally. These policies affect virtually all spheres of the economy: trade, investment, monetary policy, state enterprises, prices, industrial diversification, technology, and so on. Venezuela is atypical in that it enjoys a functioning democracy and is an oil country. It will be seen below that, in the areas mentioned above, few real threats to US interests can be found. In addition, whatever problems do arise must be balanced against the political considerations inherent in Venezuela's democracy and in her oil fields.

While in the areas of economic relations between Venezuela and the United States few real threats will be detected, it does not follow that complete harmony is the result. Normal relations will always imply a certain level of conflict, perhaps even more so when countries approach equality. (Compare the number of economic conflicts between the United States and Japan with the number between the US and any developing country.) As Domínguez notes, modern economic relations require more subtle planning and foresight than was the case in former periods. This planning must imply a long-run and integrated view of relations with any specific country. Too much attention to single-issue problems, such as a particular nationalization or Venezuela's role in the Organization of Petroleum Exporting Countries (OPEC), magnifies the negative aspects of overall relations. Individual policies could mean, for instance, the exclusion of particular US companies from the local market, discriminatory conditions of operations for foreign investors, or higher prices for American buyers of Venezuelan products. It is argued here that US policy should base itself on overall cost-benefit analysis of a range of relations, and not only on the costs of a particular action on the part of Venezuela. The past 20 years of US-Venezuelan relations show indeed that there have been significant long-run gains from a tolerant US attitude toward nationalism in Venezuela's economic policy. These are:

- Economic independence is a goal associated with the return to democracy, so that outward signs of economic nationalism tend to strengthen the popularity of democracy itself in Venezuela.

- Nationalistic economic policies tend to lend a sense of self-assurance to policy-makers when accepted by countries like the United States. This success prevents the build-up of resentments, criticism of the government by extremes of left and right, and sudden turns of policy in extreme directions in response to both the resentment and the criticism.

- Overall US–Venezuelan economic relations have in fact grown healthily, even if in some individual cases particular US interests have been set back.

- Friendly settlement of economic differences has promoted an atmosphere of mutual trust between the United States and Venezuela and has thus permitted significant political cooperation in areas of agreement.

Other points of view, of course, exist. Petras, Morley and Smith hold that Venezuelan economic nationalism has produced mainly surface changes that belie the continuation of old patterns of dependence, presenting 'the Venezuelan revolutionary left with ample evidence to rip away the mantle of nationalist legitimacy with which the current regime clothes itself'[1]. Richard Fagen interprets US–Latin American relations not as a situation of US toleration leading to mutual trust and cooperation (as US–Venezuelan relations are described above) but as a situation in which the US 'preserves and extends its political, economic and cultural influence and domination across the continent'[2]. Indeed, the dependency view in general holds that new forms of North–South accommodation tend in reality to be new forms of North–South domination. Peter Evans' refined dependency analysis of Brazil takes this view a step further[3]. Rejecting the simplistic claim that multinational corporations and their supporters have signaled the decline of governments (and hence the inability of Third World governments to cope with these foreign powers), Evans holds on the contrary that 'dependent development' in Brazil is made possible by the 'internalization of imperialism' and is associated with the 'consolidation of state power'. At the same time, local capitalists have gained 'a substantial ability to bargain'.

Finally, Evans defines dependence as 'a situation in which the rate and direction of accumulation are externally conditioned'[4]. The definition has become very broad.

Dependency theorists can rightly point out that the claim made here that Venezuelan economic nationalism poses little threat to the United States is much akin to their claim that imperial countries like the United States manage to preserve control over weaker and poorer countries despite apparent changes in forms of economic relations. But while there is a similarity in the two analyses, there is not complete agreement. Here I argue rather that there have been real changes in the balance of economic relations between the United States and Venezuela, and that Venezuelan economic nationalism does contribute to an increase in independence from the United States, but also that the United States retains a large (and perhaps natural) measure of influence in both the economic and political spheres in Venezuela. If by the 'internalization of imperialism' Evans meant that elites, and perhaps non-elites, hold to a belief in capitalism or even in American cultural values, then I must agree with Evans that Venezuela is an example of the internalization of imperialism. The difference may be in the degree to which we hold that this is a bad thing.

Robert W. Tucker argues that, as long as there is a system of sovereign states, there will be inequality among nations[5]. This is a long way from arguing that the distribution of equality or inequality is fixed, however. To the extent that Venezuela and countries like it are able to increase their relative power, the United States is constrained to accommodate to this change. The cost of non-accommodation would probably be unnecessary strains in relations caused by resistance in the face of the inevitable. Present inequalities, as the dependency theorists argue, do tend to favor the long-run interests of the United States in its relations with Venezuela; at the same time, American acceptance of the inevitable growth of Venezuelan economic nationalism is likely to further more cooperative long-term relations across all the areas of mutual concern. Domínguez points out that the internal changes taking place in many Latin American countries – changes that have created stronger and more aggressive local elites – in fact indicate success in terms of certain goals of US policy. That these elites now pursue many economic goals ostensibly prejudicial to American interests means that the United States is facing the 'hell of success'.

This chapter seeks to examine the major areas of economic contact between the United States and Venezuela in order to trace the development of nationalistic, or independence-oriented, economic policies in Venezuela and their effects on American interests. It will be seen that the Venezuelans have undergone important changes internally that have enabled them to assert their economic muscle in the last two decades. It is in this sense that a change in internal structures has led to a change in the relations between the two countries. At the same time, however, the process of change has been circumscribed by the larger structure of international relationships: auton-omous change within Venezuela has made a difference, but overall power relations still largely determine outcomes in each area to be examined. And the advantage usually goes to the strong. It should be stressed, however, that this advantage does not go to the strong because of gunboat diplomacy, high-level threats, or outright ultimata. Countries like Venezuela depend too heavily on their claims to sovereign equality to respond well to such explicit uses of power. As long as conflicts are settled without the glare of too much attention, however, outcomes are likely to reflect a rational assessment of real bargaining power. While precise measures of 'real bargaining power' will remain illusive, I shall attempt to document at least the direction of change in such power. Few will doubt that change in the world oil situation in the 1970s has contributed to a significant change in the relative bargaining positions of oil-rich and oil-poor countries. It will be seen that the graceful acceptance of the changes in internal structures in Venezuela and in external structures of world power has been more likely to produce an optimal outcome for the United States than unconsidered reactions to setbacks in particular and limited cases.

4.2 The sources of economic nationalism in Venezuela

What made the Venezuelans into economic nationalists? And when did they make the transformation? There are several sources, some of them specific to Venezuela, some more general in application. As for when they became economic nationalists, no firm date can be set because the transformation has been gradual (and incomplete); however, the overthrow of the Marcos Pérez Jiménez dictatorship in 1958 provides a convenient starting point for our analysis.

The natural lure of economic nationalism

That the government should do something to improve the economic prospects of a nation is an attractive and popular idea. As an approach to policy, it met no major opponents until the birth of liberalism, with its still counter-intuitive claim that the inhabitants of a given country will be richer when the government takes the fewest steps to ensure that outcome[6]. Despite the impeccable logic of Adam Smith and his followers, pure liberalism has never found a natural audience outside of the economics profession in Britain and the United States. The main criticism of liberal economics is that the real world does not correspond to the theoretical world of free or perfect competition. As soon as unequal competition is admitted, then optimal pricing, production and distribution are unlikely outcomes[7]. The underdeveloped countries have not been slow to point out that they play the role of the weaker party in this real world, and hence fail to reap the supposed benefits of the 'liberal' system. The natural and even the rational response from their point of view is to use state power to counteract, to the extent possible, the negative effects of the world market system. This involves what the upholders of liberalism would term 'economic nationalism'. Thus, while it has been natural for the most powerful economic actors to espouse liberalism, it has been equally natural for the less powerful to be attracted to economic interventionism.

The historical trend toward economic nationalism

There is little doubt that Venezuela has willingly snapped at the lure of economic nationalism, especially since 1958. In this, the country has been part of a broader Latin movement favoring protectionism and other statist policies, associated prominently with the thinking of Raul Prebisch and institutionalized in the UN Economic Commission for Latin America. The Marcos Pérez Jiménez dictatorship of the 1950s had been interventionist in the purely domestic sphere without, however, daring to take an aggressive line internationally[8]. The democratic government succeeding the anti-Pérez Jiménez revolution of 1958 sought to distinguish itself from the dictatorship on the basis of two main planks: its legitimacy based on popular support, and its legitimacy based on its defense of Venezuela's economic and political sovereignty. President Rómulo Betancourt, who had pursued this theme since taking the lead of the 'Generation of 28', had described the previous dictatorship, for instance, as 'A Republic for Sale'. As will be seen below, in practically all areas of economic policy, successive governments since 1958 have taken an interventionist approach, inserting the government hand into both the domestic and the international economic sectors. It should be noted, however, that this interventionism has been associated consistently with correcting the failures of the market and with stimulating local economic independence[9]. Venezuelan governments have not only rejected the pure liberal claim that the free market produces the optimal outcome, they have also rejected the neo-liberal claim that pessimistically charges governments with inevitable incompetence. In fact, there is a remarkable degree of optimism in Venezuela with respect to what the state can do when it puts its mind to it[10].

Pragmatic sources of economic nationalism

Venezuela shares with other developing countries, and with developed countries as well, the common situation in which the state is the only available agent for many projects. There is much evidence, for instance, that the creation of state enterprises world-wide results from such pragmatic considerations as that the state is the only institution large enough to manage investments in an industry requiring large-scale operations. Talcott Parsons noted also that 'the balance between governmentally controlled and free-enterprise industry is to a far larger degree than is generally held a pragmatic question and not one of fundamental principles'[11]. Jones and Mason confirm that 'countries at similar stages of development will have public enterprise sectors of similar size and similar structure'[12]. Similar pragmatic arguments exist for other aspects of state interventionism: infant industry protection, export price maintenance, employment stimulation, etc. Since most of the rest of the world thinks that statism makes practical sense, it is not surprising that Venezuela does too. There is a further feature special to Venezuela under this rubric of pragmatism – the oil industry. Like it or not, the Venezuelan government accounts automatically for about 22% of the gross domestic product by virtue of its control over oil and mining[13]. Short of giving away this income, the government has little option other than to play out its role as chief actor in the direction of the economy.

The basis for economic nationalism in country capabilities

It has already been noted that the Venezuelan government enjoys high income from the oil industry that enables it to carry out ambitious programs beyond the reach of many of its neighbors. Oil exports in 1980, for instance, were worth $17.9 billion[14]. That comes to over $1000 per person – a considerable bonanza for a developing country. In its wealth, of course, Venezuela is not typical of Latin American countries. It has one of the highest per capita incomes in the western hemisphere after the United States and Canada ($3600 in 1979), exceeded only by Trinidad and Tobago, which is also an oil-exporting country. But many other Latin American countries, like Argentina, Brazil, Mexico, and Chile, also rank high among middle-income developing countries. Above-subsistence income facilitates any program of economic nationalism by enabling the country to cover the inevitable costs of subsidies and to counter the possible effects of retaliation. Other factors, like education, may also make other countries equal to Venezuela in terms of government capacity to carry out extensive state-organized programs of economic development. This capacity depends in large part on the availability of competent personnel to carry out complex government programs. Among Latin American and Caribbean countries, Argentina, Chile, Uruguay, Jamaica, Costa Rica, Trinidad, and Cuba all enjoy higher adult literacy rates than Venezuela[15]. The conclusion is that Venezuelan state capabilities have increased considerably, but not so much that Venezuela falls into an entirely different class from its neighbors. In this volume, Grindle (ch. 3) notes for instance that Mexico has been a leader in pursuing economic nationalism in Latin America – and that its officials have demonstrated much skill in improving the government's bargaining position vis-à-vis foreign partners like the United States. Odell (ch. 5) also notes the important role of expertise and skill in determining outcomes of trade disputes between Latin American countries and the United States.

The factors underpinning the development of economic nationalism are reviewed here in order to show both the particular impulses to nationalism in Venezuela and the way in which Venezuela shares in a more general trend that cannot probably be reversed in any significant way by external pressures. What are the consequences for the United States? The next section will deal with this question on a case by case basis.

4.3   The areas of United States–Venezuelan economic relations

The direction of trade

Trade patterns have always been a sensitive issue between countries, with each country constantly assessing both political and economic vulnerabilities associated with the content, direction and volume of trade in its national accounts. With regard to the direction of trade, Clark Murdock said:

> The ideal position for a state to be in with regard to trade vulnerabilities would be for the trade it carries on to be relatively unimportant to the domestic economy and relatively important to its trading partners[16].

Latin America has typically found itself in a weak position in this respect, particularly in its trade with the United States. In 1978, 30% of Latin American exports went to the United States, and 32% of imports came from the United States. Venezuela was typical: 36% of her exports[17] went to the United States, while 41% of her imports came from the US. Meanwhile, Venezuela could hardly claim to play an equal role in US trade: she accounted for 2.6% of US exports and 2.0% of imports[18]. Needless to say, this pattern reflects profound asymmetry in trade relations, and is a typical example of a situation that tends to stimulate governmental counteraction on the part of the weaker partner.

Physical proximity tends to produce a natural link between Venezuela and the United States. In addition, the direction of trade is often highly influenced by the nationality of foreign investors, who tend to use traditional suppliers from the home country even when abroad. Thus, a government that wishes to change the patterns of the direction of trade will usually have to resort either to intervention or to indirect incentives that alter decision-making with respect to the source of imports or the direction of exports. Traditional suppliers and clients will naturally take offense at such intervention, complaining of discrimination or of 'political interference'.

Venezuelan governments have indeed sought to diversify the direction of trade, both away from the United States and, when feasible, away from industrialized countries. With respect to exports, this mainly means exports of oil should go to a more balanced group of customers, although diversification of clients for other products is also naturally to be encouraged. The Fourth National Plan (1970–74) called for 'the widening and diversification of trade with the rest of the world, particularly with other Latin American countries'; it also called for the revision of the reciprocal trade agreement of 1952, which had worked to preserve the US–Venezuela trade bias[19]. Likewise the Fifth Plan called for diversification of oil exports and development of the national capacity for marketing (more possible now that the oil industry was in government hands)[20]. This was a long step from the policy of the 1950s, which sought US assurances of preferred treatment for Venezuelan exports and which granted preferences to US goods imported as the *quid pro quo*. In 1959, Venezuelan oil minister Pérez Alfonzo (the 'father of OPEC') sought regional preferences to favor Venezuelan exports in US markets, a request repeated in the 1960s[21]. Later governments sought to disentangle themselves from the trade link with the United States. In oil this means using state-to-state arrangements to re-direct sales (sometimes in return for specific imports from the partner country), seeking out clients without the intermediary of international oil companies, and encouraging new customers with favorable terms, credits, and the like[22]. In other exports, it has meant official (but sometimes lukewarm) support for local integration efforts: the Andean Pact, the Latin American Free Trade Association, replaced in 1980 by the Latin American Integration Association, and SELA (the Latin American Economic System). In imports, the state has used government-owned enterprises to diversify import sources by using country of origin as a criterion in equipment bid evaluations. Have these efforts harmed the US? And what have been the results of American reactions?

First of all, it would seem that Venezuela's diversification efforts have had no effect on the role of the United States as a market for its exports since the mid-1960s. There have been marginal increases in the shares of some Latin countries in Venezuelan exports. In oil exports, it does not appear that the Venezuelans have succeeded in freeing themselves from their natural American market; in 1970, the US accounted for 32% of Venezuelan direct oil exports while in 1979 the figure had risen to 34%[23].

In one area of exports, iron ore, the US share of Venezuelan exports *has* fallen, but not because of Venezuelan efforts. After the nationalization of the American-owned iron ore mines, the Venezuelans hoped to continue their close sales relationship with the former concessionaires. But the American companies, particularly US Steel, have shifted purchases away from Venezuela toward captive suppliers at home and in Canada – resulting in low-profit Venezuelan sales to European buyers and the first financial losses in the Venezuelan iron ore industry since its founding.

A greater share of Venezuela's imports now comes from Japan, Canada and Spain, as well as a slightly increased share from a few Latin countries

Table 4.1 *Venezuela's principal trading partners, 1966–78*

	Share of exports (%)				Share of imports (fob) (%)			
	1966	*1970*	*1976*	*1978*	*1966*	*1970*	*1976*	*1978*
United States	36.9	38.0	39.7	36.2	50.4	48.5	43.1	40.9
Netherlands Antilles[a]	20.7	20.1	20.0	n.a.	0.5	0.3	0.2	n.a.
Canada	8.0	11.2	15.2	12.0	5.3	4.2	3.8	6.6
United Kingdom	7.1	4.8	2.3	1.4	5.5	5.1	3.8	4.0
Trinidad & Tobago	4.0	3.3	0.3	0.2	–	–	–	–
Japan	1.1	0.7	0.4	0.5	5.2	7.9	9.2	8.7
Germany	1.5	1.7	2.2	1.5	9.7	8.9	8.9	9.5
France	1.1	1.6	1.0	0.9	3.2	3.0	2.8	3.7
Italy	0.7	1.3	2.2	2.3	5.2	4.9	6.0	5.3
Switzerland	–	0.1	–	0.1	2.1	2.5	1.6	4.0
Spain	1.3	1.2	1.2	1.6	0.2	1.6	2.6	3.8
Brazil	2.4	1.8	1.2	1.0	0.4	0.5	2.0	1.9
Argentina	0.7	0.9	0.6	0.3	2.9	0.8	1.5	1.2
Mexico	–	0.2	0.2	0.3	0.6	1.5	0.8	1.0
Colombia	–	0.3	0.2	1.3	0.3	0.3	1.8	1.7
Chile	1.0	0.3	0.3	1.2	0.5	0.4	0.5	0.6
Peru	0.4	0.2	1.2	1.6	0.5	0.3	0.2	0.4
Jamaica	0.1	1.0	1.3	n.a.	–	–	0.2	n.a.
Other Latin America	5.2	5.7	6.9	n.a.	0.3	0.6	0.8	0.8
Total ($ m.)	2712.7	3204.0	8662.0	9374.0	1216.3	1780.0	3799.0	9120.0

[a] Mostly oil for re-export.

Source: IMF, *Direction of Trade Annual 1966–70, 1970–76; Direction of Trade Yearbook 1972–78.* IMF, Washington, DC.

like Brazil, Mexico and Colombia – at the expense of the United States' share (see *Table 4.1*). These changes can hardly be considered very significant from the American point of view; indeed, Venezuela accounted for 2.6% of US exports in 1978 as against about 2% in 1966[24].

Thus, one can hardly argue that there has been any material loss inflicted on the US as a result of diversification policy. Decisions now being taken to rationalize the automobile industry may shift Venezuelan imports away from US sources in favor of European countries, but the outcome is not at all clear. It is not even clear on what criteria the final decisions will be made (if they are ever made).

On the whole, American reaction to Venezuelan government efforts to get out from under the US mantle has been low key and sensible. The iron ore and automobile companies have generally had to fend for themselves in dealing with nationalistic policies. Outside of questions concerning oil, there have been no significant trade disputes between the United States and Venezuela.

Ironically, it has been in Venezuela's efforts to gain *more* access to American markets that the US has taken a negative line, with negative results for American interests. In 1970, the Rafael Caldera government requested that the US grant hemispheric preference (i.e. equal standing with Mexico and Canada) to Venezuelan oil exports. The Nixon government refused, especially in the wake of tax increases on the US oil companies (1970) and the passing of the Reversion Law (1972), the first step toward oil nationalization. American policy thus reinforced the position of Middle Eastern petroleum in its imports. As Tugwell says, 'The irony here is that when the crisis did come the tables turned so quickly that policy losses by the United States in Venezuela could not be re-couped'[25]. The US has thus strengthened the anti-American tendency in Venezuelan trade policy by such a position. It should be remembered, however, that the State Department did not support the American rejection of Venezuelan proposals for preferences; lower-level decision-making would have brought about a different result.

Basically the same story was repeated with the exclusion of Venezuela from the trade preference benefits to less developed countries granted by the US Trade Bill of 1974. Here the culprit was the Congress, while the executive branch sat helpless in its desire to recognize Venezuela's independent stance during the Organization of Arab Petroleum Exporting Countries oil embargo. While the real economic effects were virtually nil, since Venezuela exports little but oil to the US anyway, the political effects could only be to convince the Venezuelans that the United States is a perfidious trading partner on which one should not depend.

The content of trade

Standard critiques of the workings of the international economy cite a common characteristic of the content of Third World trade: high dependence on a single (usually primary) export coupled with high dependence on external sources for capital goods and manufactures[26]. Venezuela is an exaggerated example of this characteristic. Between 1959 and 1979, dependence on oil exports has if anything increased (see *Table 4.2*), although the apparent increase after 1973 reflects higher prices for oil rather than higher volumes of oil sold. Venezuela also follows the standard scheme with respect to the structure of imports: in 1959, machinery and transport equipment accounted for 38% of total Venezuelan imports, while in 1979 they accounted for 50%[27].

As with the direction of trade, the government has concerned itself with altering the structure of trade. While it can be seen from the above that positive results have been sparse, it does not follow that policy has been neutral. Like many Latin American countries, Venezuela has sought to improve the structure of its trade in two ways: (1) promotion of non-traditional exports via subsidies, state promotion of new industries with export potential, and political efforts to secure trade preferences and

Table 4.2 *Petroleum as percent of Venezuelan exports, 1959–79*

Year	%	Year	%
1959	90	1971	92
1961	91	1973	89
1963	92	1975	95
1965	93	1977	95
1967	91	1979	95
1969	91		

Source: IMF, *International Financial Statistics Yearbook*. IMF, Washington, DC, 1980.

lowered barriers in developed countries; (2) changing the structure of imports by means of import substitution policies, including tariffs, quotas, subsidies to local industry, and state production. All of these policies are apparently aimed at reducing what is perceived as dependence on the US and other developed countries. Theoretically, they would have a negative impact on American exports to Venezuela and would even lead to unfair competition, with domestic US producers competing with subsidized foreign goods.

Should the United States worry about such 'threats from the Third World' or no? Let us first look at the case of 'unfair competition' from Third World exports. As Odell argues, US efforts to justify limits on Latin American industrial exports will inevitably produce a sense of injustice and resentment. Even while one hears occasional fears about future floods of cheap Brazilian Volkswagens in the US market, it is hard to find good evidence that defensive action has any effect other than to exacerbate relations unnecessarily. In the case of Venezuela, it is hard to find any evidence at all. In 1977, *total* non-petroleum imports to the US from Venezuela amounted to $338 million, of which about 40% was iron ore[28]. In aluminum products, an area of possible export growth for Venezuela, any increases of imports into the United States are more likely to favor the Americans than the Venezuelans (a point sometimes noticed by the Venezuelans). With cheap hydroelectric power from the Guri Dam, Venezuela saw a comparative advantage in promoting an aluminum smelting and manufacturing industry, initially sponsored by the Corporación Venezolana de Guayana (CVG). In a joint venture with Reynolds Aluminum, the CVG began aluminum production with cheap energy, tax advantages, tariff protection, and other subsidies. The industry was originally oriented toward import substitution and Latin American exports, but with more recent expansion the export mission has been extended. In one recent agreement, Reynolds received a contract to buy Venezuelan aluminum at below world market prices[29]. In another agreement, the American company South Wire set up local production facilities for processing aluminum into cable for export to the US[30]. In both of these cases, America imports an energy-intensive product at subsidized energy prices. Inevitable calls for renegotiation swiftly followed these argeements.

Venezuelan exports, then, present no threat to the US as currently constituted. Indeed, a more free market approach by Venezuelans might benefit Venezuela more than the US. Might it still be argued that state intervention and local import substitution policies unfairly harm US exporters? Again, little evidence supports the charge. First of all, imports as a percentage of GDP have tended to grow since the early 1960s, averaging about 25% since 1975. As was noted above, machinery and equipment imports have taken a progressively greater share of the whole since 1950, while imports of consumer goods have fallen in relative terms. To the extent that the United States has lost some of its position in machinery and transport equipment, it would be hard to argue that this was due to anything other than normal competition from Japan, Germany and other industrial countries. In consumer goods, meanwhile, US *exporters* could be said to have lost out in the face of high protective barriers. They might even blame the pressure of the 'national bourgeoisie' seeking to displace them. This may be the case in certain industries like textiles in which there exists a national sector that has won a high level of protection. Despite such export losses, many companies maintain sales by means of 'tariff-jumping' direct investments, which cushion the effect on income, although not on home employment.

Despite its relatively weak trade position outside of oil, Venezuela has championed the cause of other Third World countries in seeking a 'new international economic order' (NIEO) in trade. There is much pride in the country's leadership in the North–South Conference, in the United Nations Conference on Trade and Development, in the Association of Iron Ore Exporting Countries, and in other international forums. Without prejudice to Venezuela's sincerity, the rich countries should realize that such a policy is almost a logical requirement for a country in Venezuela's position (relatively rich, oil-exporting) and with Venezuela's ambitions (prestige and importance in the Caribbean, Latin America, the developing countries, and, consequently, the world). Indeed, NIEO rhetoric and Third World leadership are cheap means to such prestige, and excessive discomfort at presidential pronouncements on the subject is counterproductive. So when President Carlos Andrés Pérez said things like 'The gringos have been our great teachers – what we have to do is exactly the opposite of what they did'[31], it was best not to respond. When Venezuela supports the iron ore 'cartel', what is needed is a cool analysis of the likelihood of cartel action (unlikely, as long as excess supply continues)[32].

The trade issue tends to support the observation made at the outset that manifestations of economic nationalism are inevitable and natural in developing countries. While it does not follow that industrial countries should simply acquiesce in all the claims of the developing world, the case of Venezuela indicates that negative reactions serve to reinforce that nationalism. In addition, the natural forces of the international trading system tend to persist even in the face of concerted Venezuelan efforts to counteract them. To paraphrase John Mitchell, the US should look not so much at what Venezuela says *or* does, but rather at what happens as a result. Decisions about how to react in the face of specific actions should be made in the light of the overall pattern of effects, and not in response to the complaints of particular, and perhaps limited, interests.

Direct investment

As in the case of trade, states tend to react to direct investment with what Kindleberger has called the 'mercantilist instinct'[33]. Host states feel uncomfortable with the foreigners in their midst, while home states tend to resist efforts by others to limit the investment of their nationals abroad. Of course, the hosts have many reasons to welcome the foreigners too, just as the home countries often find good reasons to restrain their protests in response to appeals for help from their nationals. The causes of negative reactions to foreign investors have been repeated often enough; complaints seem to be most vociferous among the developing countries. As Raymond Vernon said, 'The tendencies toward increased interdependence created most pain in the less-developed countries ... "dependency" seemed a more apt description of the outcome than "interdependence"'[34].

Venezuela's reactions to foreign investors have been typical of such developing countries. Through the Andean Pact, the response has been specifically Latin American and multilateral. The overwhelming presence of the international oil companies (all American, except Shell) colored the country's perception of foreign investors in general. Since nationalization, of course, non-oil investments represent the bulk of all foreign investment and a more discriminating approach is necessary. As a basically capitalist country, Venezuela does not oppose foreign investment per se. Much the same could be said of Venezuela as of Mexico by Grindle in ch. 3: foreign investment is considered an important part of development strategy (p. 76)[35]. Opinion about foreign investment ebbs and flows as governments come and go. As with New England weather, one only needs to wait a bit if the present conditions are uncongenial. Before the nationalization of oil, sensitivity in Venezuela was relatively high; the post-nationalization government of Luís Herrera Campíns has tried to project a more friendly stance toward foreign investors, although the preceding government of Carlos Andrés Pérez had earlier taken some steps to facilitate investments from abroad[36].

How should home countries, specifically the United States, react in the face of foreign investment policy in Venezuela? As in the case of trade, optimal policy would have to adjust itself to the inevitable in addition to making reasonable assessments of likely outcomes. Once again it would seem that significant anti-foreign investment moves make sense from the point of view of Venezuela, while at the same time foreign investors are likely to continue to derive significant benefits from the actual working of the system.

In Venezuela, limits on foreign investment exist mainly for three reasons. First, they have made sense for economic reasons – at a certain point, a cost–benefit analysis indicates that the country would be better off without foreign ownership in the particular industry or company. Secondly, limits have made sense from the point of view of the domestic political/economic structure: when local groups are strong enough to operate in a given industry, they are likely to argue for and to receive protection from transnational competitors. Finally, but less commonly, a government may conclude that given foreign investors interfere in some way with national policy, and this would lead it to place limits on, or even to nationalize, the offenders.

These conditions form the internal constraints on relationships between Venezuela and foreign investors. In the first case – that of rational or economically based limits on foreign investors – evidence thus far shows that patterns of control and of expropriation across many countries are similar. Stephen Kobrin finds that forced divestment in his sample of 'acts' of divestment seems to be a function of firm and industry characteristics like percentage of foreign ownership, level of technology in the industry, and relation to national security. Similar findings have been noted above in Jones and Mason. While Kobrin concludes that his findings 'refute an assertion that forced divestment is simply a manifestation of "economic nationalism"'[37], I conclude rather that a rational application of measures against multinationals is exactly what 'economic nationalism' is all about. Raymond Vernon and others characterize the rationality of such policies in terms of the 'obsolescent bargain' – the explicit or implicit arrangement between host country and foreign investor that determines the distribution of costs and benefits[38]. This arrangement tends to break down because of various factors that strengthen the bargaining position of the host country over time: sunk investments, growing managerial or technological capability, assured profits and the like. The Venezuelans clearly perceived their nationalizations in petroleum and mining in this light. Similar and simultaneous nationalizations in other countries further indicate that such moves are part of a broad and irreversible economic pattern. There is not much point in trying to stop a country from doing what will be good for it – although a discriminating policy would indeed use economic arguments to point out errors or omissions in the analysis of the host country if such exist[39].

When limits arise from the pressure of local business elites, foreign investors may again be in a position where they will inevitably have to move aside. In Venezuela, Domínguez' review of public opinion in ch. 2 (p. 35) shows that the development of a national bourgeois coalition 'suspicious of the United States and of private foreign investment' became stark in the early and mid-1970s. Some of the resentments of the period were probably deepened by the current wrangle over nationalization of the oil companies. Once accomplished, public opinion in general could settle down to 'normal' levels of mistrust, while the national bourgeoisie could ask for its normal levels of protection. In the early 1960s, the main business organization, Fedecámaras, already made it a condition of its support for foreign investment that it not cause 'unnecessary displacements or economic upsets in markets already well supplied by national capital'[40]. Additionally, it should be noted that business opposition to joining the Andean Pact was *not* based on opposition to adopting Andean Pact Decision 24 regulating foreign direct investment, but rather on questions concerning the liberalization of trade relations with future partners in the Pact[41]. Present Fedecámaras policy still reiterates the same general approach, even though certain important sectors of big business in Venezuela have pressured for a relaxation of current regulations[42].

Regardless of the Andean Pact's future, foreign investors will not fare well in areas where there is significant local capacity. For instance, Venezuela strictly limited foreign banks before entering the Andean Pact – so strictly that only one bank chose to remain 'foreign' (Citibank). Since 1970, Citibank has progressively lost its position and sunk to the bottom of the performance list in the country. Under Decision 24, Venezuelan legislation lists other areas in which national business felt strong enough to go it alone – foreigners are essentially excluded from public services, radio and TV, newspapers, advertising, and most professional services. Additionally, the discrimination against foreign firms (especially those with over 80% foreign-controlled capital) provides incentives to companies to sell some shares to Venezuelans, thus forcing the sharing of the advantages of the transnationals with local business interests. Needless to say, the result is often the use of local fronts, popularly referred to as *testaferros*.

Local business elites are also likely to continue to demand participation in areas where they can play a role auxiliary to foreign enterprise. This trend is evident especially in recent politicking over the awarding of contracts for the development of the heavy oil belt of the Orinoco area, called the Faja Petrolífera. Various groups look after local interests, like the Organization of Suppliers of Goods and Services in the petroleum industry, and the National Petroleum Federation. Such organizations routinely speak out against discrimination against local suppliers in favor of the multinationals. This sort of activity ensures that the oil companies are careful to grant a healthy number of contracts to local contractors.

Limits on foreign investors on the grounds of interference with national policy have been rare. The only obvious case in Venezuela occurred in the course of the kidnapping of the American business executive William Niehous when his company, Owens-Illinois, agreed to publish the guerrillas' propaganda in major world newspapers. In a fit of pique, President Carlos Andrés Pérez announced that the company would be nationalized – a policy never carried out. There have been veiled threats against automobile companies in Venezuela for interfering with national policy within the Andean Pact, but these have remained at the level of normal negotiating strategy[43]. Similar complaints have been lodged by the government against the management by Reynolds Aluminum in the local industry, in the wake of financial losses in recent years that required capital infusions that Reynolds balked at contributing[44]. The government took over majority control at the end of 1980.

Policy evaluation from the point of view of the foreign investor's home country must take into consideration the above trends, and allow for their inevitable development. Clearly, companies that do violate local norms should suffer for their own sins alone, as in fact various codes of conduct specify. But governments like the United States should develop their sense of restraint over individual investment issues, because overall foreign investment is often not harmed in any significant way. This has obviously been the case in Venezuela. While rational arguments did justify nationalization in the oil industry, they do not justify nationalization in many areas of American interest and expertise. Additionally, the development of the national bourgeoisie, while significant, hardly implies local competence to run all of industry alone[45].

What has actually happened to American investment in Venezuela during recent years? Grindle's review of events in US foreign investment in Latin America shows that Venezuela declined between 1960 and 1975 as a recipient of US foreign investment in relative terms (*Figure 3.1*, p. 71). This decline accompanied the changeover to the more nationalistic government installed in 1958, political instability in the 1960s, entrance into the Andean Pact, and nationalization of the foreign petroleum and iron ore companies. Since 1975, Venezuela has generally stabilized its share of investment from the United States in manufacturing, although not across all industries (see *Table 4.3*). Indeed, American investment is reported to account for 58% of total foreign investment in the country, a share greater than the American share in Venezuelan trade[46]. Expansion by US firms in Venezuela also appears to continue healthily: in 1979, capital equipment expenditures by majority-owned firms amounted to $540 million, of which $400 million were in manufacturing. The manufacturing expenditures accounted for 19% of all such spending in Latin America[47]. US foreign direct investment has fallen only slightly behind foreign investment by other countries in Venezuela. According to Venezuelan figures, overall foreign investment grew by

Table 4.3 *Venezuela's share of US foreign direct investment, 1971–79*

	1971	1975	1978	1979
All industries				
As percent of:				
World	3.1	1.5	1.2	1.1
Developing countries	11.6	7.1	5.0	4.6
Latin America	20.8	8.5	9.4	6.0
Manufacturing				
As percent of:				
World	1.5	1.2	1.4	1.3
Developing countries	8.6	6.4	7.5	6.5
Latin America	11.0	7.8	9.8	7.9

Source: US Dept. of Commerce, *Survey of Current Business*,
November 1972; August 1977; August 1979; August
1980.

20% between 1975 and 1979, while (in US data) American investments grew by almost 18% to $2.2 billion[48]. But this obscures the fact that US manufacturing investments in the same period grew by 57% against overall growth of foreign investment in manufacturing of 35%. There is no question, therefore, that American investors have had to retire in the industries where Venezuelans have seen their national interests at stake. But such a trend does not at all indicate that other investors find a particularly uncongenial climate; moreover, in Venezuela, American investments in manufacturing appear to be flourishing.

These facts indicate that the actual carrying out of policies limiting foreign investors has more bark than bite. As in Mexico, the style of policy implementation is almost as important as the policy itself[49]. The Sixth National Plan (1981–85), for instance, appears to continue with the same policy governing Venezuela since the early 1970s: priority to the entrance of high technology industries and continued insistence on local participation in company capital[50]. In the meantime, however, the government of Herrera Campíns has sponsored interviews and conferences in which government representatives have tried to signal its welcoming attitude[51].

While American policy should continue to pay attention to the *actual* effects of Venezuelan policy and to the actual implementation of that policy, it should also pay heed to more complex developments affecting foreign investment in Venezuela and elsewhere. In 1978, Bergsten, Horst and Moran pointed out that, in the raw materials area, American multinationals *cannot* be relied on to secure access to raw materials (for many of the reasons reviewed in this chapter and elsewhere) and that American policy should therefore be directed toward replacing foreign investment with management and service contracts abroad[52]. What the authors were saying in effect is that direct investment may not be the issue at all: the issue is whether the US has continued access to foreign sources of raw materials and whether American companies continue to be able to profit from their expertise and comparative advantage in areas like high technology and engineering. In Venezuela, the United States should be able to see clearly that, even in those areas where the state has intervened most drastically (oil, basic metals, professional services), involvement by foreign and especially by American companies has continued unabated. The Bechtel Corporation, for instance, has thus far acted as principal advisor in the development of the heavy oil belt; American companies have won many bids in the building of the Venezuelan steel and aluminum industries; virtually every state enterprise appears to have its management studies done by major American consultants.

The *Survey of Current Business* figure for payments for services from American companies is the balance of payments item 'Fees and royalties from affiliated and unaffiliated foreigners'. These totalled $7 billion in 1980, of which $1.3 billion came from unaffiliated sources[53]. In the case of Venezuela, payments seem to be high, although subject to continuing pressures for technological independence on the part of Venezuela. In 1979, for instance, Petróleos de Venezuela (the state oil firm) paid some $350 million in technology fees under agreements for technical support, although a renegotiation in 1980 decreased the fees to $130 million. Total payments to foreigners may not decrease proportionately when new contracts for specific projects are taken into account[54] – Petróleos planned to invest $3 billion in 1981 alone. Such figures make transfers in other industries look pale, but US companies nevertheless sell services to many industries in Venezuela, sometimes without capital investments at all. A small-scale example would be the contract held by Reynolds Aluminum to operate the state-dominated aluminum company, Venalum. In addition to income from supplying machinery and other inputs, Reynolds charges 1% of net sales as a fee for technical assistance. At full production, that would be over $3 million per year. Judging from the number of consumer products made under license, the income from sources other than direct investment in Venezuela appears to be significant.

The other positive characteristic with respect to foreign investment in Venezuela from the point of view of the United States is its continued commitment to the capitalist way of doing things. While the state is clearly the main producer in basic industries, the rest of the economy is capitalistic. There is general support of this except in a relatively small leftist sector. The business federation, Fedecámaras, started its major policy statement of 1980 with the defense of the role of private enterprise in Venezuelan society[55]. The government shares this support for private enterprise where possible, vowing in 1980 to sell off some of the companies that had been bought up over the years by the official Venezuelan Development Corporation. Such an orientation ensures that Venezuela is unlikely to turn against private enterprise, domestic or foreign, in any significant way.

The case of foreign investment confirms generally what was said at the outset about economic nationalism and its effects on the United States. Autonomous developments in Venezuela have produced a consensus about the necessity of minimizing foreign investment in strategic industries and in areas in which national interests can hold their own. In other areas, some national participation is demanded. Yet the development needs of the country inhibit stronger measures because of the concentration of technological and managerial skills outside of the country. If the United States wishes to maintain its economic position in Venezuela, Latin America, and other developing countries, its best strategy is to preserve its technological edge.

Financial relations

Perhaps because of their arcane nature, financial relations tend to be less politicized, and hence give rise to only moderate levels of economic nationalism in Venezuela. It has already been mentioned that foreign banks were virtually forced out of the local banking system in 1970[56]. This move responded to considerations more related to competition between the national bourgeoisie and powerful foreign investors than to questions of international financial relations, but it is also true that hostility to the foreign banks was brought to a head in part because of the unstable conditions in international money markets in 1969 and 1970. High US interest rates in 1969 led to capital outflows from virtually all Western countries; what was not much noticed at the time was that this caused serious problems in Latin America where capital outflows put serious strains on reserve management[57]. The Venezuelans were trying to ensure that, in the future, the disposition of Venezuelan capital would not be in the hands of foreigners, but, as we shall see, there are significant constraints on Venezuelan financial independence.

Since the price of oil started going up in the early 1970s, the popular imagination has envisioned mountains of dollars piling up in OPEC's central banks, ready to be used as blackmail against the dwindling resources of America. Saudi Arabian resources have climbed much more than Venezuela's, of course, but even Venezuela's international reserves had risen from $1.0 billion in 1970 to some $7.1 billion by the end of 1980[58]. However the example of the freezing of Iranian assets by President Carter should have alerted the public by now that the potential for blackmail also runs the other way. The only way for a country to get around this dilemma would be to hold its reserves in some currency other than dollars – but then someone *else* would have to accept the dollars.

In fact, the Venezuelans have given themselves even less freedom from the dollar than some other reserve-rich countries by continuing to tie their currency, the bolivar, to the dollar. This gives a certain stability to the local financial and trading community, which tends, for historical reasons, to get nervous whenever there is talk of a change in the exchange rate, which has been virtually unchanged since 1964. This tie to the dollar has a number of consequences. The first is that, as the dollar weakened over the last decade in relation to the currencies of its trading competitors, so has the bolivar. This gradual and downward float has thus given an advantage to American goods in the Venezuelan market, as, say, German and Japanese goods have become relatively expensive. A second consequence is that Venezuela has less flexibility in its domestic monetary policy than would be possible under a regime of floating rates. It is in this sense that the departure of the foreign banks did nothing to sever the links between Venezuela's money markets and the US. When American interest rates go up, there will be adjustments in Venezuela: (1) capital outflows, which reduce international reserves; or (2) higher domestic (Venezuelan) interest rates, which brake local economic expansion. Such a situation became acute as interest rates rose in the United States during 1980, with the prime rate over 20%. Venezuelan economic conditions called for lower interest rates to support the faltering construction industry, while international conditions called for higher rates. When the Central Bank raised interest rates in response to events in US money markets, local businessmen complained; when it delayed raising rates further, local bankers complained. When the Bank finally decided to float the rates, almost everyone complained.

The Venezuelan Central Bank has always acted as a 'good soldier' in defending the dollar. Published figures are unavailable with respect to the distribution of the official portfolio of reserves held by the Bank, but it was revealed that, in its time deposits at least, 82% of reserves were held in dollars[59]. The president of the Venezuelan Investment Fund implied that the Fund also leaned heavily toward dollars when he lamented that his money managers had not diversified out of the dollar[60]. Official and unofficial deposits by Venezuela in banks in the United States also grew. In 1970, these amounted to $735 million and by mid-1980 had reached $4.7 billion[61].

Perhaps the strongest link between the United States and Venezuela in the financial field is the debt link. Commercial loans by American banks to Venezuela have grown tremendously since 1970, and further dampen the effects of any Venezuelan efforts to free themselves from their link to the US economy[62]. (Here, of course, the tie goes both ways, since debtors do exercise a certain control over their creditors. Perhaps in no other country is that link so clearly seen as in Brazil, which owes American banks so much money that the United States would be harmed by any hint of Brazilian default.) In any case, claims by banks in the US on Venezuela were somewhat above $280 million at the end of 1970, while in mid-1980 they had reached $4.3 billion[63]. In a sense, the banks are lending the Venezuelans their own money – and making a profit by doing so. Data on all US banks world-wide show a much greater commitment of funds to Venezuela. By mid-1980, total loans from American banks and their foreign branches had reached $8.3 billion – less than loans to Brazil and Mexico, but more than loans to any other country outside of the Group of 10[64]. Almost half of these loans were to public borrowers in Venezuela[65].

In the light of such strong links with the United States, it is not surprising that a nationalistic country like Venezuela should attempt to show some independence. As we shall see, however, *la force des choses* in the international financial system led to a Venezuelan retreat. It was called to the government's attention in 1980 that the Venezuelan constitution said that contracts entered into by the government should be litigated under Venezuelan law in case of dispute. This clause had been ignored for years and never applied to foreign loans contracted by the government. But the Herrera administration decided to make a issue of it in a loan for $1.8 billion. Herrera himself commented on the question in a speech on the public debt, thus committing himself politically.[66]. In the end, however, Venezuela had to recognize that the syndicate of banks would not accept the Venezuelan courts as arbiters of any future disputes. The technicality of the law was evaded by calling the loan a 'note', and, hence, presumably not a contract within the meaning of the constitution[67].

Financial relations thus only confirm the general tendency found above in trade and investment matters. Venezuela does seek independence from the United States to the extent she can, but the structure of the external economy makes this difficult. It seems inevitable that the United States will be able to continue in its position of relative strength. Financial relations probably exemplify this situation more than any other. Any weakening of this American influence over the Venezuelan financial system is much more likely to come from US inability to control the dollar than from Venezuelan efforts alone. In oil affairs, however, the situation is reversed somewhat.

Oil relations

Norman Gall speculated some years ago that OPEC might never have been created if the American government had lent a friendly ear to Venezuelan requests for preference under the oil import quotas imposed in 1959[68]. It is probably true that the US rejection throughout the 1960s of Venezuela's requests for hemispheric preference did contribute to the deepening of nationalistic tendencies in Venezuela's international oil policy. But that is really not the issue. Pressures were growing in all the oil-exporting countries to claim a greater share of created wealth, and, despite appearances, OPEC itself seems to have been a relatively unimportant factor in the longer-run rise in oil prices. It has taken the United States some time to recognize these facts, a delay that has produced excessive conflict and recrimination. However, the conflict between the United States and Venezuela over oil never became acute, mainly because overt conflict was restricted to the rhetorical level while private and bureaucratic interests tended to recognize the real basis for long-term compatibility.

With respect to oil, there are three distinct issues that affect American interests: price, security of supply, and treatment of American oil companies. The question of the impact of nationalization on American companies has already been discussed above, and can be put aside here. The real issues are price and security of supply. During the Nixon and Ford administrations, and to a lesser extent under Carter, the United States put a mistaken emphasis on the question of price – mistaken because it rested on the incorrect assumption that oil prices were being pushed up because of the monopolistic power of the oil cartel, OPEC. A corollary assumption was that cartel action is in itself inherently illegitimate, based as it theoretically is on the principle of restricted supplies above 'free market' or marginal cost levels. Countries like Venezuela never accepted the illegitimacy of their behavior, and thus reacted with hostility to what were perceived as equally illegitimate condemnations on the part of the United States.

How did the US react? Tom Farer summed up what he called the 'anti-accommodationist' view as exemplified by Patrick Moynihan and Irving Kristol in this way:

> The Third World is attempting to extort – through economic blackmail, moral bullying, and outright theft – a portion of the West's legitimately acquired wealth. The declared justification of redistributive claims, compensation for colonial and neocolonial exploitation, has no basis in fact. … The West's failure to reject this justification simply encourages ever more arrogant, extortionate demands[69].

While the strongest versions of the anti-accommodationist view did not become official policy, the Ford administration did try a variety of methods to get a lower price for oil. That the price *was* too high was almost a matter of faith, even if that faith was based on rather poor economic theory[70]. Policy to get back to the 'real' price of oil followed a number of tracks: bilateral requests for restraint[71]; 'OPEC-busting' strategies including taxes on oil imports; multilateral arrangements for conservation and storage through the International Energy Agency. The first two tended to raise hackles in Venezuela and elsewhere. The last has been, with some reservations, accepted. The claim that somehow prices are too high persists today, however, and still holds potential for unnecessarily souring relations with Venezuela. A healthier view is to accept the many causes for rising oil prices – none of which has anything to do with Venezuelan policy. Venezuela has played, if anything, a moderating role in OPEC parleys; Venezuela's control over world supplies is marginal at best, comprising 3.8% of the production of major oil exporters in 1979[72]; Venezuela's production is constrained by her relatively limited reserves of standard quality oil rather than by any directive to hold up world prices; Venezuela, like most oil-exporting countries, depends largely on Saudi Arabian production policy and developed countries' consumption patterns in setting its oil price[73].

If Venezuela cannot affect international oil prices, then surely price should play no role in her relations with consumer countries. What of security of supply? Here, the role of Venezuela is more significant. As has often been pointed out, Venezuela has always been a faithful supplier to the American market, even though the United States Congress failed to recognize this. Today, the recognition appears to be strong, as seen in the belated repeal of the anti-OPEC clause in its application to Venezuela and in studies of US–Venezuelan relations[74]. Indeed, government agencies have generally acknowledged Venezuela's fidelity even when public appearances indicated troubled relations[75]. How important is Venezuela to US oil supplies? Less than she used to be, certainly, but perhaps less also than she will be in the future.

Formerly OPEC's largest producer, Venezuela first fell behind in 1969[76]. And, as *Table 4.4* shows, Venezuela has progressively lost her share of the United States market since the late 1950s. But as *Table 4.5* shows, the United States has maintained a relatively important position in Venezuela's

Table 4.4 *Total US petroleum imports and imports from Venezuela ('000 barrels/day)*

Year	Total petroleum imports	Petroleum imports from Venezuela	Venezuela as percent of total
1957	1574	754	48
1958	1700	711	42
1959	1780	784	44
1960	1815	832	46
1961	1917	800	42
1962	2082	907	44
1963	2123	899	42
1964	2258	931	41
1965	2468	995	40
1966	2573	1021	40
1967	2537	935	37
1968	2840	888	31
1969	3166	876	28
1970	3419	983	29
1971	3925	1019	26
1972	4742	960	20
1973	6256	1135	18
1974	6111	979	16
1975	6056	702	12
1976	7295	699	10
1977	8744	687	8
1978	8363	646	8
1979	8411	691	8

Note: Includes only direct imports from Venezuela. In 1978, indirect imports were 235 000 barrels/day.
Source: American Petroleum Institute, *Basic Petroleum Data Book*. API, Washington DC, various years.

Table 4.5 *Total Venezuelan petroleum exports and exports to US ('000 barrels/day)*

Year	Total petroleum exports	Exports to US as percent of total
1969	3411	29
1970	3468	32
1971	3282	34
1972	3074	34
1973	3150	38
1974	2751	37
1975	2085	33
1976	2137	32
1977	1964	36
1978	1942	35
1979	2095	34

Note: Venezuelan export figures to the United States are slightly different from US import figures, so this table uses exclusively Venezuela data for internal consistency. If indirect imports were included, the US market would have accounted for 50% of Venezuelan petroleum exports in 1975, and for 45% in 1978. Indirect sources for US imports are calculated by the Central Intelligence Agency, National Foreign Assessment Center, *International Energy Statistical Review*. CIA, Washington, DC, various years.

Source: Venezuela, Ministerio de Energía y Minas, *Petróleo y otros datos estadísticos*, Caracas, 1979.

total exports, amounting to 34% of Venezuela's direct exports for 1979. Thus, the decline in American imports from Venezuela has much less to do with Venezuelan efforts to decrease dependence on the American market, with which both Mexico and Venezuela should have a natural relationship, than with an overall decline in Venezuelan production and exports (see *Figure 4.1*). Most Venezuelan studies foresee that this trend will continue, as long as the country continues to depend exclusively on its traditional products. This is because the country's reserves have failed to be increased by any significant discoveries, and because domestic consumption puts a heavier and heavier burden on local production capabilities.

Proven reserves did increase until about 1965, after which they continued to fall until 1974. In 1980, they were at 19.7 billion barrels, or almost 25 years at current rates of production. Of more concern is the domestic oil consumption pattern, which diverts more and more oil from the export markets. In 1969, domestic consumption of petroleum was at 115 000 barrels a day, while by 1979 it had risen to 279 000 barrels per day, an increase of 9.3% per year at compound rates. The same pattern is repeated when only

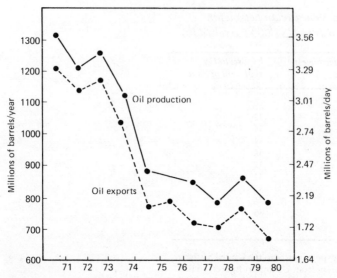

Figure 4.1 *Venezuela: volume of petroleum production and exports, 1971–80*

Source: Venezuela, Ministerio de Energía y Minas, *Petróleo y otros datos estadísticos, 1971–1978.* Caracas, 1980; Ministerio de Energía y Minas, *Carta Semanal,* Caracas, 17 July 1981.

gasoline is considered: 1979 consumption was at 157 000 barrels per day – up 9.2% per year in compound terms over 1969[77]. At the same rate of growth, Venezuela would be consuming almost 1 million barrels per day by the year 2000 in gasoline alone, and adding refinery capacity in these products has already been costly for the country.

These facts lead ineluctably to several conclusions. In the absence of unexpected new discoveries, there will be a decline in future exports, a decline in domestic reserves, and an increase in costs in the Venezuelan oil industry. Barring significant increases in the price of oil to restrain consumption, there will also be constraints on domestic expansion from a balance of payments gap. Additionally, there would be likely to be further declines in exports to the United States, and greater American dependence on the relatively less secure sources of oil outside of the western hemisphere. While such an eventuality is hardly in the interest of the United States, it is even less in the interests of Venezuela, whose democracy has thrived on healthy rates of growth to satisfy its snowballing population.

For Venezuela, there are two feasible ways out of the dilemma: a constantly rising real price of oil to maintain revenues despite falling volumes of exports, and/or new sources of production. Thus far, since 1973, Venezuela has enjoyed a more or less constantly increasing price for its oil exports. Since 1976 alone, the average price of crude imports to the United States has almost tripled. Government revenues from oil grew from $2.6

billion in 1973 to $7.7 billion in 1979, an increase of 54% in real terms, or 7% per year at compound rates[78]. But there is not any assurance that such luck will continue.

The second solution, new sources for production, implies benefits for the United States as well as for Venezuela. (Higher prices, after all, tend to benefit only Venezuela.) In this respect, it is to the advantage of the United States that production in the heavy oil belt, the 'Faja', be encouraged, and that research be carried out on how to produce refined products cheaply from the heavy oils found there. While no one knows for sure the potential recoverable reserves of the belt, state company Maraven estimated they could be 50–70 billion barrels – three to four times current proven reserves. The current program of the government calls for a cautious start, mainly because there still remains so much doubt about the future cost of production, and also because Venezuela has a long-cherished conservation policy that opposes production beyond the requirements of the economy and its absorptive capacity. Current planning overall in the industry is to boost production capacity from 2.4 million barrels per day to 2.8[79]. As has already been mentioned, American companies will probably play a significant role in the heavy oil belt. In addition, the United States has tried to encourage research through the signing of an agreement on energy research cooperation that specifies equal cost to both countries in joint projects[80]. (Venezuela also has similar agreements with Germany and Canada.)

There remains, however, the nationalistic impulse, which tends to create an aura of mistrust, particularly in the area of petroleum. The United States is popularly associated with one-sided development of Venezuelan oil, to the American advantage. There is a strong feeling that this could happen again in the belt. The government of Venezuela has already had to fight rumors to the effect that the Bechtel Corporation was being awarded a contract for over $7 billion for the belt project, a rumor that caused consternation among all local contractors[81]. Additionally, there still remains much doubt about the necessity and feasibility of current plans for the belt[82]. From the point of view of the United States and other oil-importing countries, the optimal outcome would be promoted by conservation efforts in Venezuela, greater realization by official Venezuela that increased production will be necessary to support future economic growth, and technological advances that cheapen the exploitation of heavy oils.

The case of oil highlights the main argument of this chapter. Economic nationalism doubtless fired the political will of Venezuela to take over its oil industry, to get higher prices abroad and at the same time to reduce national dependence on this single product, dependence on individual buyers, and dependence on outside technicians. Improved capabilities facilitated internal changes, while changes in the external structure further enabled the country to begin to achieve some of these goals. Oil consumers helped make it all possible. Meanwhile, events have tended to weaken the relative United

States position. Increased dependence on oil imports hardly arose in Venezuelan or any foreign nationalism. Moreover, a recuperation of relative strength will depend on the American ability to find alternative energy sources, to conserve energy, and to promote technological improvements for the use of non-traditional sources like the heavy oil of Venezuela's Faja Petrolífera.

4.4   Other considerations

Economic relations cannot be considered in a vacuum. Economics do govern much of the modern US–Latin American link, but purely political issues have not disappeared. At times, politics may even override the considerations of Mammon. Without going into great detail, a few salient characteristics of the American–Venezuelan political relationship should be reviewed. They show a basically compatible situation whose positive benefits should always be considered in the balance of any analysis of economic relations.

First of all, since 1958, Venezuela has been an upholder of democratic principles in Latin America, perhaps more than any country in its subcontinent. Starting with the Betancourt Doctrine, which forbade diplomatic relations with countries with illegitimate governments, Venezuela has constantly lobbied for the creation and preservation of democratic regimes. She has also been a strong upholder of human rights. This policy has sometimes been at odds with American policy, as in the cases of the Dominican Republic invasion, the creation of the military junta in Chile, and, to some extent, the relatively unfriendly attitude of the US to Jamaica under Michael Manley and Nicaragua under the Sandinistas. Venezuelan policy has generally been close to American policy on Cuba, although varying somewhat according to the tastes of the current president[83]. The Christian democratic government of Herrera Campíns also backed American policy on El Salvador under President Carter. While differences are likely, depending on the leanings of the respective governments of each country, the United States should realize that over the longer haul the political position of Venezuela has been salubrious for Latin America.

Other aspects of Venezuelan foreign policy should likewise be considered as positive from the point of view of the United States. The government has backed schemes for Latin American economic integration, sometimes dragging a somewhat unwilling business community behind it. While organizations like the Andean Pact or the Latin American Economic System may appear in some respects to be hostile to US economic interests, they also base themselves on principles the United States has long espoused – growth through trade liberalization starting at the regional level. Additionally, Venezuela has made more tangible contributions to Latin and Caribbean development through her extensive foreign aid program, which amounted to almost 2% of GDP in the late 1970s[84]. It has included cooperation with the United States and others in Caribbean development, cooperation with Mexico in giving aid to regional oil-consuming developing countries, and considerable multilateral aid through the Inter-American Development Bank, the International Monetary Fund, the OPEC Special Fund, and so on. While some would consider Venezuela's role in the movement to create a new international economic order to be counterproductive from the point of view of the United States, it is a policy that is congruent with the overall Venezuelan view of the world, and is unlikely to change, regardless of whether the NIEO fades as an organized form of negotiation between rich and poor. In short, even when discontent seeps into the United States –Venezuelan economic relationship, there are many reasons for the United States to consider other positive aspects of the overall and long-term connection.

4.5 Conclusions

The main conclusion of this chapter is that, in its relations with Venezuela, the United States has a great deal to gain and very little to lose. Although Venezuela is special because of the oil connection, in many ways the trends in US–Venezuelan relations appear to reflect more general trends in American relations with Latin America. In particular, the growth of economic nationalism in Venezuela reflects a much wider phenomenon found to some degree among virtually all of her neighbors. This economic nationalism, or neo-mercantilism, has grown across the board as the capabilities of the developing countries have increased, as they have diversified their internal and external economies, increased their level of living and education, gained expertise in controlling their industries and generally augmented their power of negotiation. These developments are the natural concomitant of economic progress, even if that progress is confined to only a portion of the country in question. To the extent that such changes reflect relative increases in power, accommodation makes more sense than opposition. Nowhere is this more clear than in the case of oil.

The chapter has reviewed the cases of trade, direct investment, finance and oil. In each, Venezuela displayed over time an increase in economic nationalism, mainly through government attempts to change historical patterns of dealings with the industrialized countries, especially the United States. But at the same time, each of these cases demonstrated that internal changes in Venezuela explained much of the impetus behind alterations in modern economic relations with the United States – without completely explaining the outcomes. It was found that despite many efforts to transform relations, the Venezuelans have found themselves in a situation not very substantially different from the original. The United States still plays a crucial role in Venezuela's trade, finance, and industry; despite oil nationalization, the Venezuelan petroleum industry is still very much linked to former customers, suppliers, sources of technology, and the like. This means that external structures must also be taken fully into account in explaining the present and future state of relations between the United States and Venezuela, and between the United States and Latin America. Analysis of internal structures, as in Venezuela, points to increasing capabilities in the Third World; analysis of external structures indicates that, in relative terms, those capabilities increase only very slowly. From the American point of view, this means that threats to any vital interests are unlikely.

The American ambassador in Caracas, William Luers, said, 'Relations with Venezuela are excellent at this time because there are no areas of basic conflict between us, and because the interests of both countries are the same with respect to the majority of important regional problems'[85]. He added, however, that, '...if we fail to give adequate attention to these relations, problems could develop in the future'. But what is adequate? In the realm of economic relations, there is little indication that high-level attention would actually improve matters; it might even serve to call attention to questions best handled routinely. Abraham Lowenthal pointed out correctly that 'Because the United States is so privileged, what may appear to be mutually advantageous from Washington's perspective may seem exploitative from a Latin American standpoint'[86]. While Luers claimed in his speech that US–Venezuelan relations were free from suspicion, he was really describing a wish rather than a complete reality. The Venezuelans are likely to remain suspicious, and to continue to nurture their economic nationalism in self-defense. On a day-to-day level, however, they are likely to continue to deal with the United States on the basis of realities, lacking as they do the willingness to assume the role of martyrs of any revolution. There is one exception to the rule that American–Venezuelan relations should flourish most strongly when handled most routinely, and that is at the level of purely diplomatic relations. Presidential and other high-level visits in both the north and south direction, public affirmations of admiration, and overt recognition of areas of mutual agreement are happily accepted by the Venezuelans, and actions that imply that the United States places more emphasis on relations with Mexico or Brazil seem to create discomfort. Knowing how accommodating they have been to American policy-makers, the Venezuelans naturally resent it when the US appears to forget. That is why there was so much unhappiness when Venezuela was excluded from the preferences offered by the American trade bill.

This review of Venezuelan–US economic relations allows for considerable optimism about the future, not only for the specific case in question, but also for American relations with the many countries of the Third World actively pursuing nationalist policies in the economic sphere. Certainly,

US–Venezuelan relations cannot be categorized as an example of the inherent harmony of interests among nations, but, nevertheless, a high degree of harmony was found to exist below the rhetorical level. Narrow bureaucratic interests do not seem to play an excessively heavy role in relations between the two countries, although any analysis of such relations must surely consider the particular non-governmental sources of influence, in both Venezuela and the United States. Nor does an uncritical dependency approach provide a sufficient explanation for the evolution of relations, because it was found that Venezuela enjoys a high degree of autonomy in its foreign policy, in both the economic and political arenas. Dependency theory does, however, point to certain profitable areas for research, since it stresses the persistence of the historical pattern of asymmetrical relationships. We have found here both inequality and some conflict among states penetrated by external interests – but overall outcomes still seem to be more the result of the balance of power resulting when states pursue their general interests. Suffice it to say that, at a certain point, arguments over labels can turn into unjustified substitutes for arguments over questions of substance. Let us simply hope that future American and Venezuelan policy-makers concentrate on the substance of their relationships, and recognize that they have many possibilities for common gain. Let us hope also that they put aside preconceptions that might turn the distant stroke of a hammer into a thunderclap.

Notes

1 James F. Petras, Morris Morley and Stephen Smith, *The Nationalization of Venezuelan Oil*. Praeger, New York, 1977, p. 156.

2 Richard R. Fagen, 'Comentario al artículo de L. R. Einaudi'. In J. Cotler and R. Fagen (eds), *Relaciones políticas entre América Latina y Estados Unidos*. Amorrortu, Buenos Aires, 1974, p. 291.

3 Peter Evans, *Dependent Development: The Alliance of Multinational, State and Local Capital in Brazil*. Princeton University Press, Princeton, 1979, p. 11.

4 ibid., p. 27.

5 R. W. Tucker, *The Inequality of Nations*. Basic Books, New York, 1977.

6 R. A. Gilpin, *US Power and the Multinational Corporation*. Basic Books, New York, 1975, pp. 21–33.

7 The literature of criticism of liberal economics is vast. Noteworthy is the work of Gunnar Myrdal. See for instance his *Economic Theory and the Underdeveloped Regions*. Oxford University Press, London, 1957.

8 Government spending between 1950 and 1958 grew by 201%, while GDP grew by 112%. In the meantime, Pérez Jiménez maintained oil income as a more or less constant percentage of tax revenues, in contrast to his democratic successors who steadily leaned harder (and depended more) on the foreign oil companies. See Banco Central de Venezuela (BCV), *La economía venezolana en los últimos treinta y cinco anos*. Caracas, 1978.

9 For instance, President Carlos Andrés Pérez of the Acción Democrática party said, in this outgoing annual message of 1979, 'The patriarchal state is incompatible with the goal of modernization and social justice' (*Mensaje al Congreso*, 1979, p. VI). Meanwhile, President Herrera, of the Christian Democratic party (known by its initials COPEI), has promised that his new government would be an 'estado promotor', which would 'stimulate the social and individual initiative of all Venezuelans' (p. 15). For instance, in the industrial sector, he would continue

'direct and massive state investment' in certain industries like minerals, while leaving aside areas in which private enterprise was capable on its own (p. 272). See Luís Herrera, *Mi compromiso con Venezuela: Programa de Gobierno para el período 1979–84*. Caracas, November 1978.

10 The pessimistic liberal position is best seen in Milton Friedman, *Capitalism and Freedom*. University of Chicago Press, Chicago, 1962, Ch. 13. That Venezuelans can be at once highly critical of their government while still optimistic is argued by Enrique Baloyra, 'Criticism, Cynicism and Political Evaluation: A Venezuelan Example'. *American Political Science Review*, 73 (4), December 1979, pp. 987–1002. A recent poll in Venezuela confirms such a view: even as President Herrera slipped to Carter-like levels of popularity, a large portion of respondents expressed the belief that a president could be capable of solving most of the country's ills.

11 Quoted in Leroy Jones and Edward S. Mason, 'The Role of Economic Factors in Determining the Size and Structure of the Public Enterprise Sector in Mixed Economy LDCs'. Paper presented at the conference on Public Enterprise in Mixed Economy LDCs, Boston Area Public Enterprise Group, 3–5 April 1980, p. 6.

12 ibid., p. 50.

13 As of 1978. BCV, *Informe económico*. Caracas, 1978.

14 International Monetary Fund (IMF), *International Financial Statistics Yearbook*. IMF, Washington, DC, 1979.

15 ibid., for income figures. For literacy rates, see World Bank, *World Development Report, 1980*. Washington, 1980, pp. 110–11. The IMF may understate population by as much as 2 million.

16 Clark Murdock, 'Economic Factors as Objects of Security: Economics, Security and Vulnerability'. In Klaus Knorr and Frank N. Trager, *Economic Issues and National Security*. Regents Press of Kansas, Lawrence, 1977, p. 83.

17 This understates real Venezuelan exports to the US, since total oil exports to the US, including oil refined elsewhere, are about 35% higher than direct oil exports alone. Thus some 45% of Venezuelan exports really go to the US.

18 IMF, *Direction of Trade Yearbook*. IMF, Washington, DC, 1979.

19 República de Venezuela, *IV Plan de la Nación 1970–74*. Caracas, 1971, pp. 117–19.

20 República de Venezuela, Cordiplan, *V Plan de la Nación*. Paz Pérez, Caracas, n.d., p. 175.

21 Franklin Tugwell, *The Politics of Oil in Venezuela*. Stanford University Press, Stanford, Calif., pp. 67–73.

22 See Franklin Tugwell, 'The United States and Venezuela: Prospects for Accommodation'. In Robert D. Bond (ed.), *Contemporary Venezuela and Its Role in International Affairs*. New York University Press, New York, 1977, p. 212.

23 República de Venezuela, Ministerio de Energía y Minas (MEM), *Petróleo y otros datos estadísticos*. Caracas, 1979, p. 84. By volume.

24 IMF, *Direction of Trade Annual 1966–70*; *Direction of Trade Yearbook 1972–78*. IMF, Washington, DC.

25 Tugwell (note 21), p. 138.

26 For a typical Venezuelan academic exposition of the problem, see Eduardo Carlos Schaposnik, *Las relaciones económicas internacionales y América Latina*. Universidad Central de Venezuela, Facultad de Derecho, Caracas, 1978, Ch. 4.

27 1959: BCV, *Memoria 1959*; República de Venezuela, President, *Primer mensaje al Congreso de la República, 1980*, Caracas, Table 45.

28 US Department of Commerce, *Survey of Current Business*, April 1978, p. 26.

29 Author's interview, Aluminio del Caroní (Alcasa), 9 May 1979.

30 República de Venezuela, Corporación Venezolana de Guayana, *Informe quinquenal 1974–78*. Caracas, 1979, p. 90.

31 *El Nacional*, 16 June 1978.

32 See for instance, Dennis Pirages, *Global Ecopolitics*. Duxbury Press, North Scituate, Mass., 1979, p. 161.

33 Charles P. Kindleberger, *Power and Money: The Politics of International Economics and the Economics of International Politics*. Basic Books, New York, 1970. p. 117.

34 Raymond Vernon, *Storm over the Multinationals: The Real Issues*. Harvard University Press, Cambridge, Mass., 1977, p. 9.

35 These were the exact words of the Superintendent of Foreign Investment. See interview in *Número* (Caracas), 3 August 1980, p. 21.

36 The Pérez changes were new interpretations of Andean Pact Decision 24 with respect to limits on re-investment. See República de Venezuela, President, De-

creto No. 2442, 8 November 1977 in *Gaceta oficial*, no. 2100 Extraordinario, 15 November 1977.

37 Stephen Kobrin, 'Foreign Enterprise and Forced Divestment in LDCs'. *International Organization*, 34 (1), Winter 1980, p. 85.

38 Raymond Vernon, *Sovereignty at Bay*. Basic Books, New York, 1971, p. 47; see also Theodore Moran, 'The Evolution of Concession Agreements in Underdeveloped Countries and the US National Interest'. *Vanderbilt Journal of Transnational Law*, Spring 1974.

39 The nationalization of the iron ore industry in Venezuela points to the difficulties of official intervention and argues further for a hands-off policy by the home country. (US policy in this case was indeed non-interventionist). Strict economic analysis would have indicated that the Venezuelan iron ore industry would lose a good share of its American market after nationalization, thus removing or reducing the supposed benefits of the act. Intervention by the government might have taken the route of pointing out this likely outcome. But at the same time, the American companies expropriated were actually happy to create the impression that their large purchases of ore would continue after nationalization, and they signed long-term purchase contracts to this effect. Knowing nationalization to be inevitable, they thus fostered an amicable settlement to ensure maximum remuneration for their assets. Later they declared their inability to live up to the contracts on the grounds of market conditions.

40 Fedecámaras, 'Carta económica de Mérida', XVIII Annual Meeting, May 1962.

41 For a review of the national debate see Instituto de Comercio Exterior de Venezuela, *Venezuela y el Pacto Andino, documentos y controversia*. Información Documental de América Latina, Caracas, 1974.

42 See, for example, interview with Gustavo Vollmer, 'El capital foráneo es beneficioso'. *Número*, 3 August 1980, p. 18.

43 For instance: 'Revela Ministro de Fomento: Empresas transnacionales presionan para impedir el desarrollo del programa automotriz del Pacto Andino'. *El Universal*, 20 August 1977; or 'Asegura el Canciller Consalvi: Las transnacionales han in-terpuesto sus grandes intereses para perturbar el proceso del Pacto Andino'. *El Universal*, 28 July 1978.

44 *Monthly Report*, Editora TMR, Caracas, 30 June 1979.

45 It is not possible to review here all of the factors that condition a state's capacity to control foreign investors. One of the best catalogues is found in Alfred Stepan, *The State and Society: Peru in Comparative Perspective*. Princeton University Press, Princeton, 1978, pp. 237–48. Stepan presents four categories of variables, two reflecting what are here called internal structure and two reflecting external structures. These are: (1) factors stemming from the internal characteristics of the state; (2) factors involving the characteristics of the domestic public and private sectors; (3) economic background variables; (4) variables rooted in the political and economic relationship of the state to the international economic system.

46 *El Nacional*, 16 July 1980. This shows a slight increase in the American share of 56.6% in 1977 reported in Ministerio de Hacienda, *Memoria (1977)*. Caracas, pp. 84–7.

47 US Department of Commerce, *Survey of Current Business*, March 1980, p. 27.

48 Venezuelan figures of the Superintendent of Foreign Investment reported in *Número*, 3 August 1980, p. 25. US data: *Survey of Current Business*, August 1977 and August 1980. While the two series differ as to totals, growth rates should be relatively comparable.

49 For a review of the weaknesses of implementation of foreign investment control, see Moisés Naim, 'Ideology, Dependence and the Control of Multinational Corporations: A Study of Venezuelan Policy on Foreign Investment and Technology Transfer'. MIT Working Paper, Alfred P. Sloan School of Management, Cambridge, Mass., 1977, pp. 18–48.

50 *El Diario de Caracas*, 28 December 1980.

51 Among these, representatives of the government gave this message at a Council of the Americas seminar on the Andean Pact in May 1980, as well as frequent interviews with the national and international press. See *El Nacional*, 16 July 1980; *El Diario de Caracas*, 7 May 1980; *Número*, 3 August 1980.

52 C. Fred Bergsten, Thomas Horst and Theodore Moran, *American Multinationals and American Interests*. The Brookings

Institution, Washington, DC, 1978, p. 454. For similar views, see Albert Hirschman, 'How to Divest in Latin America and Why'. In his *A Bias for Hope: Essays on Development and Latin America*. Yale University Press, New Haven, 1971; Theodore Moran, *Multinational Corporations and the Politics of Dependence: Copper in Chile*. Princeton University Press, Princeton, 1974, pp. 255–60.

53 US Department of Commerce, *Survey of Current Business*, March 1980, p. 50.

54 Petróleos de Venezuela, *Informe anual*, Caracas, 1970, 1980. On renegotiation, see MEM, *Carta semanal*, Caracas, 26 April 1980.

55 See Fedecámaras, Consejo Nacional, XXXVI Annual Assembly, 'Carta de Maracaibo', 1980.

56 *Ley general de bancos y otros institutos de crédito*, 20 December 1970, BCV, *Revista*, October–December 1970. Foreign-owned banks (those with more than 20% foreign capital) could not increase their capital, and could not increase deposits beyond the level of six times capital (Art. 33–34).

57 See *Latin America Political Report*, 18 July 1969. On the overall situation, see, for example, *The American Banker*, 8 July 1969.

58 IMF, *International Financial Statistics Yearbook*, 1980; *International Financial Statistics*. Washington, DC, May 1981. Foreign currency assets of the Venezuelan Investment Fund and of Petróleos de Venezuela would add over $6 billion to official reserves.

59 End of October, 1980: *The Monthly Report*, 25 November 1980.

60 Interview with Leopoldo Díaz Bruzual, *The Daily Journal*, 23 October 1979.

61 *Federal Reserve Bulletin*, March 1972; August 1980.

62 This link reflects the 'privatization' of financial relations as noted by Barbara Stallings, 'Peru and the US Banks: Privatization of Financial Relations'. In Richard Fagen (ed), *Capitalism and the State in US–Latin American Relations*. Stanford University Press, Stanford, 1979, pp. 217 –53. Venezuela, however, does not fit the model of the indigent country in the banks' thrall, as does Peru.

63 *Federal Reserve Bulletin*, March 1972; August 1980.

64 US Comptroller of the Currency, Federal Deposit Insurance Corporation and Federal Reserve Board, 'Country Expo-

sure Lending Survey', Joint News Release, 24 November 1980.

65 Unfortunately, it is impossible to know to what extent Venezuela is indebted to other countries' banks or in other currencies than the dollar because official Venezuela data are too spotty. Total claims on Venezuela through the Eurocurrency market reached $13.1 billion at the end of 1978, while Venezuelan deposits in the same market were $9.4 billion, according to the Bank for International Settlements, *Annual Report*. Basle, Switzerland, 1978 –79.

66 *El Universal*, 30 September 1979.

67 See 'El Estado se sometió a las leyes de Nueva York'. *Número*, 7 September 1980.

68 Norman Gall, 'The Challenge of Venezuelan Oil'. *Foreign Policy*, Spring 1975, p. 45.

69 Tom J. Farer, 'The United States and the Third World: A Basis for Accommodation'. *Foreign Affairs*, October 1975, p. 89.

70 The text of Project Independence speculated that OPEC could maintain a $7.00 per barrel price with minor cutbacks in production, while maintaining an $11.00 world price would require major cutbacks (p. 4). US Federal Energy Administration, *Project Independence: A Summary*. US Government Printing Office, Washington, November 1974. Still, $7 oil would lead to excess supply by 1985 (p. 41). The most outspoken economist on the artificiality of the price of oil was M. A. Adelman. See, for instance, his 'The World Oil Cartel: Scarcity, Economics and Politics'. *Quarterly Review of Economics and Business*, 16 (2), Summer 1976. That depletable natural resources are not priced by cost factors alone was an idea promoted by Robert Solow of MIT, although the classic exposition is usually attributed to H. Hotelling. For a review of these theories, see P. S. Dasgupta and G. M. Heal, *Economic Theory and Exhaustible Resources*. Cambridge University Press, Cambridge, 1979.

71 The Shah of Iran rejected bilateral overtures with this famous retort: 'No one can wave a finger at us, because we will wave a finger back.' See *New York Times*, 27 September 1974. Kissinger is reported to have put heavy pressure on Venezuelan Foreign Minister Calvani in early 1974 under the Caldera regime; President Pérez reacted six months later with an 'Open

Letter to President Ford', published in the *New York Times*, 24 September 1974, defending the justice of the then current price level. Tariffs were supported by Federal Reserve chairman Arthur Burns, *New York Times*, 28 November 1974. Various academic schemes included the Houthakker Tariff, as well as other plans for a national oil-purchasing board operating by soliciting sealed bids from potential suppliers.

72 US Department of Energy, *Monthly Energy Review*, September 1980, p. 91.

73 For views on oil price determination, see V. H. Oppenheim, 'The Past: We Pushed Them', and Theodore H. Moran, 'The Future: OPEC Wants Them'. *Foreign Policy*, Winter 1976–77; Robert Pindyck, 'OPEC's Threat to the West'. *Foreign Policy*, Spring 1978; Robert Stobaugh and Daniel Yergin (eds), *Energy Future*. Random House, New York, 1979, especially pp. 31–41, on the key role of Saudi Arabia; Resources for the Future, *Energy: The Next Twenty Years*. Ballinger, Cambridge, Mass., 1979, pp. 13–16, which takes an agnostic view, but tends toward the position that prices are in line with current market realities.

74 From the beginning, President Reagan emphasized that he would seek out closer relations with the two US neighbors, Canada and Mexico. This recalls former attempts to give preferences to these countries while excluding Venezuela, which in many ways shares the same naturally close relations with the United States as the other two countries.

75 For a review of the positive attitudes in the United States, in business as well as in the State, Treasury and Defense Departments, see Petras, Morley and Smith (note 1), Ch. 3.

76 John Blair, *The Control of Oil*. Pantheon, New York, 1976, p. 102.

77 MEM, *Petróleo y otros datos estadísticos*. Caracas, 1979. Excludes consumption by the oil industry and bunkers.

78 ibid., p. 5. Revenues were deflated by the price index of imports from the United States according to BCV, *Informe económico*. Caracas, 1979.

79 *El Nacional*, 27 December 1980.

80 *The Daily Journal*, 23 October 1979.

81 For the Minister of Mines' denial, see *Carta semanal*, 5 December 1980.

82 Carlota Pérez, 'Pronóstico del ingreso fiscal petrolero de Venezuela (1980–2000)'. Centro de Estudios para el Desarrollo, Universidad Central de Venezuela, Caracas, 1980, presents a doubtful view on the net contribution to the Venezuelan economy from Faja development. Optimistic views tend to be expressed by outside interests and by the oil industry itself. See, for instance, a Bechtel Corporation study indicating that heavy oil sands operations would produce a 15% return on investment after taxes to private enterprise at cost levels of $22 per barrel in 1979 prices. The implication is that from the Venezuelan point of view, the exploitation of the Faja would be easily profitable now. But the Venezuelans know that such pre-profit cost figures can be inflated considerably in the course of implementation. Bechtel, 'Economic Review of Advanced Fuel and Power Technologies', October 1979.

83 Venezuelan relations with Cuba have been poor since the early 1960s, when Castro backed revolutionary activity in the country. Relations were opened in the early 1970s and improved slowly, but have been once again soured under the government of Herrera Campíns.

84 According to the American ambassador in Venezuela (1980), William Luers. See his speech before the Center for Interamerican Relations in New York, 19 November 1980, published in *El Nacional*, 22 December 1980. Venezuela's foreign aid program fits most of the categories noted by J. Stephen Hoadly in 'Small States as Aid Donors'. *International Organization*, **34** (1), Winter 1980, p. 136, especially in the heavy reliance on aid to multilateral agencies, in the emphasis on the most needy and in the high percentage of aid in relation to GDP.

85 Luers, *El Nacional*, 22 December 1980.

86 Abraham Lowenthal, 'Jimmy Carter and Latin America: A New Era or Small Change'. In Kenneth Oye, Donald Rothchild and Robert J. Lieber, *Eagle Entangled*. Longman, New York, 1979, p. 300.

Latin American industrial exports and trade negotiations with the United States

John S. Odell*

In the western hemisphere, as in other regions, the traditional relation between richer and poorer countries has been undergoing an accelerating transformation in the last decade. Whereas developing countries traditionally imported manufactures and exported primary commodities, they are now clearly emerging as serious competitors in a range of manufactured products. One of the highest foreign policy priorities of Latin American governments is increasing industrial exports. An example of the shift in this direction is discussed in the chapter on Mexico in this book (ch. 3). Some Latin American industries are leaders in the shift toward rivalry with US producers. Meanwhile, at the same time demands for import restrictions have been increasingly heard in the older industrial countries[1].

One result is that bilateral bargaining between governments to regulate trade and market shares has become a common but inadequately studied element of the North–South diplomatic agenda. Despite all our discussion of the international economic order, our knowledge of this type of bilateral conflict is quite sketchy. What are the outcomes of such industrial trade disputes between governments? Which parties are most likely to achieve their objectives? Do outcomes vary from one case to another, and, if so, what accounts for the difference? Can the negotiator's choice of strategy influence the result? An investigation of inter-American interactions on this issue can shed light on an international phenomenon that is likely to recur in this hemisphere and elsewhere for some time.

5.1   The record

An inter-state dispute or conflict is here defined as a process in which a government resists or rejects a request from another government or takes harmful action against another state. The emphasis is thus on overt behavior rather than on the degree of underlying conflict of interests or compatability of interests between states[2]. An industrial trade dispute begins with either the first inter-governmental request or the tentative announcement of a possible restrictive trade action, and ends with the final action, inter-state

* Assistant Professor of Government, Harvard University

agreement, or cessation of intergovernmental communication on the matter. A list of such conflicts between Latin America and the US beginning and ending between 1960 and 1978, presented in *Table 5.1*, has been compiled from US Treasury and State Department records, periodicals, and previous research[3]. Data on the size, growth, and product composition of Latin American industrial exports to the US are presented in an Appendix.

Of the 25 conflicts, 19 are countervailing duty proceedings. United States law allows citizens to file complaints against 'unfair' foreign competition made possible by governmental subsidies to exporters. Export subsidies are used by many states, including the United States. The US procedure was administered by the Treasury Department during the period of this study. If the Treasury ruled that a foreign government was paying a 'bounty or grant' on exports to the US, an equivalent countervailing duty was imposed. During its investigations, Treasury negotiated with representatives of the foreign government to try to force it to eliminate or reduce the subsidy. Thus a ruling of 'no bounty or grant' may reflect more than a technical study. In these negotiations Treasury took the position, understandably, that it had very little to give up. We shall see, however, that, as usual, technical determinations require assumptions, which can be adjusted and offset. The US countervailing duty law was unusual internationally in that it had been exempted from the GATT rule that serious injury to domestic industry from the imports must be shown before a state can countervail. The US has been virtually alone in using countervailing duties against less developed countries. Before the Trade Act of 1974, the Treasury normally used indefinite delay to exempt them, but at that time the Congress imposed time limits on investigations[4]. The subject of export subsidies and countervailing duties was central to the Tokyo Round multilateral trade negotiations (which were concluded in 1979). To encourage an agreement limiting the use of export subsidies, the 1974 Act gave the Treasury Secretary some discretion to waive the enforcement of countervailing duties until 4 January 1979. The waiver was authorized if a Geneva agreement was reasonably likely, if imposition of the countervailing duty would probably have jeopardized the negotiations, and if 'adequate steps' had been taken 'to reduce substantially or eliminate' the 'adverse effect' of the subsidy[5]. This temporary waiver authority enlarged the scope for inter-state bargaining in bilateral disputes.

The other disputes listed in *Table 5.1* arose in a variety of ways. In 1966, US producers of instant coffee complained that the Brazilian practice of charging a tax on green coffee exports to them, while selling green to Brazilian processors at a lower price, constituted unfair competition. The 1971 Nixon–Connally surcharge on dutiable US imports set off an outcry from Latin America, with which the US customarily has a trade surplus. In 1973, Argentina came into conflict with US restrictions on trade with communist countries when she demanded that US-owned auto firms in

Table 5.1 *US–Latin American disputes concerning Latin American industrial exports, 1960–78*

Year begun	State	Product	Current import value ($m.)	Latin American strategies	Outcome[a]
1966	Brazil	Soluble coffee		Technocratic; allies	C: Brazil provided some tax-free green coffee to US processors; US dropped demand for export tax on soluble
1971	Many	(US 10% surcharge)		Protest	L: US abolished surcharge but not because of Latin American action
1972	Mexico	Steel plate (CVD)	23 ('71) 1 ('74)	Technocratic	C: US ruled small bounty but waived duty; Mexico agreed not to increase it; CVD revoked 10/78
1973	Argentina	Vehicles for Cuba		Threat	L: US approved sale
1974	Colombia	Cut flowers (CVD)		Protest	U: Colombia eliminated subsidy for cut flowers
	Brazil	Non-rubber footwear (CVD)	81+	Technocratic; allies; threat	C: US imposed 5% CVD in 1974; in 1976 Brazil reduced subsidy for shoes
	Argentina	Non-rubber footwear (CVD)	24	Allies	U: Argentina abolished subsidy for shoes; US ruled no bounty
1975	Many	(US Trade Act of 1974, GSP)		Protest	U: No US modifications
	Brazil	Handbags (CVD)	5	Allies	C: US 14% CVD; later waived when Brazil agreed to phase out subsidy for handbags
	Brazil	Soybean oil		Allies	U: Brazil agreed to phase out subsidy for soybean oil; US agreed not to initiate investigation
	Brazil	Processed castor oil (CVD)	1	?	U: US 11% CVD
	Mexico	Processed asparagus (CVD)	2	Technocratic	L: US ruled no bounty; no Mexican concession
	Brazil	Specialty steel	3	Protest	U: US quota imposed
1976	Brazil	Scissors and shears (CVD)	1	Protest	U: US 16% CVD
	Brazil	Cotton yarn (CVD)	3	Technocratic; allies	U: US 20% CVD

Year	Country	Product	No.	Strategy	Outcome
1977	Uruguay	Handbags (CVD)	3	Yield; technocratic	U: US 17% CVD waived; Uruguay abolished subsidy for handbags for all markets and agreed to abolish it for all exports by 1983[bc]
	Uruguay	Non-rubber footwear (CVD)	12	Yield; Technocratic	U: US 23% CVD waived, on the above conditions[bc]
	Uruguay	Leather apparel (CVD)	17	Yield; technocratic	U: US 12% CVD waived on above conditions[bc]
	Colombia	Handbags (CVD)	6	Technocratic; allies	C: US 5.5% CVD waived; Colombia agreed to halve key export incentive
	Argentina	Non-rubber footwear (CVD)		Technocratic	L: US 0.86% CVD
	Argentina	Leather apparel (CVD)		Technocratic	L: US ruled no bounty; no Argentine concession
1978	Colombia	Textiles and clothing (CVD)		Technocratic	L: US ruled no bounties except on leather garments; ITC ruled no injury from these; no CVD
	Argentina	Textiles and clothing (CVD)		Technocratic	L: US ruled no bounties except on wool garments; US 3% CVD on these
	Brazil	Textiles and clothing (CVD)		Technocratic	C: US 37% + 35% CVDs waived; Brazil pledged major reduction in subsidy programs for all exports and support for multilateral subsidy code; US agreed to require proof of injury in future CVD cases
	Uruguay	Textiles and clothing (CVD)		Technocratic	U: US CVDs of 17%, 39% and 43%[c]

[a] Classification of strategies and outcomes is discussed in the text.
CVD = countervailing duty
ITC = US International Trade Commission
U = outcome substantially more favorable to initial objectives of the US government than to Latin American objectives
L = outcome substantially more favorable to Latin American objectives
C = compromise outcome

[b] The Treasury revoked this waiver on 13 November 1978 on the grounds that since January Uruguay might have granted exporters forgiveness from a social security tax, considered a bounty; further negotiations were underway at the close of 1978.

[c] Uruguay's CVDs were revoked in March 1979 after the government of Uruguay pledged to collect an equivalent export tax on its shoes, handbags, leather apparel and textiles shipped to the United States.

Sources: Unpublished US Treasury and State Department records, the *Federal Register*, periodicals, previous research, interviews in Washington.

Argentina export vehicles to Cuba. The passage of the 1974 Trade Act was received in Latin America with vocal protests aimed at limitations on its general system of preferences (GSP) for developing countries, its exclusion of Ecuador and Venezuela from GSP, and the fear that the law's procedures would stimulate more protectionist measures in the US. Under its escape clause (section 201) an investigation of specialty steel imports resulted in 1976 in the imposition of US quota restrictions on Brazil's exports. Finally, in 1976 the US threatened to begin proceedings against Brazilian subsidies on soybean oil exports as unfair competition against US exporters in third markets (section 301 of the Trade Act).

Table 5.2 *US anti-dumping cases concerning Latin American industrial exports, 1960–78*

Year begun	State	Product	Current import value ($m.)	Outcome[a]
1960	Cuba	Rayon staple fiber		No injury
1961	Dom. Rep.	Portland cement		No injury
1969	Brazil	Pig iron		No SLFV
1971	Mexico	Sulphur	4	*AD duty*
1972	Brazil	Pig iron	4	No SLFV
	Brazil	Printed vinyl film		*AD duty*
	Argentina	Printed vinyl film		*AD duty*
	Mexico	Steel reinforcing bars	4	No injury
1973	Mexico	Picker sticks		*AD duty*
1974	Brazil	Vehicle seats	0.5	No SLFV
1975	Mexico	Portland cement	3.5	No injury
1976	Mexico	Lithographic plates	0.2	No injury
1977	Brazil	Methyl alcohol		No injury

[a] No SLFV = finding of no sale at less than fair value
AD duty = anti-dumping duty imposed

Sources: Unpublished summary supplied by US Treasury, supplemented by Tariff Commission published reports.

Latin American industrial exports were also subject to 13 US anti-dumping investigations during the same period (see *Table 5.2*). Governments sometimes express strong opinions about anti-dumping cases, and these cases need to be kept in mind. But they are excluded from the analysis of inter-state bargaining below because in practice their outcomes owe very little to inter-state communication or bargaining. While the US countervailing duty law is directed at foreign government policies, here in contrast the target is foreign companies' pricing practices. The US Antidumping Act provides that when a foreign company sells goods in the United States 'at less than fair value', and when these imports injure or are likely to injure US producers, the Treasury shall levy anti-dumping duties equivalent to the dumping margins. In the event of a complaint from an American, the

Treasury calculates whether less-than-fair-value sales have taken place, normally by comparing data on home market prices with prices charged in the US market, and the ITC determines injury. Nine of the complaints against Latin American firms were dismissed, and duties were assessed in four cases involving Argentina, Brazil, and Mexico. To include these cases in the present analysis would misleadingly raise one's estimate of Latin American government bargaining influence[6].

In a third set of cases, also excluded below, action against Latin American and other trade was begun by a sub-unit of the US government but was later abandoned unilaterally, rather than as a result of inter-state negotiations. In 1970 an effort to repeal section 807 of the US tariff schedules failed. This section has encouraged the establishment of plants in Mexico, Central America and the Caribbean for the partial assembly of US-made components to be exported back to the US for further processing. In four escape clause investigations – concerning Mexican processed asparagus, Brazilian and Argentine footwear, and Brazilian ferro-chromium exports – the ITC recommended import restrictions, and President Ford and President Carter rejected those recommendations as far as Latin America was concerned[7]. Though these decisions are of great interest in several countries and may influence policy-makers' calculations on other occasions, the political process involved seems to fall outside the category of international negotiation, which is the direct subject of this chapter.

The disputes listed in *Table 5.1* may appear to be minor, judging from the value of imports at issue at the time of the dispute. Indeed, these disputes should be considered in the context of total Latin American manufactured exports to the United States. That is, from 1970 to 1976 Mexico increased her total manufactured exports to the US from $398 million to $1944 million; Brazil registered a sharp rise from a very low $63 million to $541 million. Over the same period, totals for Argentina rose from $47 million to $142 million, and for Colombia from $24 million to $105 million (see the Appendix). Despite some US trade restraints and a few early disputes, a number of Latin American countries were able to begin expansion of these exports to the huge American market.

This background does not indicate, however, that these official disputes are trivial. They have both economic and political consequences, and their significance, particularly to the exporting side, is larger than is indicated by the size of product trade at the time of the dispute. Current trade figures in *Table 5.1* are not a valid measure of potential or future trade. Some of the Latin American industries involved were only barely off the ground. Manufactured exports are central to many developing countries' long-term plans for development. Therefore trade actions against those exports, if they diminish hoped-for future trade flows, strike at the foundation of national economic plans for the long term, not to mention efforts to escape immediate balance of payments and debt crises. The rates of increase in

Latin American total manufactured exports are less impressive when one considers how low the levels remain, when compared either to US consumption of the product or to total exports of the exporting country.

A successful attack on a line of exports, or even the act of filing a complaint, may depress exports by that industry and also more generally by raising new uncertainty about the US market. Such disputes may discourage Latin American investors from beginning new export industries they would otherwise have launched. Signals that the US government intends to resist export subsidies may affect private investment plans in industries other than the one at issue. In that industry itself, the filing of a complaint raises uncertainties in the minds of US importers, which may lead them to shift to other suppliers abroad or at home in order to avoid having their business delayed by US customs procedures. There is some evidence supporting these suppositions. A comparison of US imports across industries found that the more frequent the *complaints* of 'less-than-fair-value sales' in an industry, the slower the import growth rate[8]. Moreover, exports to markets other than the United States may be affected. Yielding to US pressure to abolish a subsidy program for products going to North America might be considered an invitation to other importing states to make similar demands, which in some cases would affect larger trade flows.

Finally, such disputes have political consequences. US pressures and sanctions are considered insulting and unfair. Conflicts can be expected to strengthen those in Latin America who oppose US foreign policy as being imperialistic, and thus to increase incentives for their governments to demonstrate independence from the United States, on economic or non-economic issues. These cases normally involve top officials in the Latin American country, and some have involved cabinet officers and the President of the United States. The symbolic value of these cases probably exceeds their monetary value.

5.2   Conflict outcomes and Latin American strategies

Considering a set of industrial trade disputes, what pattern of outcomes should be expected? One general hypothesis might hold that in any bilateral conflict with a Latin American state, the United States enjoys such an overall superiority of international power and relative invulnerability that it is able to achieve its objectives in virtually every case. In such an imbalanced international power structure, no real bargaining takes place; the US states its demands, and Argentina or Colombia finds little alternative but to comply. Since there is little they can do to hurt the United States, Washington can reject demands contrary to its objectives. An amended version of this general argument might place some emphasis on variations among Latin American states: Brazil and perhaps Mexico should achieve their objectives somewhat more often than the smaller states, providing a few exceptions to the general rule[9].

In contrast, other general views or hypotheses lead one to expect results significantly more favorable to the Latin American states. The structure of a particular bargaining situation may be subject to some influence. According to what has been dubbed an 'unorthodox dependency' perspective on inter-American relations[10], the relation is basically unequal and conflictual, but the hegemonic state is not a monolithic entity. The pluralism and contradictions of the United States allow peripheral or semi-peripheral states some room for maneuver and autonomy except during crises. This approach sensitizes one to the distribution of US domestic political forces relevant to a given trade issue, and it raises the question whether Latin American governments have been able to bring into the bargaining structure domestic groups having interests in common with them. In conflicts with the United States, Canada has mobilized transnational corporations having subsidiaries in Canada or parts of the Washington bureaucracy as allies inside the US policy-making process, thus shifting outcomes in favor of Canada[11]. On this second view, then, one would expect that by using such a strategy Latin American governments achieve some relatively favorable outcomes, although in most cases the outcome will be closer to the initial objectives of the United States government.

Third, within a given power structure, other negotiating strategies and tactics could theoretically be used to bring about some greater success for the weaker party. Several considerations suggest means for retaliation available to Latin American states and the use of threats of retaliation as bargaining moves. In the first place, the uncertainty of power relations in a given situation might lead at least to more such attempts than power analysts would expect. Pressures in domestic political systems might also encourage such attempts. In its coverage of trade disputes, the newsletter *Business Latin America* often raises the fear that Brazil or other states would retaliate against US-owned firms in the event of a trade war. In 1971, tiny Malta aggressively negotiated with Britain the terms of continued use of Malta's military facilities and managed to triple the rent being paid while making other gains as well, even though technological change was reducing the value of its chief asset to NATO. Malta's prime minister implicitly threatened to deal instead with Libya and the Soviet Union, among other tactics[12]. In principle, developing countries owing debts to the industrialized world have available the threat to repudiate the debts. In 1972, during talks over relief from earlier debts, the government of Ghana actually repudiated some of them and raised its demands. The final debt settlement in 1974 was more favorable to Ghana than the terms that had been acceptable to the creditors before the repudiation[13]. Following the 1973 success of the oil-exporting countries, it was argued that developing countries now have or will increasingly acquire the capability and inclination to pose serious threats to the United States[14]. In sum, this assortment of examples, while not amounting to a coherent prediction of a pattern of outcomes, does suggest a reason for expecting greater Latin American success than under the first perspective.

Of the 25 cases shown in *Table 5.1*, 12 ended with either unrequited concessions by the Latin American government (e.g., abolition of its export subsidy) or unilateral sanctions by the United States (e.g., imposition of a countervailing duty). These outcomes can be classified as substantially more favorable to the initial objectives of the US government than to those of the Latin American government. Six disputes ended in what I classify as a compromise. For example, in the 1974 case of Brazilian shoes, Brazil maintained its programs, the US imposed a countervailing duty, but in response to Brazilian arguments the size of the duty was fairly small, given the nature of the footwear trade. In these six cases, each side settled for less than its initial demand, but the US concession was usually to accept a lesser degree of Latin American compliance or to waive a possible new sanction, rather than to retreat in response to a Latin American initiative. The seven remaining disputes ended in outcomes more favorable to the initial objectives of the Latin American government than to the US.

If these rough classifications can be taken as meaningful, the results at least cast doubt on an overall power structure perspective. The US side achieves clear success in nearly twice as many cases as Latin American governments taken together, but Latin American successes and compromises are frequent enough to require investigation. Nor do negotiation outcomes seem to vary clearly with basic power differences among Latin American states. While Brazil's record is clearly more favorable than that of Uruguay, at the same time Mexico, Argentina, and Colombia each achieved greater success than Brazil[15].

None of these disputes can be understood adequately from an examination of aggregate data alone, but before moving to case studies let us note that, generally, negotiation outcomes are associated with the type of strategy used by Latin American governments. Five types of strategy were used, singly or in combination.

In a set of three cases handled simultaneously in 1977–1978, Uruguay essentially *yielded* to the demand for an end to its export subsidies and even agreed to abolish them not only for the products in question but for all exports within five years. Three years before this case, Economy Minister Alejandro Vegh Villegas had begun a daring free-market economic policy that had not, however, swept away these export subsidies. The American demands fell upon a military government that was ideologically receptive to such changes. In another five disputes, the Latin American government did no more than *protest*. Protests were ineffective in all the cases. The United States tended to have its way in four of them; the outcome of the fifth case was more favorable to Latin America but for reasons unrelated to these protests.

But when each of the other three types of strategy was employed, the pattern of outcomes was more favorable to the Latin American states. In at least seven disputes *allies within the United States* were mobilized. The allies have included both groups with a common economic interest and agencies with a supportive international political objective. The six cases involving economic allies tended to end in compromise. In three cases the Secretary of State or National Security Council (NSC) staff weighed in with political arguments on behalf of the Latin state. The effort failed in two large cases but helped Colombia somewhat in a third. A strategy of *retaliation or threat of retaliation* against the United States was usually avoided, but two examples do appear in these conflicts; the outcomes in those cases were compromise and 'pro-Latin', respectively. A fifth type of strategy has been used a number of times, though not always; namely, careful *technical preparation and technical argument* at the administrative level in Washington. Such arguments have helped shift the outcome to compromise or Latin American 'victory' in 10 out of 15 cases.

Protest

In a number of trade disputes, the Latin American exporting country or countries are viewed from Washington as peripheral to the main bargaining and trade between the US and other major powers, the results of which have been simply imposed on the western hemisphere parties largely as an afterthought. In late 1971, the Nixon–Connally import surcharge was removed, but in response to protests and exchange-rate concessions by major financial powers, not in response to Latin American complaints. Protests over the 1974 Trade Act elicited no concessions from the United States. In 1975 an avalanche of criticism of the Act's new authorities for import restrictions fell upon the State Department, which responded with the basic position that the Act would ultimately benefit Latin America by authorizing US leadership in global negotiations to liberalize trade. The Department also attempted to assure Latin Americans that the executive branch would apply the new provisions flexibly in a way that would not harm the region[16].

But the 1975–1976 case of specialty steel restrictions was not reassuring. Brazil was a very small supplier to the US market, and her *imports* of specialty steels from US firms exceeded her exports. The US negotiated an orderly marketing agreement with the government of Japan and other major suppliers, and simply imposed a basket quota on all small suppliers, fixed at a level lower than shipments for the previous year. The Brazilian embassy filed a protest note complaining that the action froze the market share of small suppliers at a meager 8% of US imports and failed to provide special allowance for the expansion of developing countries' exports, a principle ostensibly accepted by the United States[17].

Mobilizing allies in the United States

At first glance, the notion of Colombia or Argentina building a coalition strong enough to swing Washington politics in its favor seems a bit quixotic. Indeed this is likely to be a rare feat on occasions when major lobbying groups and political figures are actively involved and public attention is focused on the issue. But many US policy actions affecting Latin America are handled through a much less visible process, and most industrial trade issues are likely to make potential allies out of at least some US groups. When those groups are strong and skillful enough, Latin Americans may benefit as well, whether or not the activity is triggered by a Latin American initiative. A provision in a US tax bill before Congress in the early 1970s would have ruled out tax deductions for American convention meetings held outside the country. The provision would have significantly hurt economies of Caribbean countries, but it was dropped when US firms owning hotels there lobbied against it[18]. Often the effects of such activity are difficult to assess, but in industrial trade disputes a few known attempts have failed, while allies' activities seem to have made secondary contributions to the Latin American side in a few other cases.

Mobilizing State Department or NSC allies is more difficult on countervailing duty cases than on some other issues where the State Department routinely chairs the decision process (e.g., on the question of Argentine vehicle exports to Cuba) or where the President has explicit authority to waive a sanction on broad foreign policy grounds. Some leeway for 'foreign policy' flexibility in countervailing duty cases was permitted before 1974 by the absence of time limits on investigations, and from 1974 through 1978 by the waiver authority during multilateral trade negotiations. The largest Latin American cases before 1978 reached their decision during 1974, however, when producer groups were able to scuttle the delay option by court action and by holding the pending Trade Act hostage in Congress. The Treasury opened several new cases less than a month after Secretary of State Henry Kissinger had pledged to a conference of Latin American foreign ministers that the US would refrain from new restrictions on Latin American access to US markets. With their large shoe exports to the US under attack, Brazil and Argentina pressed the State Department to plead their case for friendly treatment. The Brazilian government was 'hopping mad' over the investigation and called for an immediate halt, fearing that it would open a 'Pandora's box' of attacks on Latin American export incentives. Minister of Commerce and Industry Severo Fagundes Gomes declared bitterly, 'The shoe probe is an aggression'[19]. Secretary of State Henry Kissinger was persuaded to present the case himself, but Secretary of the Treasury George Shultz refused to make concessions on 'foreign policy' grounds, and chastized Kissinger for improperly poaching on Treasury authority[20].

In 1978, with the waiver authority in effect, another 'foreign policy' intervention took place, this time with perceptible effect. As part of his campaign for the Panama Canal treaties, President Carter met in Washington with each Latin American head of state. President López Michelsen of Colombia was sufficiently concerned about the pending countervailing duty case against Colombian leather handbags to include this matter on his agenda with Carter, who then instructed his National Security staff assistant, Robert Pastor, to follow the matter. Other high Colombian officials, including the directors of the Foreign Trade Institute (Incomex) and Proexpo, flew to Washington to lend their hands to an intensive effort to prevent measures harmful to this industry[21]. NSC participation was probably beneficial to the Colombian position in the negotiations, given the administration's interest in favoring democracies as exemplars in Latin America. The outcome was a compromise, including Colombian incentives reductions and a waived countervailing duty[22].

A strategy of mobilizing US allies with an economic rather than a 'foreign policy' interest can claim somewhat better success in industrial trade disputes. Such economic allies include not only firms with business in the country and importer associations, but also members of Congress whose constituents are affected. Senator Russell Long is well known for his advocacy of protection for US producers under pressure from imports. But Long's state also happens to include a major importer of rubber footwear; on that item Long has spoken up for fair treatment for East Asian exporters[23]. US economic allies are sometimes overpowered. During late 1976 and early 1977 the Treasury was considering a countervailing duty against Brazilian cotton yarn. The Brazilian government took a hard line, refusing to reduce export incentives in this case. They argued that, because this trade was already limited by US textile quotas, no further restrictions were justified. A Massachusetts firm depended on these lower-cost imports, and Senators Edward Kennedy and Edward Brooke opposed countervailing on the grounds that it would cost some 400 jobs for Americans[24]. But these two were no match for the very strong demands from Southern representatives of competing yarn producers that a countervailing duty be imposed. A new administration had just taken office, and wider pressure organized by the Brazil–Massachusetts side might have tipped them in favor of granting a waiver. Instead a heavy countervailing duty was levied.

In other cases, however, economic allies have contributed to compromise outcomes at least in secondary ways. In the case of Colombian handbags, a gentle campaign was organized to demonstrate the presence of US interests other than import-competing producers. The US Chamber of Commerce in Bogotá was active in arranging for its member firms to contact Washington agencies other than the Treasury to make clear that they wanted fair consideration for Colombia. These firms included Singer, Goodyear, and Braniff Airlines, which ships the handbags to the US[25]. This allied campaign probably contributed to the compromise outcome.

Midway through the lengthy interchange concerning Brazilian soluble coffee, the Brazilian government's hand was strengthened when the US coffee industry association reversed itself and came out against measures to penalize Brazilian exports. Some of the US companies thus abandoned General Foods to carry on the fight thereafter and became tacit allies of the Brazilian negotiators, perhaps because some, like Nestlé, had soluble coffee and other interests in Brazil and decided that retaliation in Brazil constituted the greater threat to their interests. This shift at least seriously undercut efforts to persuade the Brazilians that their inaction could lead to crippling attacks on the International Coffee Agreement, as well as efforts to paint a picture of general domestic harm from imports[26]. Later in the mid-1970s a formal US–Brazil Business Council was established, including on the US side the chiefs of firms like Goodyear, Caterpillar, and Citibank. Such a link between Brazilians and firms with interests in Brazil could be used to facilitate transnational coalitions to influence policy decisions.

Threat and retaliation

Most general perspectives on US–Latin American relations would expect a Latin American strategy of threat or retaliation either to fizzle out or to backfire, hurting the Latin American side the most. Governments in most cases have avoided this strategy, but two examples do appear among these industrial trade disputes, and two other related instances will help illustrate possibilities. To the extent that a conclusion is possible, the strategy seems to have been relatively successful in these few applications.

In the 1976 Brazilian cases, the threat was subtle and the effect difficult to estimate, given the complexity of these interactions. In January, while the ITC recommendation for shoe quota restrictions was pending before the President, in Brasilia Finance Minister Simonsen allowed himself to be drawn briefly into a public discussion of the means Brazil would have for retaliation if shoe quotas were imposed[27]. That spring, Treasury Secretary William Simon made a personal trip to Brasilia to negotiate a resolution of several trade disputes. The result, in brief, was that Brazil made concessions on shoes, handbags, and soybean oil exports. Simon waived a countervailing duty on handbags and withdrew threats of other measures, and he added a public endorsement of Brazil to encourage foreign bankers and investors. This was a time when Brazil's increasing foreign debt was causing nervousness abroad, a major concern in Brasilia. *O Estado de São Paulo* regarded the Simon–Simonsen agreements as valuable to Brazil for the demonstration that the US accepted Brazil as a partner[28]. Whether the more serious, high-level treatment of Brazil in these cases owed something to a subtle threat of retaliation, or to private expressions of concern from potential Wall Street allies, could not be determined conclusively.

In 1973 and early 1974 Argentina was more explicit. The Juan Perón government, faced with leftist violence at home, combined a purge of leftists from his cabinet with a foreign policy intended to appeal to the left. Economy Minister José Gelbard led an effort to increase Argentina's independence by diversifying its external economic ties. Gelbard travelled to Eastern Europe to arrange trade deals and provoked a serious dispute with the United States by opening relations with Cuba. In August 1973 Argentina and Cuba agreed to a six-year plan for Cuban purchases and Argentine credit totalling $1.2 billion. Cuban delegations then approached US auto firms and others in Argentina about contracts, but some of the firms dragged their feet. The US government's embargo policy required export licenses for US citizens to trade with Cuba, and until this time licenses had been refused except for food and medicine on an emergency basis. By early 1974 Washington was delaying granting the licenses, and Gelbard threatened expropriation of the vehicles in the name of Argentine sovereignty over its trade if cooperation were not forthcoming[29]. On 18 April the State Department announced that the licenses would be issued. Secretary Kissinger explained that the decision did not indicate that the embargo of Cuba had been changed, but that the US needed to allow its firms to comply with the laws of their host country[30].

Mexico practiced retaliation after a 1972 dumping case, but the move had no known effect on US policy. At the time of this sulphur case, the US complainant, Freeport Minerals Company, was also seeking an asbestos venture in Mexico. When the US announced anti-dumping duties, National Properties Minister Horacio Flores de la Peña angrily denied that Mexico's sulphur was being dumped, and the government blocked the Freeport asbestos project. At the same time the government nationalized the US-owned share in the Mexican sulphur firm, linking the move to the dumping action. It is likely, however, that this latter move would have taken place anyway for other reasons[31].

In contrast, in an earlier trade dispute with Canada the Mexican government incorporated a calculated threat of trade retaliation into the negotiation process with telling effect. Though this case did not involve the US, it is useful as an illustration of possible trade bargaining outcomes. During 1968, textile producers in Quebec raised a cry for protection from Mexican cotton yarn imports. Ottawa insisted that Mexico limit its exports, but Mexico refused and expanded them in 1969, though even then the trade was flowing at the rate of only $1.5 million a year. Canada then imposed a 50% surtax on Mexican yarn, sufficient to price it out of the market. Ottawa argued that without a bilateral restrictive agreement with Mexico, Canada would risk the collapse of its system of such textile pacts with larger suppliers. The Mexicans at this point agreed to talk, but adopted a highly aggressive bargaining strategy. Their textile industry took out full-page advertisements in Mexico City newspapers condemning the Canadian sanctions. The Secretary of Industry and Commerce informed Mexican importers of the principal Canadian exports to Mexico that no more import licenses would be granted for Canadian goods. The message was transmitted informally, and the Secretary was later able to deny having done so at all. Meanwhile these importers panicked, 'calling the Canadian embassy every 20 minutes'. Mexican government agencies suggested to Canadian officials that their purchases in Canada would be reconsidered or discontinued. Canadian negotiators were shocked and were anxious to reach a harmonious settlement on what they regarded as a relatively minor matter to avoid a wider trade war. Under the multilateral Long-Term Textile Arrangement, Canada could have insisted on a ceiling on Mexican yarn imports as low as 150 000 pounds per year. The final agreement did impose a quota, but the level was 1 824 000 pounds per year[32].

In short, the strategy of threat or retaliation in these trade disputes seems to compare with the strategy of debt repudiation in North–South bargaining over debt relief. Each is seldom used, but each is capable of improving the outcome from the weaker state's point of view.

The technocratic strategy

The Latin American strategy used to greatest effect, but not anticipated at the beginning of this study, could be called the technocratic strategy. This strategy requires mastering the technical details of the relevant business and related laws, precedents, and institutions, and using this mastery to persuade middle-level officials in the US to accept a favorable technical argument or interpretation. Taking the initiative in suggesting terms for a possible compromise settlement can be an element in this strategy. Many less developed states have not yet acquired this capability to operate as a technocratic equal, but Brazil and others have been using it for some time and more will do so in the future. The strategy is used not only in quiet cases relatively unnoticed in the US but also along with other strategies in publicly controversial ones. Despite the rather factual and automatic appearance of the US countervailing duty procedure, Latin American states have found through experience that, even aside from flexibility permitted by the waiver, Treasury officials are open to arguments to persuade them that an export subsidy is less than it may seem. Careful efforts to formulate such arguments and present them effectively have sometimes failed, but in a number of cases they have contributed to outcomes more favorable to Latin American objectives. In practice, the distinction between a technocratic strategy and mobilizing US allies may seem hazy, for example when a foreign government retains a Washington law firm both to deal with government trade lawyers and simultaneously to mobilize interest groups or 'foreign policy' allies. But the technocratic strategy is distinguished in principle by use of economic and legal research and persuasion directed at officials below the top levels.

The soluble coffee dispute was finally settled in 1971 on the terms of a technical compromise proposal suggested by Brazil earlier in the conflict. The US had protested that Brazil's practice regarding soluble coffee was inconsistent with the International Coffee Agreement. Because of the Argeement, the reasoning went, Brazil was able to collect a large tax on the value of its green coffee exports. US processors of instant coffee had to pay the tax to get Brazilian green, but Brazilian processors could buy it at the internal price, giving them an unfair advantage. The US insisted that Brazil impose an export tax on Brazilian soluble coffee. Brazil rejected this solution, denying the relevance of the ICA and pointing out, among other things, that US soluble producers did not in fact use green coffee from Brazil on the whole. The 1967 Brazilian proposal was basically an offer to provide a quota of green coffee free of the export tax to US soluble producers, in an amount equivalent to US purchases of Brazilian soluble during a base period. Thus the damage to Brazilian soluble exports would be minimized, particularly to third markets. After the US coffee industry association reversed its position and began to oppose sanctions against Brazilian soluble, and after the White House and Brazil's Finance Minister became involved, the US and Brazil agreed on the 1967 Brazilian scheme[33].

The contrasting outcomes in the 1974 shoe cases suggest strongly the effect of the technocratic strategy. During that year in Argentina Juan Perón died, José Gelbard was replaced, and the rapidly inflating economy was developing a massive payments deficit. Argentina's foreign policy generally began a shift toward mending fences with the United States in order to get desperately needed help. In response to the countervailing duty proceedings, the Argentine ambassador in Washington tried the traditional strategy of enlisting State Department support. When this failed, Argentina simply agreed to abolish its incentive program for footwear exporters, and their exports ground to a halt[34].

Likewise Brazil loudly protested the investigation, citing US encouragement to developing countries to diversify their exports and US acceptance of the principle that developing countries should receive special treatment to permit their industrialization. Meanwhile the Brazilian shoe export industry (and later the government) also retained a seasoned Washington law firm to work with their own highly trained trade officials. The firm put forward the argument that Brazil's products were in no way harming US shoe producers, since the Brazilian share of US shoe consumption was only 1.8%[35]. The North American complaint held that Brazil's program of giving tax credits to exporters constituted unfair competition. The Brazilians and their lawyers conducted a survey of exporting firms and used the information to convince the US Treasury that the actual utilization of the tax credit program was less than anyone realized, amounting to just 4.8% of the export value for most of the trade. Thus Brazil continued its incentive program and the United States imposed a countervailing duty of 4.8% on most of the trade bound for the US. At that time, Finance Minister Simonsen maintained that this duty would not reduce shoe exports, and Brazilian exporters were reportedly satisfied, having expected a much heavier blow. Thereafter their shipments to the US increased[36].

The governments of Brazil and Mexico have impressive capabilities for economic and legal analysis, as the Mexicans demonstrated in countervailing duty cases involving their steel plate and processed asparagus. In both cases, Mexico made use of Treasury's long-standing position that rebates to compensate exporters for indirect taxes paid do not constitute a bounty or grant under US law, while rebates of direct taxes and over-rebating of indirect taxes are countervailable. In the steel plate case, Mexico, advised by the same law firm that represented Brazil's shoe exporters, gathered information on indirect taxes paid by steel exporters to show that the total amount would cover a 5% export rebate. The Mexican government then reduced the rebate from 10% to 5% to escape an affirmative 'bounty' ruling. They also successfully countered two other elements of the complaint without changing any programs, but Treasury did find that a railroad freight rate differential constituted a small subsidy. Mexico agreed not to increase the nature and size of this program, and the Simon Treasury waived the countervailing duty[37]. For the processed asparagus case, Mexican technocrats compiled evidence that the exporting firm was paying indirect taxes equal to the full 10% export rebate[38]. Mexico got this case dismissed without any compromise.

Colombia was presented with an eight-count complaint against its policies on leather handbag exports in 1977. While US allies were being mobilized at higher levels, technical maneuvers were also underway. Colombia and its Washington counsel persuaded the Treasury that seven of the programs should not be judged countervailable, including preferential export financing, exemptions from import duties on capital goods and raw materials used to manufacture exports, and transportation subsidies. The key program granting 12% tax credit certificates upon export was clearly a 'bounty', Treasury said. But its final determination set the size of the subsidy and the countervailing duty at less than 6%, as a result perhaps of high-level non-economic concerns, but also because of arguments that several factors offset the benefits of the subsidy. As with Mexico, Treasury agreed to deduct for indirect taxes paid by exporters but not rebated, since these taxes could have been rebated without creating a countervailable subsidy. Another successful technical argument pointed out that exporters in practice experienced long delays in receiving cash for their certificates, reducing their real value. The US code did not specify that the Treasury must adjust for such offsets, but they were considered highly important by Colombia's leadership and by angry US producers. In order to get a temporary waiver of the countervailing duty, the attorneys then argued that a country with a miniscule 0.5% share of the US market could do no harm to US producers and should qualify for a waiver on that basis, since the language of the law refers to subsidies that have an 'adverse effect'. But Colombia was nevertheless required to phase out roughly half of its 12% program in order to receive the waiver[39].

5.3 Conclusions

In summary, by the 1970s Latin American industrialization and export expansion had progressed to a point at which a substantial number of dyadic industrial trade conflicts with the United States began to occur, given the competitive problems of various US industries. Several other potential international conflicts were suppressed by the President and other advocates of open trade in the United States. Those that reached the international level were often salient and irritating in Latin America, while the share of the US market supplied by the Latin American party in many cases was quite small.

Judging conventionally from the great disparity in international power between the United States and each Latin American state, one might expect that their international negotiations over trade restrictions would in reality show the northern colossus achieving its objectives virtually every time. Instead, this investigation of 25 such cases has found results confirming some earlier studies of bargaining between the strong and the weak, and its evidence is consistent with an 'unorthodox dependency' perspective on inter-American relations. Latin American states have had little success in rolling back barriers to the US industrial market, and in these discrete conflicts the initial US objectives were achieved more often than were the Latin American. The more dependent were less successful, but they were not without bargaining assets and strategies.

The strategy of attempting to shape the structure of the bargaining situation by bringing in domestic American allies did not have dramatic effects in these cases, but in some cases it played a quiet part in diluting the impact of producers' demands for protection. In a few cases there is a hint that economic allies are more effective from the Latin American viewpoint than agencies having a foreign policy concern, although both can be overpowered in Washington. Not surprisingly the coercive strategy of retaliation or threat to retaliate was not common on the Latin American side. But the instances of Argentina's exports to Cuba and Mexico's conflict with Canada show that, when pursued, this strategy can be relatively effective.

Finally, I have proposed that familiar theories of bargaining need to be modified by adding the concept of the technocratic strategy. The approach Latin American policy-makers have been employing most often, and one of the more successful with issues of this sort, has been the use of economic and legal norms, interpretations, and research to persuade US administrators to adopt proposals more favorable to their states. The suggestions that simply providing information can make more than a trivial difference in international relations, and that policy outcomes might depend on perceptions and honest interpretations of legal or other cultural norms as well as narrower self-interests, are often rightly greeted with skepticism by well-informed analysts. Such possibilities deserve more serious attention, however, perhaps on some types of issues and in some cultures more than others, even if technocratic argument is developed in other cases only as a *post hoc* rationale for decisions taken for other reasons. To the extent that developing countries' use of a technocratic strategy in foreign economic policy reflects the gradual development of technical and administrative capabilities, we can expect its use to increase in frequency and sophistication in the future. Its application will of course depend on the degree to which legislation and higher authorities restrict the discretion of administrators. On this score countervailing duty proceedings in the United States may not be the most fruitful area of application in the future. The Trade Agreements Act of 1979 and subsequent administrative changes narrowed the range of discretion in this area. The new statute itself contains an illustrative list of practices to be considered subsidies; the time allowed for investigations is reduced substantially; and administrators are required to release more information and entertain greater participation by the parties in the process. Subsequent regulations moved authority over this field to the Department of Commerce. In addition, under the new rules, after the US government has reached a tentative finding that exports are subsidized, but before a final determination, importers are required to begin immediately posting a cash deposit or bond equivalent to the alleged subsidy on all further imports.

More generally, subsidies and countervailing measures were only two of many practices that may be affected by the 1979 conclusion of the Tokyo Round multilateral trade negotiations (MTN). We may speculate, in conclusion, about the effects of these 1979 multilateral agreements on US-Latin American bilateral bargaining and commerce.

The Tokyo Round produced tariff reductions, new international rules covering non-tariff barriers (NTBs) to trade, and decisions by Colombia and the Philippines to join GATT, the international trade organization, for the first time. Latin America's non-members in 1980 were Mexico, five Central American states (excepting Nicaragua), Venezuela, Ecuador, Bolivia, and Paraguay. These non-members can nevertheless benefit from any tariff concessions granted by member countries on a non-discriminatory basis. During the Tokyo Round, 13 Latin American and Caribbean states also reached new bilateral trade agreements with the United States.

Of the new codes covering non-tariff barriers, the most important was the code on subsidies and countervailing measures in industrial trade. The new elements include an enlarged list of prohibited export subsidies, a joint commitment to use domestic subsidies only in ways that avoid serious prejudice to other countries, requirements to make such subsidies more visible, and a new dispute settlement procedure. The code recognizes that subsidies are integral to plans of developing countries, but it specifies no special protection for programs that 'cause serious prejudice' to other signatories. The code permits countervailing measures only when material injury to a domestic industry can be shown to have resulted from subsidized exports. The major American concession during the MTN was agreement to change US law to require such an injury test. The US administration made it clear, however, that this benefit would be withheld from states that refused to sign this code. Other new codes aim to regulate import licensing procedures, discriminatory government procurement, customs valuation systems, and the effects of safety and pollution standards. Agreement was not reached on proposed new rules to cover the use of 'safeguards' such as quotas and orderly marketing agreements.

What are the political and economic effects of the MTN? As to political effects, developing countries, led by Brazil, first secured adoption of a new general 'enabling clause' legalizing 'differential and more favourable treatment' for developing countries' trade. Examples would be lower tariffs or waivers of obligations. In the future, Latin American states might be able to improve their concrete bargaining outcomes by appealing to this rule. This seems doubtful, however. Many developing countries had already received non-reciprocal treatment under existing rules. Furthermore, the industrial countries supported this rule only after inserting a 'graduation' clause stating that, as developing countries advance, they expect to lose this special treatment. This graduation clause is quite vague, but bilateral bargaining between the United States and Brazil in 1978 gave it some concrete meaning. The US chose the Brazilian export subsidy programs as a prominent target, and with considerable persuasion succeeded in extracting a tacit commitment by Brasilia to phase out completely the leading subsidy programs, and to sign the subsidy code, as part of the MTN package. On the other hand, Mexico rejected similar pressures and decided against both signing the code and joining GATT.

Secondly, it is often said, after the Kennedy Round experience, that a multilateral trade negotiation provides a rationale for governments to resist taking protectionist steps, as long as talks continue. On this hypothesis one might have expected that the talks' end would release a flood of new petitions and restrictive measures. This does not seem to have happened, at least as regards Latin America and the US. During the Tokyo Round itself, there were already a number of complaints, some of which were turned back while others led to protection. Then after the negotiations, 1980 was 'one of the quietest years in a long time', in the words of a ranking Latin American representative in Washington. And in 1981 the US ended earlier footwear restrictions. The Tokyo Round thus differed in this political respect from the Kennedy Round.

Passage of the 1979 MTN legislation in the US did have a different political effect. Fearing opposition to general trade liberalization, the Carter administration agreed to measures designed to defend the steel and textiles industries. In February 1978, a 'trigger price' mechanism began to set an effective minimum price for steel imports. In March 1979, the administration promised the textile and garment industries that it would reduce the ability of foreign exporters to shift their production between categories and between years. Neither of these measures had led to disputes in Latin America by early 1981, however. The burden of the textile deal fell on East Asia.

Early estimates of the likely commercial effects of the Tokyo Round on developing countries ranged from glum to gleeful. As for the tariff cuts, Latin American and other developing countries worried that they would lose exports to the industrial countries as the latter lowered tariffs on products where they had earlier given special duty-free treatment to developing countries. Estimates by both the Organization of American States and others indicated, however, that such losses due to eroding preferences would be more than offset by export gains due to reductions in tariffs on other products[40]. In general, the trade effects of further tariff cuts are expected to be small, since average tariff rates in industrial countries were already low before the Tokyo Round.

The Economic Commission for Latin America (ECLA) was especially disappointed with the results on non-tariff barriers. In the ECLA view, the most widely used NTB is the import quota, which was not the subject of any new code. Their report found that 542 categories of American imports are subject to non-tariff barriers, and that the US agreed to modify such barriers covering less than 10% of its eligible imports (weighted by value). ECLA objects to the graduation clauses in the new codes[41]. Most Latin American governments had declined to sign most of the new codes by early 1981. Mexico, for one, made the calculated decision to forgo the advantage of the American injury test and risk bilateral conflicts in particular industries, rather than make a commitment to avoid export subsidies generally.

Whatever the consequences of the 1979 changes, we are warranted in assuming that industrial trade, a relatively new issue in Latin American–US relations, will continue to be at least as salient or more so in the future, globally as well as in the western hemisphere. Global shifts in comparative advantage are likely to continue manifesting themselves in inter-state bargaining and conflict. Much of the attention devoted thus far to North –South international relations has been directed at multilateral negotiations. More of that attention should be directed at the causes and consequences of bilateral encounters such as these in the western hemisphere. In bilateral North–South relations we are likely to find some of the most important political responses to shifts in the structure of the world economy.

Appendix

Latin American industrial exports to the United States, 1970 and 1976 ($ m.)^a

Country	1970	1976	
Mexico	398.0	1943.7	
Electrical machinery			722.6
Non-electrical machinery			188.5
Clothing and accessories			165.9
Brazil	62.6	541.0	
Footwear			140.5
Electrical machinery			97.2
Iron and steel			51.9
Chile	117.7	154.0	
Non-ferrous metals			132.1
Footwear			5.2
Fertilizers			3.7
Argentina	47.1	142.2	
Leather – bovine, nes			54.9
Iron and steel			19.3
Organic chemicals			15.1
Peru	162.2	107.8	
Non-ferrous metals			101.5
Textiles			2.3
Wood and cork products, nes			1.2
Colombia	24.4	104.5	
Clothing and accessories			26.3
Precious stones			23.6
Textiles			19.3
Haiti	14.2	104.0	
Clothing and accessories			33.3
Misc. mfrd. articles, nes			29.4
Electrical machinery			17.1
Jamaica	66.9	90.5	
Dominican Republic	0.9	88.4	
El Salvador	1.0	67.1	
Uruguay	7.2	53.4	
Surinam	20.8	36.7	

Country	1970	1976
Bahamas	22.3	34.6
Costa Rica	3.6	27.2
Trinidad and Tobago	21.3	26.6
Venezuela	9.1	24.7
Bolivia	0.8	19.2
Barbados	4.0	14.9
Nicaragua	0.4	10.6
Guatemala	1.7	9.4
Honduras	1.5	8.4
Belize	0.7	6.0
Ecuador	0.9	4.8
Guyana	3.5	4.1
Paraguay	1.3	3.5
Panama	1.5	2.5
Cuba	0	0

[a] Industrial products are defined as Groups 5–8 of the US Census Bureau import commodity code. For selected countries the three largest two-digit product groups in 1976 are shown.

Nes = not elsewhere specified.

Source: US Department of Commerce, *US General Imports*. FT-155, Washington, DC, US Government Printing Office, 1970 and 1976.

Acknowledgements

I am grateful to the Harvard Center for International Affairs and the US Department of State for support, and to participants in trade negotiations who spoke to me candidly and anonymously. I also benefited from critical comments on an earlier draft made by Jorge Domínguez, Albert Fishlow, Gary Gereffi, Janet Kelly, Stephen Kobrin, Edward Morse, Stanley Nehmer, Neil Nevitte, and Donald Wyman. Jaime da Silva was an able research assistant. The author alone is responsible for the contents.

An earlier version was published in *International Organization*, **34** (© 1980 by the Board of Regents of the University of Wisconsin System), pp. 207–228. Reprinted with permission.

Notes

1 On manufactured exports by less de-
veloped countries (LDCs), see Hollis
Chenery and Donald B. Keesing, 'The
Changing Role and Composition of LDC
Exports'. Staff Working Paper No. 314,
The World Bank, Washington, DC, 1979;
UNCTAD, *Trade in Manufactures of De-
veloping Countries and Territories: 1974
Review*, UN Document TD/B/C.2/161,
New York, 1976; UNCTAD, *Dynamic
Products in the Exports of Manufactured
Goods from Developing Countries to De-
veloped Market-Economy Countries, 1970
–1976*. UN Document ST/MD/18, New
York, 1978; Stephen B. Watkins and John
R. Karlik, 'Anticipating Disruptive
Imports'. *New International Realities
(National Planning Association)*, Fall
1978; *The Economist*, 10 June 1978, pp.
84–5; Kathryn Morton and Peter Tullock,
Trade and Developing Countries. Croom
Helm, London, 1977; Lorenzo L. Perez,
'Export Subsidies in Developing Coun-
tries and the GATT'. *Journal of World
Trade Law*, 10, 1976, pp. 539–45; Tho-
mas K. Morrison, *Manufactured Exports
from Developing Countries*. Praeger, New
York, 1976; Hal B. Lary, *Imports of
Manufactures from Less Developed Countries*. Columbia University Press, New
York, 1968; Joseph Grunwald (ed), *Latin
America and the World Economy: A
Changing International Order*. Sage Publications, Beverly Hills, Calif., 1978. On
protectionism, see IMF, *The Rise in Protectionism*. Pamphlet No. 24, Washington, 1978; IMF, *Annual Reports on Exchange Arrangements and Exchange Restrictions*. Washington; GATT, *International Trade*. Geneva, yearly; Susan
Strange, 'The Management of Surplus
Capacity: or how does theory stand up to
protectionism 1970s style?' *International
Organization*, 33, 1979, pp. 303–34.
2 See Joseph Nye, Jr., 'Transnational Relations and Interstate Conflicts: An Empirical Analysis'. *International Organization*, 23, 1974, pp. 961–96.
3 In order to make the research more man-
ageable, I exclude from this study the
negotiation of 'orderly marketing
agreements'; these are covered by current
work.
4 19 U.S.C. S1303; 'A Roadmap to the
Trade Act', *Law and Policy in International Business*, 8, 1976, pp. 171–4;

Donald L. Wyman, 'US–Latin American
Relations and the Cases of the Counter-
vailing Duty', in US Commission on the
Organization of the Government for the
Conduct of Foreign Policy, *Appendices*.
US Government Printing Office,
Washington, DC, 7 vols, 1975, vol. III,
pp. 234–42.
5 19 U.S.C. S1303(d).
6 19 U.S.C. S160–173; 'A Roadmap to the
Trade Act' (note 5). pp. 166–71; 'Anti-
dumping Duties', in US Commission on
International Trade and Investment Policy, *United States International Economic
Policy in an Interdependent World*, US
Government Printing Office, Washington, DC, 1971, vol. I, pp. 395–408. Several interviewees maintained that anti-
dumping proceedings are more 'cut-and-
dried' than countervailing duty proceedings and, despite an original intention to
include them, I found no examples of
anti-dumping cases whose outcomes could
be attributed to anything other than
routine application of standard operating
formulas by US agencies. Some anti-
dumping cases may arise because American businesses, feeling successful foreign
competition, lack the capacity to conduct
their own investigations of prices charged
in the foreign market, and hope mistaken-
ly that activating a US government investigation might produce data favorable to
them. A study of anti-dumping complaints involving state-owned firms or major powers or larger amounts of current
trade might reveal a different political process, however, as suggested by the Ford
administration's subtle handling of the
huge complaint against automobile imports in 1975–76.
7 In the case of Mexican processed asparagus, the ITC was evenly divided on the
question of injury, and President Ford
determined that the imports had not
caused serious injury. In the large 1976
shoe case, the ITC unanimously found
injury, and five of the six commissioners
recommended some form of import restriction. The cabinet was pressured both
by American shoe producers and by consumer groups, and failed to reach an
agreed recommendation to President
Ford. The Departments of State, Treasury, Defense, the Office of Management
and Budget, and Council of Economic

Advisers took the consumer-oriented free
trade position; the Departments of Labor
and Commerce and the Special Trade Representative favored trade restrictions. At
the time, the domestic shoe industry was
experiencing a brisk recovery. Ford decided against import curbs and in favor of
adjustment assistance to firms and workers. Later in the year the footwear case was
re-opened at the request of the Senate
Foreign Relations Committee. The ITC
sent President Carter a recommendation
for a tariff-rate quota restriction. Carter
decided in early 1977 to reject that recommendation, to negotiate orderly marketing
agreements with Taiwan and South Korea,
to warn other suppliers against surges of
imports, and to provide new adjustment
assistance to domestic industry. Later that
year the ITC held that ferro-chromium
imports threatened to injure US producers
and recommended raising tariffs. South
Africa, Brazil, and Yugoslavia were the
main suppliers. In rejecting import relief,
President Carter held that it would mainly
benefit the dominant firm in the US industry, that absence of relief would not lead
to job losses, and that relief would be
inflationary and might encourage protectionism against US exports.

8 J. M. Finger, 'The Industry–Country Incidence of "Less than Fair Value" Cases in
United States Import Trade'. Paper prepared for an NBER–FIPE Conference in
São Paolo, Brazil, March 1980, p. 21. The
cited finding is only preliminary and partial evidence on this question. A thorough
investigation of the economic effects of
these disputes and barriers in various sectors is needed, but would extend far
beyond the feasible scope of the present
effort.

9 The image of a very unequal relationship is
shared by many who have analyzed inter-
American relations in terms of
'dependency', despite the other sharp differences between this view and traditional
power analysis. Though dependency
analysis does not often deal directly with
discrete diplomatic disputes, it might lead
one to expect that the United States uses
those occasions as another means of
domination and exploitation of Latin
America.

10 See Jorge Domínguez, 'Consensus and
Divergence: The State of the Literature on
Inter-American Relations in the 1970s'.
Latin American Research Review, 13,

1978, pp. 106–8. An example of an 'unorthodox dependency' perspective is
Helio Jaguaribe, *Political Development: A
General Theory and a Latin American
Case Study*. Harper and Row, New York,
1973, pp. 371–86. While my reference to
dependency perspectives pertains to their
vision of international relations, dependency analysts themselves are equally
concerned with conflicts within dependent
states, and the connections between external and internal forces.

11 See Nye (note 2).

12 W. Howard Wriggins, 'Up for Auction:
Malta Bargains with Great Britain, 1971'.
In I. William Zartman (ed.), *The 50%
Solution*. Doubleday, New York, 1976,
pp. 208–34.

13 John S. Odell, 'The Politics of Debt Relief: Official Creditors and Brazil, Ghana,
and Chile'. In Jonathan Aronson (ed.),
*International Debt and the Less De-
veloped Countries*. Westview Press, Boulder, Co., 1979.

14 See C. Fred Bergsten, 'The Threat from
the Third World'. *Foreign Policy*, 11,
Summer 1973, pp. 102–24, and 'Coming
Investment Wars?' *Foreign Affairs*, 53,
October 1974, pp. 135–52; Mahbub ul
Haq, *The Poverty Curtain*. Columbia
University Press, New York, 1976, chap.
9.

15 With rough classifications and a relatively
small number of cases, no sophisticated
data analysis will be possible. But here and
at other points, evidence casting some
light on a question can be mentioned.

16 *Business Latin America*, 8 January, 22
January, 5 February, and 30 April 1975.

17 US State Department unclassified files.

18 Robert Pastor, 'Congress's Impact on
Latin America: Is There a Madness in the
Method?' In US Commission on the
Organization of the Government for the
Conduct of Foreign Policy (note 4), vol.
III, p. 267.

19 *Footwear News*, 1 April 1974; *New York
Times*, 4 August 1974, p. F6. Severo
Gomes was known as relatively weak in
Brazilian policy-making, but this issue
also elicited a difference between the
Foreign and Finance ministries in Brasilia,
with the Foreign Ministry favoring the
harder line. 'Ultimately, the president resolved the difference on terms somewhat
more favorable to Itamaraty than would
have been the case in the preceding
administration' (Ronald M. Schneider,

Brazil: Foreign Policy of a Future World Power. Westview Press, Boulder, Co., 1976, p. 110.

20 Interviews with former US officials. The compromise outcome in Brazil's case is better explained by other factors, noted below.

21 Interviews; *Business Latin America*, 10 May 1978, p. 152.

22 It is difficult to judge conclusively how much effect the NSC role had, since other actors and strategies were at work as well.

23 Interview with a former US official.

24 Interviews with former US officials.

25 Interviews in Washington.

26 A Coca-Cola subsidiary producing instant coffee in New Jersey found its own solution to the international conflict, by acquiring control of a freeze-dry soluble plant in Brazil in 1969, putting it on the winning side either way (*Business Latin America*, 13 March 1969, pp. 82–3). The reversal of the National Coffee Association's position was not sufficient by itself to halt efforts by US leaders, particularly Congressman Wilbur Mills, to press for Brazilian concessions. (Richard J. Bloomfield, 'Who Makes American Foreign Policy? Some Latin American Case Studies'. Harvard University Center for International Affairs, Cambridge, Mass., 1972).

27 American embassy Brasilia to Department of State, unclassified cable 0945, 3 February 1976.

28 *O Estado de São Paulo,* 13 May 1976. Also see joint communiqué by Simonsen and Simon, 11 May 1976; *Journal of Commerce*, 12 May 1976; *Business Latin America*, 26 May 1976; *Latin America Economic Report*, 28 May 1976.

29 Edward Milenky, *Argentina's Foreign Policies*. Westview Press, Boulder, Co., 1978, pp. 55–9, 72, 123–4; *Business Latin America*, 12 December 1973 and 8 May 1974; *Latin America Economic Report*, 11 January 1974 and 17 May 1974; *Washington Post*, 13 January 1974, p. A29; 19 April, p. A1; 20 April, p. A12; and 22 April, p. A22; *Business Week*, 13 April 1974, p. 80.

30 US Department of State *Bulletin*, May 1974, pp. 517, 544.

31 *Business Latin America*, 29 June 1972, pp. 201–2. During the anti-dumping proceedings the Mexican firm hired Joseph Califano as counsel and was supported by the Anti-trust Division of the Justice Department. Testifying before the Tariff Com-

mission for the US producers, however, were Senator Russell Long of Louisiana and Representatives Hale Boggs, F. Edward Hebert, and Joe Waggoner of Louisiana (*Chemical Marketing Reporter*, 3 April 1972).

32 Robert W. Butler, Jr., 'Trade Conflict: The Mexican–Canadian Yarn War of 1969 –1970'. *Inter-American Economic Affairs*, **25**, 1971, pp. 21–30. Colombia recently protested Japan's trade surplus with Colombia by banning imports of Japan's electronic products, consumer durables, and cars (*Economist*, 5 August 1978, p. 66).

33 See Bloomfield (note 26).

34 *Journal of Commerce*, 26 November 1974; *Footwear News*, 3 February 1975; Wyman (note 4), pp. 238–9. In 1978, Argentina used technocratic strategies and achieved its objectives more fully.

35 *Footwear News*, 17 June 1974; *New York Times*, 4 August 1974, p. F6.

36 Interviews in Washington; *Footwear News*, 16 September 1974; *Business Latin America*, 18 September 1974 and 26 May 1976.

37 US Congress, House, Committee on Ways and Means, *Waiver of Countervailing Duties on Certain Mexican Steel Plate*: *Communication from the Assistant Secretary of the Treasury*. House Doc. 94–406, 94th Cong., 2d sess., US Government Printing Office, Washington, DC, 11 March 1976; interview in Washington. In any case the Mexican government imposed a temporary embargo on steel exports in late 1972 due to the strength of domestic demand in Mexico, and the flow of steel plate to the US fell sharply (*American Metal Market*, 21 December 1972).

38 *Federal Register*, **41**, 1976, p. 1299.

39 Interviews in Washington; *Federal Register*, **42**, 1977, p. 57201 and **43**, 1978, pp. 18659–61; *Business Latin America*, 10 May 1978, p. 152.

40 *Business Latin America*, 16 May 1979 and *passim*. See also Bela Balassa, 'The Tokyo Round and the Developing Countries'. *Journal of World Trade Law*, **14**, March/April 1980, pp. 93–118; UNCTAD, *Multilateral Trade Negotiations: Evaluation and Further Recommendations Arising Therefrom*, New York, 7 May 1979; and John A. Mathieson, *The Tokyo Round Trade Agreements: What Effect on the Developing Countries?* ODC Communiqué 1979/3, Overseas Development Council, Washington, DC, 1979.

41 *Business Latin America*, 29 October 1980.

The transformation of US–Latin American technology transfer relations

Debra L. Miller*

Technology has been increasingly recognized as an important factor in the development of a strong and growing economy. One of the ways in which states seek to strengthen their technological capacity is by importing technology – the so-called transfer of technology. Although technology has been transferred across national borders for centuries, the transfer process and the rules and norms governing it have become more politically salient during the past two decades, as states have come to appreciate the importance of technology and the seriousness of the 'technological gap' that exists between industrialized and developing countries, and as developing countries have come to recognize that technology is the engine of economic development and industrialization.

During the 1960s and most of the 1970s, the protagonists in conflicts about technology transfer were American. Latin America imports most of its technology from large US-based corporations, mostly through direct foreign investment or, to a lesser extent, licensing. Until recently, transferring 'non-strategic' technology from North to South was almost completely a private commercial transaction: the terms and conditions of transfer were set by the recipient and supplier firms. Governments interfered little, if at all, and only a few very limited international conventions affected the process. For a variety of reasons discussed later in this chapter, suppliers of technology usually had more bargaining power in relationships with recipients. Thus, developing countries alleged, contracts were written more with a view to protecting the proprietary nature of the firm's technology or its ability to make a profit than with the aim of increasing the technological capacity or the export potential of the recipient firm and country.

Given the importance to Latin American states of developing a technological capability and an export potential for finished goods, and given an ambivalent attitude toward direct foreign investment, as is detailed in other chapters in this volume, it is not surprising that technology transfer became a politicized issue. Some Latin American intellectuals and policy-makers believe that, like other international economic issues, problems with technology transfer stemmed from an international political system that was dominated by strong advanced, industrialized states that were able to make

* Assistant Professor, Political Science, Barnard College, Columbia University

and enforce economic rules and norms that discriminated against the developing world to the advantage of the industrialized world. Others stressed the role that the international spread of capital and capitalism played in underdevelopment, dependence, or dependent development. Those who saw problems in the North–South transfer process agreed that somehow supplier-skewed relationships must be changed to the benefit of recipients.

The first time in the post-World War II era that a Latin American country raised the issue of technology transfer in a political context was in 1961 at the United Nations General Assembly in New York. There, the Brazilian delegate argued that the patent system might have a deleterious effect on economic development and called for a study of this possibility[1]. In the 1960s, the focus of contention was the Paris Convention on Industrial Property of 1883 and its subsequent revisions. The attack on the patent system by developing countries produced a strong counter-attack, led by the United States. The result by the end of the 1960s was a strengthened convention, more signatories, and the elevation to United Nations specialized agency status of the international organization that dealt with intellectual property.

By this time, however, Latin Americans had come to believe that other aspects of the transfer process, including the involvement and the behavior of multinational corporations, were as important, if not more so, than patent rules. Discussion and negotiation of matters concerning technology transfer blossomed at a number of international organizations: the World Intellectual Property Organization (WIPO), as noted above, the United Nations Industrial Development Organization (UNIDO), and the United Nations Conference on Trade and Development (UNCTAD). Despite the key roles the American states played in technology transfer, surprisingly little regional or bilateral dialogue took place among Northern and Southern American governments. This is partly because technology transfer has global implications, partly because most developing countries tend to believe that they will have more 'power' and 'influence' to change political economic relations in international organizations (especially in UNIDO or UNCTAD) than they would on the bilateral or regional level, and partly because an unfortuitous set of diplomatic circumstances and *faux pas* surrounding another economic issue (trade) resulted in the cancelling of previously scheduled inter-American meetings on technology transfer.

International efforts to change technology transfer relationships were supplemented by 'local' national efforts. During the 1970s, Latin American governments began to intercede in negotiations between foreign suppliers and local recipients so as to influence the outcome of the negotiations and to change the dynamic of the negotiating relationship itself. Those governments that became effectively involved in the negotiating process were usually those that had strong national bourgeoisies in the country[2].

This chapter discusses conflicts and discussions the United States and

Latin America have had on technology transfer issues with particular reference to the settings in which conflicts took place and the strategies each side used to achieve its aims in disputes. First I shall discuss the reasons Latin Americans believed they were not getting a 'good deal' when they imported technology, the policies they enacted to rectify the situation, and the US response. Second, I analyze what happened when governments began to intervene in the transfer process at the local level and explain why some states are more effective than others in this intervention. Third, I examine the reasons developing countries had for going to international organizations for changing technology transfer relationships and discuss the progress to date made in these forums. Finally, I offer some alternative ways in which both the US government and Latin American states may wish to look at technology transfer relations.

I make three arguments in this chapter about the transformation of US–Latin America technology transfer relations in the 1970s. First, the involvement of Latin American governments in technology transfer relationships in order to promote local, autonomous development has had both costs and benefits – fewer costs than multinational corporations have alleged and more limited benefits than developing country governments and UNCTAD have suggested. Second, and contrary to conventional wisdom and even counter-intuitively, Latin American states have had only limited success in using international organizations to change the structure of technology transfer relationships. National strategies have yielded far better results in this area, and international strategies, if pursued in the future in this area, may erode gains made on the national level. Third, as long as the US government does not intercede on behalf of multinationals, US multinationals have circumscribed power in confrontations with Latin American governments and will have even less power as their market share in sectors declines in Latin America. At international organizations, however, the US government has been quite effective and influential in negotiations on the restructuring of technology transfer relations, and has safeguarded its interests as the leading supplying state in the world and the interests of its multinational corporations.

6.1 Perspectives and policies

Latin America

Latin American leaders believe that technology is crucial for economic development. Economic studies have shown that technology is a major factor for achieving development and increased industrial output, both of which have been major policy objectives of Latin American states at least since the 1960s. Building up a state's technological capacity requires the development of indigenous capabilities, relying on the state's own resources perhaps through governmental incentives or direction, or importation of technology from foreign sources. Although the strategies should not be thought of as mutually exclusive, and some efforts have been undertaken in Latin America to build a technological base using the first strategy[3], more attention has been concentrated on importing technology from abroad. It is alleged, however, that many problems attend the latter strategy.

First, it is argued, technology simply costs too much. Purchasing it uses precious foreign exchange and exacerbates already troublesome balance of payments deficits. It is very difficult to obtain reliable figures on how much Latin American states pay for technology imports. In the 1960s, Latin American governments did not keep track of how much they or their firms paid for technology. Writing in 1972, Francis Masson and R. Hal Mason noted,

> [O]nly in Mexico are reports received by a balance of payments unit from individual business firms. The other balance of payments depend upon information from the exchange control authorities. Brazil (since 1958) and Colombia (since 1967) have required that payments in foreign exchange for royalties and technical assistance be based on a written agreement and that the agreement be referenced in exchange transactions. Peru and Argentina are developing such systems, although they will cover only new contracts. However, a large number of payments and intrafirm transactions (especially payments in kind, in local currency or intrafirm transactions which may involve claims against residents of these countries and therefore are balance of payments transactions) are not picked up by the statistical systems of these countries[4].

This relates to private transfers only. Government-to-government or public sector transfers are rarely accounted for. Masson and Mason found that none of the five Latin American countries they visited identified the technical assistance components of loans and grants for accounting purposes[5]. Nor did the US Agency for International Development, the Inter-American Development Bank or the World Bank segregate goods from services that are financed in connection with the execution of many projects[6].

Technology is often transferred in package form. Along with the requested technology, recipient firms pay for related or tie-in purchases such as machinery and equipment and related technical know-how and marketing guidance. The packages are not itemized, so that the firm may not know how much it is paying for technology.

Developing countries purchase between 3% and 10% of technology that is exported. UNCTAD predicts that these costs will grow each year by 20%, which means that developing countries that paid $1.5 billion by the end of the 1960s would pay about $9 billion by the 1980s, or, estimates

UNCTAD, about 15% of developing countries total foreign exchange payments[7]. Given that accounting practices for technology imports are primitive, the absolute amounts offered should be considered as estimates. Given that these figures are based primarily on royalties and fees reported to governments, the growth rate UNCTAD predicts is also suspect. During the 1960s and 1970s, developing country governments began to tighten up on the freedom with which corporations were allowed to repatriate profits. Royalties and technical assistance agreements suddenly cost more, but this was merely an accounting device used by firms to get profits out of the country. Nevertheless, one of the primary complaints Latin American states have about foreign technology is that they must pay too much for it.

Some characteristics of the market for technology contribute to its high price. There is very little information about the existence or price of technology or about alternative suppliers. During the 1960s there was even less information about the market than there now is because Latin American firms did not share any information they did have with each other. In addition, the market for technology in Latin America has been very concentrated, although this situation is slowly changing. In some cases it was alleged that suppliers had 'monopoly power', either because they were in fact the only supplier or because no knowledge existed about alternative suppliers. And certainly packaging and patenting practices tend to increase the price of technology to the buyer.

Some Latin American writers have suggested that, given that using or 'working' technology does not diminish its availability, technology should be thought of as a public (not a private) good, and that, accordingly, recipients should have to pay less than they pay for it now, the current price of which is based on the notion that it is a private good[8]. But technology is not really a pure public good; there are costs involved in developing and commercializing it; widespread diffusion and working of it tend to diminish the profits users reap from its commercialization. Thus, even though the use of technology does not limit its inherent availability to anyone else, there are certain characteristics about technology that make it a private good. Nevertheless, developing countries still argue that, like the seabed, technology is the universal heritage of mankind and that supplier and recipient relationships should change accordingly[9].

Because of the market power of suppliers and developing countries' perception that technology is crucial for development, suppliers were seen as having the ability to stipulate the conditions under which technology will be transferred. It is alleged that multinational firms engage in unduly restrictive practices when transferring technology. These practices include tie-in sales, package deals, excessive royalties, price-fixing, restriction of volume or structure of production, prohibitions on the use of competing technology, grant-back provisions (where improvements or R & D results are returned to the supplier), and export restrictions. It is also alleged that licensors provide insufficient guarantees for the reliability and suitability of the technology transferred.

The two practices that have been considered the most pernicious and serious are tie-in and package deals and export restrictions. In answer to an UNCTAD questionnaire, Argentina, Chile, Ecuador, Mexico, and Peru responded that their firms were forced to make tied purchases of equipment and spare parts when buying technology[10]. Vaitsos found, in a study of licensing agreements in Bolivia, Ecuador and Peru, that 67% of the contracts required tied purchases[11]. Again, the major complaint against tie-in sales is that they result in higher prices because they make for non-competitive market conditions.

Export restrictions are even more prevalent than tie-in clauses in contracts. In the same UNCTAD study referred to above, it was found that exports were completely prohibited in 90% of contracts in Peru, 62% in Mexico, 38% in Chile, 93% in Bolivia, and 98% in Colombia[12]. Export restrictions are antithetical to Latin American states' industrialization and export promotion policies. The rationale for import substitution and development of the manufacturing sector, key parts of Latin America's development programs in the 1960s, was to make Latin American states competitive in the international trade of manufactures. Latin American states argue that export restrictions prevent them from doing this. The Economic Commission for Latin America (ECLA) substantiates this claim: '[US] manufacturing subsidiaries [in Latin America] sell more than 90% of their output on Latin American markets and about 8% to Canada and Europe'[13].

It should be pointed out, however, that the deletion of export restriction from contracts between suppliers and recipients may have no significant effect on the exports of developing countries. If the recipient is a subsidiary, the parent firm may wish the subsidiary to gear production to the domestic market; management does not have to specify this in a contractual agreement in order to have its wishes carried out. On the other hand, if the recipient is an independent licensee, and the technology transferred is patented, the export by the licensee of the product of the worked technology to markets where the licensor has patent protection will be considered infringing.

The foregoing, then, are a sample of some of the economic problems alleged to be experienced during the transfer process. Beliefs about the grave nature and causes of these problems have no doubt been influenced by elite views about the relationship between development in Latin America and a liberal, capitalist international economic system. These views vary. Some are presented below.

The UN Economic Commission for Latin America is a very influential proponent of what one might call structuralist views. Specifically, it is posited that 'the fundamental ... reason for Latin America's backwardness ... lies with the international trading system in which Latin America has become involved...'[14], and that the structure of economic relationships arising from this system discriminates against the interests of weaker developing countries in favor of stronger industrialized countries. Thus, the development efforts of Latin American states in the 1950s and 1960s were thought to be impeded by relations with industrialized states. A major key to correcting this problem was thought to be governmental intervention in economic affairs. ECLA advocated at various times policies such as import substitution, sectoral planning, export promotion, and governmental regulation of direct foreign investment. Regarding the latter, one of ECLA's reports in the late 1960s stresses that 'Experience of industrial development in Latin America shows more and more clearly that the expansion of multinational firms' industrial activities must be oriented to fit into the framework of over-all development strategies'[15].

ECLA did not advocate severing relationships between Latin America and the industrialized countries. Indeed, ECLA found that those sectors that were the most dynamic in Latin America in the 1960s were those where there was direct foreign investment[16]. Rather, ECLA suggests reforms that would promote equity within the existing international economic system, compensating for the current discrimination against Latin America with national governmental regulation.

ECLA's suggestions reflect the twin values of development and autonomy in the choice and direction of the course and speed of development. Many scholars argue that this is not possible because of Latin America's involvement in the international economy. These scholars are less concerned about the laissez-faire nature of this system than ECLA political economists seem to be; rather, they believe that the fundamental underlying problem is that the system is capitalist, and that, consequently, the relationships between North and South (or supplier and recipient of technology) are inherently and by definition characterized by dependence and exploitation.

These scholars write in the Marxist–Leninist tradition. Some such as Paul Baran or Andre Gunder Frank have argued that the spread of international capital and capitalism produces stagnation in developing countries and causes their underdevelopment[17]. Recently M. A. Trevor has argued in a similar vein regarding technology transfer, suggesting that no real transfer occurs between suppliers and recipients and that the end product is dependent underdevelopment and the satellization of industries[18]. Lynn Mytelka notes that multinational corporations do very little research and development in developing countries. OECD statistics bear this out: they estimate that only 2% of R & D is done outside the industrialized world[19]. Mytelka also notes that, when technology is imported into Latin America, the skills people gain from working it are not transferable to other sectors of the economy, nor are they sufficient for making the product without foreign participation. Moreover, in the Andean Pact countries, Mytelka has found distressingly little indigenous development of R & D by the government or the private sector. The suggestion is that a heavy reliance on imported technology and little or no effort to develop an indigenous technological capability are linked, perhaps causally[20].

Others see the dependence created by external relations as producing more dynamism than stagnance. Consider Fernando Enrique Cardoso and Enzo Faletto's argument:

> The basic economic conditions of development are an open market, the exclusion of the dependent economies from the markets of the most developed countries, and the continuous transfer of new units of external capital in the form of advanced technology, which are more appropriate to the intrinsic needs of the mature economies than to those of the relatively backward economies. The combination of these conditions with the ideologies and legal relations among social groups makes possible 'industrial economies in dependent societies.' Whether the structural barriers to development remain or are overcome will be determined by how these economic conditions are used in the power game rather than by the particular economic conditions themselves. In this sense, we suggest that present or potential opposition may vitalize the industrialized and dependent countries of Latin America[21].

Peter Evans carries Cardoso and Faletto's argument even further. He notes that 'dependent development implies both the accumulation of capital and some degree of industrialization on the periphery .. [it is] the emerging antithesis rather than the main theme of classic dependency'[22].

Structuralist and 'dependencia' thought have had influence on the direction of technology transfer policy. ECLA, Cardoso and Faletto, and Evans all suggest that the state plays an important role in transformations of political economic structures and relations. In the early 1970s, states began to screen and regulate the importation of technology. This made the host state a bargaining partner in negotiations on technology transfer with multinational firms (or other suppliers). It was hoped that state participation would change the character of relations between suppliers and recipients. This national strategy was consistent with other development strategies suggested by ECLA. As Albert O. Hirschman notes,

> ECLA gave expression and direction to feelings that are diffuse among important intellectual and middle-class circles in Latin America: first to various resentments against the US and in particular to the suspicion of exploitation; and second, to the idea that the cure for society's ills lies in empowering the state to deal with them[23].

Another strategy Latin American states employed in the 1970s was to seek reforms in the international rules and norms that governed technology transfer. They called for changes in the international patent and trademark systems, and the creation of an all-inclusive legally binding code of conduct to govern technology transfer to be negotiated at UNCTAD. Later, these reforms were demanded again in the Programme for a New International Economic Order[24]. Given that Latin Americans believed that problems with technology transfer were in part rooted in the character of international political economic relations and the nature of the system itself, international measures were seen as an integral part of the effort to change technology transfer relations. These measures had three fundamental goals: altering the conduct of technology suppliers, legitimizing national action, and inducing other states to adopt legislation similar to Latin America's. They will be examined in section 6.3.

National measures

Argentina, Brazil, Mexico, and the Andean Pact (including Bolivia, Chile, Colombia, Ecuador, Peru, and later Venezuela) passed national legislation or ratified regional agreements to control flows of technology into their countries. Initial legislative action took place during 1970 and 1973. Prior to the passage of these laws, states did not *directly* regulate technology transfer[25]. Payments were indirectly regulated in some states through 'foreign exchange controls by central banks, royalty commissions set up primarily for balance of payments discipline and review boards for granting industrial incentives to qualifying firms'[26].

The Andean Pact countries were the first in Latin America to regulate technology transfer through the passage of Andean Common Market Decision No. 24 in 1970. Legislation of states that are not members of the Andean Pact closely parallels the regional group's Decision[27]. Such legislation *prohibits*, among other things, tying clauses in contracts that designate or restrict sources of technology, goods or services, or that either require acceptance or limit access to additional technology; restrictions that set territorial or quantitative limits or require prior approval for exports; designation of persons to be employed by the licensee; restrictions on adaptation and development of appropriate technology by the licensee. In addition, some states have set limits ôn the amounts of royalties to be charged by the licensor and have forbidden the importation of technology that is already available nationally. Finally, some states took measures to decrease the amount of equity that foreign firms owned or could obtain in local firms. Each state provides that all technology contracts be submitted to a national registry for *prior* approval before the contract goes into effect. Frequently, the state sends the contract back to the licensor for revisions so that its terms will be in line with national regulations. Sometimes contracts are rejected.

Latin American legislation is, in part, modelled after United States and West European anti-trust laws and also, in part, after Japanese regulation of foreign investment and licensing practices. However, several significant differences exist between Northern anti-trust legislation and Southern technology transfer regulation.

The rationale for industrialized state anti-trust law is the promotion of unregulated markets and competition[28]. In contrast, a primary rationale for Latin American legislation that 'looks like' anti-trust law is to make the state a partner in dealings with foreign multinational firms so that host state nationals can get the best deal possible when purchasing technology and on terms that are in line with the economic and social development objectives of the state. Eduardo White writes:

> [Latin American] state intervention ... is based on the view that in the case of agreements between foreign enterprises and their local subsidiaries, there is generally no contract in the economic sense because the two parties involved are not separately autonomous; and, in the case of agreements between independent enterprises, these reflect an inequality in the negotiating power of the two parties. Consequently, the principle of intervention is not aimed at eliminating negotiation, but rather, at strengthening it by making the government either a 'party' (in cases where there is no other way of representing the national interest) or a 'protector' of the local enterprises with a view to increasing their bargaining power having regard to its own interests and certain national objectives[29].

As a standard for enforcement, industrialized state anti-trust authorities use 'a rule of reason' under which licensing practices are judged in terms of whether they are for a legitimate business purpose and are not unduly broad or long in light of the technology right on which they are based. Although some practices are considered per se illegal, many practices that are generally banned may be considered legal in special circumstances[30]. In contrast, Latin American authorities screen all contracts prior to their conclusion, reject many practices out of hand regardless of technology rights, and judge the intent of the practice in terms of its effect on the autonomous economic development of the country, rather than on competition.

In light of the differing rationales for anti-trust laws and technology transfer legislation, it is not surprising that there is a different scope of enforcement in the South. In general, developing countries have not prosecuted national firms for anti-trust violations. Instead, they concentrate on prosecution of foreign firms. Lawrence Ebb notes,

> [T]he general cultural factor underlying this minibody of [Latin American] antitrust law [is], namely, that it is directed expressly and specifically against the foreign licensors – the multinational company – and is aimed at protecting local business enterprises as well as the domestic consumer . . .[31].

Industrialized state anti-trust authorities prosecute their national firms more than foreign ones and, in any case, do not discriminate against foreign firms.

Latin American regulations also pertain to intra-corporate transactions.

Industrialized state anti-trust legislation, for the most part, does not. One American anti-trust authority explains why:

> It is the usual rule in both American and [West European] Common Market antitrust that a corporation cannot commit a violation of such law by commanding its branches or divisions to avoid competition with each other. This result is explained either by stating that there is no conspiracy taking place because there are no independent conspirators to conspire or by arguing that it is virtually impossible to try to have the law command that offices, factories, or divisions under common ownership and perhaps even their common management should vigorously compete with one another …. It is clear that the general rule is that antitrust laws are not intended for the governance of intra-corporate relations[32].

The effectiveness of national legislation in Latin America will be considered in section 6.2.

The viewpoint of the United States

US policy on technology transfer represents, and has always represented, an uneasy accommodation among the interests of US business, liberal ideology, and the position of the United States as the largest and one of the very few net exporters of technology in the world. The policy is international in that US relations with different countries or regions are, in most cases, not taken into account during policy formulation. The relationship with the Eastern bloc is an obvious exception to this general rule. In addition, policy on the transfer of military or strategically related technology is formed by different bureaus and in response to a different set of interests.

Officially, the US government states that its policy on the transfer of non-military technology is neutral – that it neither encourages nor discourages its transfer[33]. The government suggests that it has been inclined to view all trade and investment, including technology transfer, as a private activity that the government should either leave alone or for which it should merely create a favorable climate. However, an examination of US policy reveals that its neutrality is arguable. The bulk of technology transferred from the US to other countries is effected in three ways: through foreign aid programs, through US firms' direct investment abroad, and through patent licensing. US government policies on each of these activities ultimately *encourages* transfer, with strong support for proprietary rights and supplier discretion.

US foreign assistance programs grew rapidly after World War II. Technical assistance was a major part of President Truman's Point IV program, and the rationale offered for it then continues to be accepted in many parts of the US government today.

The U.S. is preeminent among nations in the development of industrial and scientific technique. The material resources which we can afford to use for the assistance of other people are limited. But our unponderable resources in technical knowledge are constantly growing and inexhaustible[34].

Most of the technology transferred under foreign aid programs is primarily agricultural rather than industrial in nature. The trend toward transfers of technical assistance rather than large material outlays has continued, and reflects the US's position as the world's technological leader[35].

Most industrial technology is not transferred by governments. Multinational corporations transfer about 80% of all technology, usually through direct foreign investment (DFI). While the US government has exercised only very limited direct control over how much technology (of a nonmilitary nature) is transferred by US multinational corporations (e.g., to Cuba), US policies on direct investment abroad have an impact on the amount of technology transferred: the more DFI, the more technology transferred. The US government takes the position that its policies on DFI are also neutral. Robert Gilpin argues to the contrary:

American tax policy, the insistence that American subsidiaries in the [West European] Common Market be treated as European corporations, and, much later, the creation of O.P.I.C. (1969) to insure foreign investments are but three examples of measures designed to foster corporate expansionism[36].

The US government's century-old policy on patents also promotes the transfer of technology[37]. One incentive for an inventor to transfer technology is strong industrial property protection in the importing country. In the late nineteenth century, the US, along with a dozen other countries, signed the Paris Convention, which provides for, among other things, national treatment of foreign patents in host countries, thus ensuring that foreign inventions will be as much protected as national patents in the country of licensing[38]. The US has also pushed for two programs conducted by the World Intellectual Property Organization that will make patent protection stronger – the Model Laws on patents, written to aid developing countries in formulating strong patent laws, and the Patent Cooperation Treaty of 1970[39]. Ultimately, these programs should also foster the transfer of technology.

Thus, intentionally or unintentionally through its policies on foreign aid, foreign investment, and patents, the US government has promoted the transfer of technology. Sometimes the transfer was a result rather than an explicit purpose of a policy. In regard to foreign aid, technical assistance programs were a means to achieve certain political and humanitarian ends of foreign assistance programs. Technology transfer is a by-product of direct foreign investment, not an end in itself. Lastly, industrial property protection was to do simply that – prevent the pirating of US technology by other states or foreign firms – not to promote the transfer of technology. Nevertheless, all three government policies acted as spurs to the transfer of US technology abroad.

The United States has reconsidered its policies on technology transfer because developing countries insisted in the 1970s on more access to the advanced technology of industrialized countries on better terms, and on a legally binding international code of conduct to govern the transfer of technology. US policy on these recent issues has largely been the creation of the Economic and Business Bureau (EB) of the State Department, which has traditionally represented the interests of American business abroad. The State Department's historical position for the preservation of open markets is reflected in their technology transfer policy, which is fairly conservative, and generally opposed to changes in the status quo[40].

Because the US is the largest and until the mid-1970s was the only net exporter of technology, exporting ten times as much technology as it imports[41], private interest groups in the United States tend to be concerned with safeguarding the US technological lead, thought to be crucial to the health of the US economy. This concern has been heightened during the past 10 years because of US economic problems. Some groups and individuals have argued that technology transfers by multinational corporations have meant a loss of jobs for the American workforce, and the issue has become highly politicized. Jack Baranson contends:

> The new generation of management service contracts coupled with evolving corporate strategies for maximizing returns on technology assets, may result in a further erosion of US production jobs in key industries such as automotive, aircraft, consumer electronics, and chemicals[42].

Other groups and individuals have more generally voiced concern about US firms' investment activities abroad. While direct foreign investment and technology transfer used to be considered quite profitable for the US economy, some skeptics now argue that the situation has changed. Robert Gilpin predicts that, because of a counter-offensive by host states of multinational corporations, the US will lose its economic and technological superiority, that competition for markets and resources will become increasingly more fierce, and that growth rates will drop[43].

While the views of private interest groups have not forced the US government to change its position that the transfer of proprietary, non-military technology ought not to be regulated by the government, neither have calls by developing countries for more access to the private technology of the US been successful. Both private US interest groups and developing country recommendations contradict traditional US government policy and it is doubtful that the government would try to satisfy the demands of the latter at the expense of further alienating the former.

State Department positions on technology transfer have been influenced by two factors that have tended to have the effect of exaggerating the pro-business bent of its policy on technology transfer. First, the policy has been formulated in response to developing country initiatives taken at the United Nations Conference on Trade and Development. Second, developing country proposals on changing technology transfer transactions are a part of the developing country Programme for a New International Economic Order (NIEO). Both UNCTAD and the NIEO are perceived with suspicion at the State Department. UNCTAD is thought to be a lobbying group for the demands (sometimes considered radical by industrialized states) of the developing countries for economic development and preferential treatment within the international economic system. Thus, the US government often suspects the motives of UNCTAD regarding the implementation of any agreed-to programs[44]. Accordingly, the US has insisted that any codes of conduct successfully negotiated under UNCTAD auspices be voluntary guidelines rather than legally binding strictures on behavior[45]. These negative attitudes have not been fully consistent with US positions on codes of conduct written under other international organization auspices. For instance, the US has pushed for a legally binding code of conduct on illicit payments under United Nations Economic and Social Council auspices.

That proposals for technology transfer reform are a part of the Programme for a New International Economic Order, sponsored by developing countries in the United Nations, has also added to US negativism. If the negotiations on the transfer of technology were not a part of the NIEO, there might have been less politicization of the issue. Except for a very brief period of time around the Seventh Special Session of the UN General Assembly when Secretary of State Henry Kissinger was more conciliatory about some NIEO programs, the State Department, Congress, and other interested agencies have viewed the NIEO as a threat to the free enterprise system and an open, competitive international economy[46]. NIEO programs call for more state intervention in the economy than states with laissez-faire attitudes and orientations are comfortable with. The NIEO favors the value of equity in international economic relations more than the value of efficiency. The companion document to the NIEO, the Charter of Economic Rights and Duties of States (CERDS), asserts the supremacy of developing country law in expropriation disputes and endorses the right of developing states to engage in primary commodity cartels such as OPEC. US official policy is strongly opposed to these programs and values.

As noted earlier, the New International Economic Order also calls for changes in the international patent system, changes that Latin American states strongly favor[47]. The United States believes that these changes may lead to abrogations of the industrial property rights of inventors, and thus does not favor them.

In some respects, it is unfortunate that general negativism toward UNCTAD and the NIEO has influenced State Department policy on technology transfer. A good part of the UNCTAD code on technology transfer as proposed by the Group of 77 (the developing country group) might actually enhance international competition, which is theoretically one of the US government's goals, and harmonize approaches, as will be shown below. Moreover, having a set of guidelines on technology transfer would tend to make the environment in which US businesses invest more predictable and stable, also a goal of the State Department.

The Economic and Business Bureau is not the only agency involved in the formulation of policy on the transfer of non-military, proprietary technology. The State Department's Bureau of Oceans, International Environmental, and Scientific Affairs (OES) also makes policy on aspects of technology transfer, and the State Department's Bureau of International Organization Affairs (IO) monitors the activities of international organizations involved in technology transfer issues. However, these two bureaus have little influence on the aspects of technology transfer policy that have been discussed in this chapter. This is so for several reasons. First, these technology transfer policies have largely been cast in economic and commercial terms. Thus, in a functional sense, the Economic and Business Bureau is thought to be more equipped and better able to handle policy-making than OES or IO. EB also serves as a conduit for the expertise and opinions of major American firms directly involved in the commercial technology transfer process. Second, EB is one of the more prestigious bureaus of the State Department and thus has been invested with considerable policy-making power. In contrast, OES is a relatively new bureau whose policy-making impact has yet to be felt in many issues that have both scientific and economic components[48]. IO has little policy-making power on any issue that is also handled by either a functional or a regional bureau. It is mainly limited to procedural or technical international organization issues rather than substantive ones. Had OES been given more responsibility for the technology transfer problems discussed in this chapter, policy might have been different – but attempting to determine what it would have been would be highly conjectural.

Other governmental agencies do have policy-making responsibilities for those aspects of technology transfer discussed in this chapter. Along with the delegates from EB, the Department of Commerce Patent Office and the Department of Justice Antitrust Division send representatives to the UNCTAD negotiations that have been taking place since 1975 on a technology transfer code. But these bureaus have different missions, and hence somewhat different goals for the negotiations. The Patent Office wants to ensure the protection of industrial property rights. The Antitrust Division wishes to ensure competition. The Economic and Business Bureau believes that the protection of the interests of US firms should be paramount. These goals are not always compatible, and there is no evidence that any agency has triumphed in disputes over the goals of US technology transfer policy. Rather, the policy on the code of conduct reflects a curious mixture of all of these positions, philosophies, and goals.

The perspectives from which Latin America and the United States view technology transfer are quite different and can only lead to conflict. The Latin Americans consider that greater access to the advanced technology of the United States is vital to their economic development; the US government argues that it has no political or ideological basis upon which to act to satisfy demands for more access. Latin American states view technology as an investment problem, and believe that they have problems in acquiring technology because they must deal with multinational corporations who have more bargaining power; the US government considers this to be a problem of the market for which it has little or no responsibility. Latin American states argue that international action is necessary to reform the process of technology transfer; the US counters that actions taken to reform the international patent system or other aspects concerning negotiations can only discourage technology transfer and hurt chances for revitalizing an open international economic system. Given these differences, it is hardly surprising that the US and Latin America have had conflicts about technology transfer during the past decade.

6.2 Conflicts and strategies

It might be presumed in a paper on the US–Latin America technology transfer relationship that the focus would be on hemispheric or bilateral relations. Yet, although the issue was discussed at the inter-American level under the auspices of Kissinger's 'New Dialogue' at a ministerial conference in Tlateloco in 1974 and later in Atlanta, none of the proposals or initiatives discussed in those contacts has ever come to fruition. A regional commission was to be established to look into US–Latin America cooperation and conflict on technology transfer, but the Latin Americans scrapped the idea because the 1974 Trade Act passed by the US Congress withdrew certain Latin American states' right to most favored nation trade status for participating in OPEC (even though those countries did not participate in the OPEC boycott of the United States), and because of the conflict at the time over the Panama Canal Treaty.

Latin American states have generally been hesitant about participating in regional activities concerning changes of technology transfer relationships because they have not wanted to detract from UNCTAD activities in the area, where they assumed that they had more power and more to gain. Thus, the lack of regional activities on technology transfer does not mean that there is no interest in the subject; rather, the US fumbled in its efforts to undertake some sort of cooperative program with the Latin Americans, and the Latin Americans themselves thought they could achieve their goals more easily by acting on an international or purely national level. Therefore, this section examines the US–Latin America conflicts about aspects of technology transfer on only two levels: first, the US multinational corporation–Latin American state technology transfer relationship; and, second, the North–South technology transfer relationship.

Latin American states vs. US multinational corporations

If one were interested in comparing the relative power of states and transnational actors, the experience of US multinational corporations with Latin American states on issues of technology transfer would be an interesting case study. With one notable exception, the United States has not interfered with Latin American states' attempts to regulate the conduct of US multinational corporations' transfer activities. Thus, inter-state relations do not 'cloud' the case study and some interesting insights concerning the strategies of states and transnational actors in achieving their goals on a conflict-ridden issue might be developed.

As noted before, Latin American states passed regulations during the period 1967–75 to change the behavior of multinational firms when transferring technology. These regulations are still in existence and still enforced. Other developing countries have followed Latin America's lead and have enacted similar policies for the regulation of technology importation. Three questions are commonly asked about the impact of this legislation. First, did the behavior of multinational corporations change as a result of the legislation when they transferred technology to Latin America? Second, what were the costs and benefits involved to the states in implementing these regulations? Third, when the costs outweighed the benefits, did the behavior of the state change toward multinationals?

When confronted with new legislation on technology transfer, multinational corporations had three basic choices. First, they could continue investing or licensing in and transferring technology to Latin America, changing their behavior to conform to the new legislation. Second, they could stop or curtail technology transfer to Latin America. Third, they could enlist the aid of their home governments.

Appraisals of the effects of these laws and the behavior of multinational firms are at variance with one another. Studies sponsored by business groups tend to argue that the stringency of the laws has forced multinational corporations to curtail investment, licensing and technology transfer to Latin America. Evidence tends to be anecdotal in nature. Consider the following offered by Business International, SA:

> [One firm noted that] 'We decided against setting up local manufacture [in Ecuador] because of local equity requirements. Going in in those circumstances would have exposed our technology to third parties.'

In Venezuela (and also in Colombia) the government asked for conditions that a major electrical firm would not accept and so it did not go ahead with a proposed project ... Particularly bothersome were requirements for full export freedom for the licensee and very low royalties that would not even cover the licensor's costs. Under such conditions the company decided not to make the transfer[49].

The message from business is clear: national regulations on technology transfer cause a net reduction in transfers to Latin America.

However, business groups also point out that, when firms decide to remain in Latin America despite the national regulations, firms are careful to comply with governmental contractual regulations. The International Group of the American Chamber of Commerce did an informal survey of several companies that had invested or licensed in Latin America and found that each of the companies interviewed (among others, Allied Chemical, Tecumseh Products, Owens-Illinois, Genesco, and Kayser-Roth) was forced to renegotiate existing agreements, some of which had been in effect for five to ten years, to comply with new national legislation[50].

Interviews and information provided by Latin American governments offer a different picture. They point out that technology transfer regulations have reduced the number of restrictive clauses in technology transfer contracts, reduced the price Latin American recipients must pay for technology, and shortened the validity of contracts. The evidence they present is statistical. For example,

From the second half of 1967 to June 1971, the Comité de Regalías of Colombia had evaluated 395 contracts of technology commercialization. Of these 334 were negotiated, modified and finally approved and 61 were rejected. In the process of negotiations, payments of royalties were reduced by about 40% or about US ... $8 million annually .... Also during the latter part of 1970 and the beginning of 1971 negotiations by the Colombian Comité de Regalías
   1) Reduced by 90% the tie-in clauses in the purchase of intermediates
   2) Eliminated by 100% the restrictive export clauses
   3) Eliminated by 80% clauses on minimum royalty payments
   4) Prohibited payments on taxes by the licensee on royalties remitted to the licensor
   5) Established maximum percentage royalty rates by sectors[51].

Statistics provided by the National Registry of Mexico illustrate a similar trend. The Registry claims that in 80–85% of the cases where firms were found to be charging too much for technology, contracts were changed to suit the Mexican authorities. The Registry also claims to have reduced export restrictions and grant-back clauses in contracts by about 20% and limitations on production volumes by about 40%[52].

UNCTAD published a study in 1980 corroborating the claims of individual national governments. Its format was also statistical and based on information provided by Brazil, Mexico, India, Argentina, Colombia, Peru, Venezuela, and the Philippines. UNCTAD concluded that national regulations had a substantial impact on the price of technology, the incidence of restrictive practices found in contracts, and the length of contracts. They also noted that:

> The inflow of technology to countries with a regulatory framework has not been hindered or prevented ... The number of agreements annually submitted for registration or approved shows generally a constant or rising trend over time. Direct foreign investment flows – another measure of technology inflow into the countries in question – have generally grown more after the regulations on technology transfer were implemented than before ...
>
> Growth rates of transfer of technology payments in the 1970s have been lower than in the 1960s and such payments represent a lower proportion of some countries' exports than at the beginning of the last decade. The changes produced in Latin America regarding intrafirm payments are particularly striking[53].

One thing seems to be clear, then. If firms decide to transfer technology to Latin America despite national regulations, they have complied with regulations regarding the content of technology contracts. Business groups imply, however, that national regulation has produced a loss of transfers to Latin America; Latin American governments and UNCTAD argue that technology transfer to Latin America has increased. Why the discrepancy?

An empirical study done by Joel Bleeke, a consultant with McKinsey and Company, and Professor James A. Rahl of Northwestern University Law School, gives a clue. They suggest that some firms that used to *license* technology to Latin America have curtailed their licensing because of national laws:

> National registration laws in developing countries, however, have significantly reduced technology flows. Nearly 40% of respondents state that regulations in the Andean Community have affected the quantity of know-how which they have licensed to unaffiliated licensees. Of the respondents, 25% indicated that national registration regulations in Mexico and India have had an impact upon the quantity of technology transferred[54].

It is probably the case that overall technology transfer agreements have increased in Latin America, as UNCTAD and Latin American governments suggest, but that firms are more reluctant to make such agreements with independent firms in Latin America. Firms prefer to transfer technology through the vehicle of direct foreign investment than licensing.

The reason for the preference is that it is much more difficult for Latin American governments to control what occurs between parent and subsidiary than between two independent (unaffiliated) firms. For example, a parent firm may be forced by the host government to delete export restrictions from its technology contracts with its subsidiary in Latin America. But management decisions by the parent may have the effect of gearing the subsidiary's production to its local market anyway. For instance, the product might not be competitive in the international market. Or suppose that a national registry strikes from a technology contract certain tie-in clauses. A subsidiary may continue to accept what would have been tied purchases anyway because local managers may feel compelled to by corporate headquarters.

Independent licensors do not have the same power that parent firms do. The deletion of an export restriction may, in some cases, be meaningless to an independent licensor if the licensor has registered industrial property rights in markets where the licensee wishes to export, but this may not always be the case. Or, Latin American governments may lower the allowable royalty rate suppliers can charge for the use of technology to recipients. In an intra-corporate transaction, profits can be repatriated in other ways, through accounting maneuvers. The same is not possible for an independent licensor.

Thus, many firms suggest that they are more wary of licensing technology to Latin America than before. This is not to say that the only changes Latin American governments have been able to effect in intra-corporate transfer are cosmetic. But the laws should be thought of as a qualified rather than an unmitigated success.

The record indicates that of all of the Latin American states that have some kind of laws on the importation of technology, Mexico and Brazil have been more consistently successful in achieving their goals than other states. The Andean Pact was the first jurisdiction to pass a law on technology transfer (Cartegena Decision No. 24, 1970), but not all of the states ratified it then (e.g., Bolivia) and many states did not have or create effective machinery with which to implement the Decision. Many members of the Pact suffer from economic weakness, political instability, or a weak bureaucratic infrastructure. Although Mexico and Brazil passed laws on technology transfer several years after Decision 24 was enacted, they had fewer problems with the adequacy of administrative machinery, and thus were able to enforce the law efficiently. In Brazil and, under Echeverría, in Mexico, the administrative machinery of the national registries was fairly autonomous and insulated from other economic ministries of their governments. Only in these two states have technology transfer authorities had complete control over decisions to approve or deny contracts on technology. In other states, the head of the technology registry must report to an inter-agency ministerial group that is empowered with ultimate decision-making. Thus, the Brazilian and (in the early and mid-1970s) the Mexican registries were not subject to pressure to relax enforcement of their laws in response to bad economic times or even outside pressures.

Some US-based firms have claimed that the Mexicans and Brazilians have been more flexible in the enforcement of their laws and have been willing to negotiate more with firms. They also claim that Andean Pact countries have been more rigid in the interpretation of their laws and that particularly 'bothersome' restrictions on equity have forced firms to do business elsewhere[55].

But, aside from questions of adequate and insulated administrative machinery, and the flexible interpretation and enforcement of national legislation, two other factors appear to have been responsible for the success or failure of governments in changing the behavior of multinational corporations while maintaining a high level of technology inflows. These have more to do with market conditions than enforcement procedures or relative stringency of laws. For one, both Mexico and Brazil are very attractive markets for foreign investment – large, stable, growing and relatively developed. Thus, investors have been more willing to put up with new regulations there than in Ecuador or Colombia, where markets are intrinsically less attractive. However, in Argentina, also a relatively attractive market, this was not the case: the second technology law passed there was so restrictive that, according to the Argentina government, net investment in the country dropped, as did imports of technology. Thus, while size and development of the market are important factors in a firm's decision to invest in and transfer technology to a country, it appears that restrictive legislation can still cause a firm to do business elsewhere.

A second factor that seems to have had an impact is the degree to which European firms have been willing to replace American firms that decide to pull out of a country instead of changing their behavior to conform to national laws. US supremacy as the leading technological supplier to Latin America began to decline in the early 1970s. Although the US was and continues to be the only country that is a net exporter of technology, West Germany, Switzerland, and Japan began to transfer increasing amounts of technology to Latin America in the 1970s. And, a few new Latin America multinational corporations began to transfer technology. The advent of non-US direct foreign investment in Latin America was a boon to the bargaining position of the Latin Americans. If the US firms backed off from investing in Latin America because of restrictive host country legislation, European and Japanese firms were often ready to fill the gap. '[T]he very fact that the Europeans and Japanese are latecomers to the area gives them a valuable freedom of maneuver: they can tailor their deals to the prevailing political climate'[56].

But, European and Japanese firms did not always fill the gap, Latin American multinational corporations were few in number, and attractiveness of the market did not always compensate for stringent legislation. However, even in those countries where investment and technology flows tapered off because of the legislation, there has been no retreat from the principle of screening. Why? Eduardo White has argued,

> [R]estrictive practices [regarding technology transfer] were considered not as much from the angle of the private cost/benefit balances they entailed for the parties to a contract – in fact, it may be assumed that, in many instances, technological dependence laid the foundation for a recipient enterprise's competitiveness in the local market – but rather in terms of the extent to which they might affect the economic and social interests of the countries in which they were applied[57].

Thus, because the importance of technology transfer was viewed in terms other than traditional commercial ones (in that it was seen as important in an economic, social, and political sense), no government that has passed legislation has ever abandoned the idea of regulating and screening the importation of technology. Putting technology transfer into the domain of government regulation meant that the state would have greater bargaining power with the heretofore unchecked multinational corporation. Latin American states hoped that the success of state intervention in technology transfer would spill over into other areas of regulation of multinational corporation activity, so that they would reap political gains as well as economic ones.

It must be remembered that this issue is only a part of a much larger package of issues on North–South economic relations. Many Latin American leaders believed that structural international economic imbalances had to be remedied in the 1970s in order to achieve their goals of economic development and industrialization. Regulating technology transfer on a national level was only a starting point. If reforms could be made on the national level, they might also be accomplished at the international level. Indeed, the Latin Americans were leaders in this effort, as will be shown later.

That Latin American states will not cease in their efforts to regulate the activities of the multinational firm in transferring technology does not mean that the laws that exist today will go unchanged. In some countries where legislation has had adverse effects on investment and technology transfer, governments have changed their laws. This has been the case in both Chile and Argentina. Chile withdrew from the Andean Pact in 1976 and now has 'liberal' regulations on technology transfer. Argentina, a country that experimented first with a law similar to Mexico's, then a second, much more stringent law, recently passed a third law on technology transfer, more permissive than the second. In the introduction of the new legislation, Law No. 21,617, is the statement:

The enactment of Laws 19,231 and 20,794 had a negative effect on this most important aspect of national activity, due to the fact that its immediate consequence was to stop the flow of modern technology toward the country, a state of affairs which it is essential to reverse within the shortest possible time.

The negative experience gained as a result of the enactment of the laws referred to above was due basically to an extremely restrictive attitude adopted by enforcement authorities; in addition to the exaggerations included in the second of those laws, the effect was to diminish the willingness of foreign suppliers of technology to cooperate with our country[58].

Future revision of technology transfer legislation will probably occur in those states where the technology registry has little autonomy, when investment and technology flows drop dramatically, or when changes of national regime also dictate a change in national ideology regarding state –business relations. However, unless there are significant changes in economic conditions and political-economic ideological orientation, Latin American states will probably not give up the idea of regulating inflows of technology in the future. These new conditions did obtain in Argentina in 1981 and they repealed their law.

Strategic implications

At the outset of this discussion it was noted that the experience of US multinational corporations with Latin American states on issues of technology transfer was an interesting case study because inter-state relations do not substantially cloud the experience and because some insights concerning the strategies of states and transnational actors in achieving their goals on a controversial issue could be developed. During the next few pages three questions are addressed. First, why didn't the United States intervene when Latin American states regulated the conduct of US multinational corporations? Second, why were the Latin Americans able to achieve a degree of success through their efforts? Third, what resources did multinational corporations have at their disposal to ensure that they could continue transferring technology on profitable and otherwise acceptable terms?

Latin Americans have long been suspicious of the supportive relationship between the US government and US multinational corporations. It might have been surprising to them that the US government did not try to change, either diplomatically or through 'gun-boat diplomacy', Latin American technology regulatory policies. In fact, it appears that the US has intervened only once. Acquaintance with the reasons for this intervention will shed some light on why the US has not intervened at other times, and will help explain why Latin American states have been successful in having their policies accepted, at least by other states.

In 1975, the Mexican government passed a Law on Inventions and Trademarks. Although the portion of the law that deals with inventions was not a radical departure from established industrial property law, the portion that deals with trademarks was:

> The Mexican Law ... does not nationalize the foreign trademark, but makes it mandatory that it be used in the domestic market associated with a local trademark ... The intention of the provisions ... is that the Mexican licensee obtains good will for one of its own trademarks together with the foreign trademark, so that it might continue to market the products with its own trademark, both in the local and foreign markets, in the event the owner of the foreign trademark attempts to establish an excessive royalty or to establish unacceptable conditions harmful for its interests or in the event it simply does not wish to renew the license[59].

Reaction to this law by American business was extremely negative. The law was viewed by many companies as tantamount to an expropriation of industrial property rights. Members of the business community in the US turned to the US government for support in their efforts to prevent the passage of the law, and European firms turned to their home governments for support. These governments and the Mexican government then had discussions concerning the new law. As a result, implementation of the law has been postponed, and officials of the Mexican Registry confide that they believe that the law will never go into force[60].

When this law is compared to other laws passed by Latin American states on technology transfer, an immediate difference is observable. Other laws on technology transfer (including the Mexican law concerning registration, screening, and regulation of technology transfer agreements) concern the exercise of industrial property or technology rights. However, none of the laws ever abrogates or expropriates those rights. The US itself has anti-trust and other laws affecting the exercise of industrial property rights. Although there are significant differences in Latin American and US law, the US had very little precedent or international law justification for intervening in the activities of Latin American states concerning the exercise of industrial property rights, and in fact had tolerated a similar strategy by Japan in screening technology. No international conferences had ever been held on the exercise of industrial property rights; no international agreements had ever been concluded. However, international conventions are in force concerning the *sanctity* of industrial property rights – the Paris Convention on patents and the Berne Convention on trademarks and subsequent revisions. For almost a century, the United States has been a leader in arguing that industrial property rights must not be expropriated. Thus, the Mexican law regarding foreign trademarks was considered to be inconsistent with international conventions and antithetical to US policy on industrial property rights. Therefore, the US government took the liberty of making known its position and US business reaction to the new Mexican law.

From this episode it is possible to conclude that the reason that the United States did not intervene in Latin American efforts to change the transfer process and the reason that Latin American states were successful, in part, in changing the process of technology transfer through their legislation was because the legislation concerned the exercise of industrial property rights, an area in which there have been no international agreed-to norms or rules. Latin American states could pass legislation in this area, then, without fear of international condemnation. Without US government backing, US multinational corporations had either to conform to new rules or to refuse to invest in and transfer technology to Latin America.

As noted above, however, US multinational corporations have sometimes 'voted with their feet' instead of conforming their behavior to Latin American strictures. This has caused relaxation of some of the laws. Moreover, multinational corporations sometimes changed their contracts so that they would be legally acceptable to technology registries, but only in cosmetic ways. Obviously, not all changes in laws are cosmetic, and Latin American officials purport to be pleased with the operation of the new laws. But success in this area is hard to measure.

The South vs. the North

The second significant set of conflicts between the US and Latin America on the transfer of technology has centered on the formulation of a legally binding international code of conduct to govern the transfer of proprietary technology. Negotiations took place initially because of initiatives by developing countries, led by Latin American states and India; the US only grudgingly participated in the exercise, unconvinced of the need or value of a code.

The idea of an international code of conduct was both an outgrowth of the 'movement' at the national level for legislation on technology transfer and the continuation of a long battle conducted by developing countries at the United Nations to change political economic relationships between industrialized and developing countries, and particularly regarding this issue, with a view to promoting the development and autonomy of the Third World.

The main purpose of the code was to change the terms of transfer to the benefit of recipients by establishing binding legal principles and rules that would endorse and embrace the philosophy and substance of national legislation on technology transfer already existing in some Latin American states. Among other things, it was believed that a universal code would solve the main problem some Latin American states faced when they implemented their national legislation – that is, loss of technology imports when firms decided to relocate in other less regulated environments. The code was also designed to legitimize the idea of screening and regulation by the state and reduce the threat of Northern intervention. Before India and the Latin American countries enacted their laws, the only Northern state that had taken a similar course was Japan. Japanese regulation was tolerated by the United States in the 1950s and early 1960s when it was most restrictive because the US had a strategic interest in building up the economic strength of Japan[61]. Latin Americans saw no reason to believe that the US government would continue to tolerate regulation of American firms. In fact, as noted previously, the US and other Northern governments did protest when Mexico attempted to implement a law on trademarks that was thought by foreign firms to abrogate the industrial property rights of suppliers.

Developing countries that did not yet screen and regulate technology were also in favor of the code idea. They noted the success that countries with national legislation had had in changing terms of technology transfer. While screening and regulation were perceived as useful strategies, many developing countries would not adopt necessary legislation because of domestic political circumstances or because there was no effective bureaucracy to enforce rules[62]. A code that was legally binding and international would solve this problem, it was believed. In addition, there was nearly unanimous consensus among developing countries that an international code was necessary even if a developing country had national legislation because the basic international 'rules of the game' regarding trade and investment relations had been established by the North and its enterprises. In order to gain more bargaining power, it was thought that new international rules that took into account the South's needs must be written[63].

Pressure for a code was built in stages. First, the UN Conference on Trade and Development did a series of studies on the feasibility of a code and suggested its possible shape; then numerous inter-governmental organizations such as the UN General Assembly, the Interparliamentary Council, the UN Advisory Commission on the Application of Science and Technology for Development, the UN Conference on Trade and Development, and the UN Economic Commission for Latin America passed resolutions supporting the idea of a code. The Programme of Action for a New International Economic Order also called for formulation of a code[64].

At UNCTAD III in 1972 it was resolved that work would commence on a code by an Intergovernmental Group of Experts (the IGE). Initial meetings of the IGE could not produce a draft, since the positions of the developing country group (the Group of 77), the industrialized country group (Group B), and the socialist country group (Group D) were too far apart.

The first draft of a code was actually written at the 1973 Pugwash Conference on International Affairs by a group of technology transfer experts almost exclusively from developing countries, many of whom had helped draft or implement their own national laws. The chairman of the working group that produced the Pugwash code was Miguel Wionczek of

Mexico, who was also chief negotiator for the Group of 77 at the UNCTAD IGE[65]. After consultations with the UNCTAD Secretariat's technology transfer section and with the Group of 77 of the IGE, the modified Pugwash code was offered to the IGE as a whole by the Group of 77. Group B and Group D waffled for almost 18 months before each of the two groups countered with their own drafts. The IGE held a total of six negotiations between 1975 and 1978. In addition, full UN conferences on this subject were held in November 1978, March 1979, November 1979, April/May 1980 and March/April 1981. No code has yet been agreed to, but progress has been made. The three groups have modified their initial positions and sections of composite (and even agreed-to) text exist for most of the code's chapters.

The original Group of 77 draft code contained chapters on principles, definitions, and scope of application, regulation of restrictive business practices, national regulation of technology transfer, responsibilities of source and recipient enterprises (sometimes known as 'guarantees'), international collaboration and special measures for developing countries, and applicable law and settlement of disputes. A final chapter stressed the binding legal nature of the code[66].

The Group of 77 proposed code embodied a whole series of principles basic to the New International Economic Order and to Latin American technology transfer policies. From the NIEO principles came the emphasis on special measures for developing countries, and the concept that technology should be viewed as the common heritage of mankind, and that national regulation of technology transfer should be recognized as a fundamental right of each state. From the Latin American background came the concept that technology should be transferred in an unfettered, unpackaged manner designed to employ local materials and personnel, and that the suitability and performance of technology should be guaranteed by the supplier. Consistent with the Charter of Economic Rights and Duties of States, the proposed code provided that all technology disputes should be settled entirely under the local law of the recipient country and that international rules should be binding except when national officials of recipient states chose to make an exception in line with their national development interests. In the longest chapter, based especially on the Latin American experience, the code provided that 40 restrictive practices committed by multinational enterprises or other suppliers should be prohibited (including export restrictions, tie-in clauses, and grant-backs, as well as restrictions on adaptation of technology to local conditions, on the use of local personnel, and on acquiring and using technology from competing sources). Many of the practices listed as improper were considered legal by industrialized countries, such as 'obliging the recipient to convert technology payments into capital stock'[67]. The Group of 77 draft code was to apply to relationships not only between suppliers and non-affiliated recipients but also between parents and subsidiaries. In addition, the code was to be legally binding on both states and enterprises.

In 1974, most members of Group B viewed the code as a radical proposition. The US was especially opposed to the idea, arguing that a legally binding code was neither feasible nor desirable. Group D countries positioned themselves somewhere between Group B and the Group of 77, rhetorically supporting a code but, during the substantive talks, stressing adequate protection for the rights of technology suppliers[68]. Despite their negative reaction to Group of 77 proposals, Group B countries have participated fully in the negotiations. The original version of their code was consistent with existing US and European Community anti-trust and contract law. They stressed a need for fairness and stability in national regulations. Group B's list of restrictive business practices to be prohibited was much shorter than the Group of 77's, since it included only practices that were judged to be anti-competitive (rather than injurious to economic development). The original version of Group B's code was not intended to apply to intra-corporate relations. The code was envisaged as a set of guidelines rather than as a legally binding instrument. Finally, the guarantees chapter was to feature mere 'best efforts' obligations, combined with emphasis on little more than adhering to the exact terms of contracts[69].

UNCTAD has put together a composite text for all of the chapters of the code, bracketing words and phrases that continue to be sources of disagreement. As it stands now, the preamble of the code is almost completely agreed to. It recognizes the need to facilitate the adequate transfer of technology, especially to developing countries. The chapters on objectives and principles (chapter 2), national regulation (chapter 3), special treatment for developing countries (chapter 6), and international collaboration (chapter 7) are nearly finalized. Little bracketed text remains in the first half of the guarantees chapter (chapter 5), which is on the negotiating phase of technology transfer agreements, and some progress has been made in removing brackets from the second half of the chapter that covers the contractual phase. With the exception of the export restrictions provision, a relatively clean text has been produced for the first 14 practices in the restrictive practices chapter (chapter 4). Finally, during the last two years, the groups have agreed on the type of international institutional machinery that will exist to implement the code (chapter 8)[70].

Significant areas of disagreement do remain, however. Some may be resolved by more negotiation, but others reflect fundamental philosophical, political, legal, or economic differences among the groups that may prove to be impossible to resolve. The ultimate legal character of the code remains in question, as does the definition of an international transfer of technology. Agreed text has not been completed for the last six practices in the restrictive practices chapter, largely because these practices are not considered anti-competitive by Group B. No agreement in that chapter has been made on the exceptions clause that would provide criteria for states to waive prohibition of the practices, and no overall criteria have been established for judging what constitutes a restrictive business practice.

An issue that has proved nearly impossible to resolve has been the extent to which the code's rules will cover parent–subsidiary transactions or transactions among subsidiaries of the same corporate parent. This issue has also been problematical for the negotiators of the UN's general code of conduct on multinational corporations and the UNCTAD restrictive business practice code. In the negotiation of the technology transfer code, the issue is manifested in three separate contexts. The first concerns the definition of an international transfer of technology. Developing countries argue that a transfer from a local subsidiary of a foreign parent to another local enterprise should constitute an international transfer of technology and thus be subject to the code. Industrialized countries are adamant that this type of transfer is not international at all and that coverage of it would disadvantage firms with foreign ties by subjecting them to stricter commercial standards than those imposed on other local firms.

The second place this issue arises is in the guarantees chapter. The question has been posed whether affiliated firms should have fewer obligations toward each other than unaffiliated firms. Language may be inserted into the chapeau of the chapter to state that economic affiliation of the parties should be considered when assessing whether suppliers and recipients of technology have treated each other fairly in negotiating and carrying out contracts.

By far the most troublesome manifestation of this issue is in the restrictive practices chapter. In fact, a number of participants believe that the impasse here seems so intractable that completion of the code may be precluded. Group B has argued that many of the practices that are listed as undesirable are perfectly legitimate among affiliated firms. Their position is based on the general policy that the purpose of this chapter is to prohibit anti-competitive behavior, as their own national anti-trust or competition laws do. Intra-enterprise restrictions are in most cases excluded from anti-trust laws. The Group of 77 has insisted that intra-enterprise activities should be covered by the rules of this chapter. This view is based on their position that the purpose of the chapter is to prohibit any practices that are injurious to the development or export interests of the recipient country, just as their own national laws on investment and technology transfer do. Consequently, at least 30 chapeaux for the chapter have been written and submitted for negotiation, all of which have been ultimately rejected.

The conference held in the spring of 1980 brought the groups closer together on chapter 5 on guarantees. At one point, it appeared that a compromise text would be agreed to, but the Algerian delegate insisted that the compromise did not accurately reflect Group of 77 desires and the negotiations fell through. Currently, the Group of 77 is standing fast on its position that planks on both performance guarantees and price and price specification be inserted into the chapter. Group B is against this.

Chapter 9 on applicable law and settlement of disputes is in the worst condition. This chapter was also considered at the spring 1980 conference, after a long period of no active negotiation. Nevertheless, the groups have fundamental differences about what the chapter should say, which negotiation did not resolve. Group B insists that, if chapter 9 is to exist, it should give firms the right to choice of applicable law and the national forum to which disputes will be brought. They would also like to see the concept of arbitration promoted. The Group of 77 counters that 'the law of the acquiring country shall be applicable to matters relating to public policy and to sovereignty'[71]. This position, of course, is consistent with Latin American adherence to the Calvo Doctrine. Since the positions of the groups are diametrically opposed to one another, and since the wording regarding arbitration has been so difficult to solve (although, using a draft written by the Chinese, some progress was made in this area in spring 1981), there is some talk of dropping the chapter entirely. Group B decided in 1978 that this was probably the only feasible solution to the problem and, by 1980, the Latin Americans came to the same conclusion. The Africans, specifically Madagascar, Zambia, Nigeria, and Algeria, reputedly do not wish the chapter to be dropped and still insist that language that is consistent with the Calvo Doctrine be inserted into the code.

In sum, the areas of disagreement that do remain are critical. No progress whatsoever was made on the code in the 1981 negotiation and the future of the code remains in doubt. The American delegation, and even certain sectors of the US business community, are much less disinclined to accept a code and could even be characterized as favoring a code. On the other hand, many members of the Group of 77 seem disgruntled with the current state of negotiations; others have lost interest. An examination of the code in its current incarnation reveals why the initiators and proponents of the negotiations, members of the Group of 77 and mostly Latin Americans, are less interested in reaching agreement on the code than they previously were. One can divide the Group of 77 into two groups: those that have national laws on technology transfer and those that do not. Those that do have national laws were interested in the code for two principal reasons: to legitimize the idea of regulating technology transfer, and to harmonize regulation. Those states that do not have technology transfer legislation were interested in the code either as a model for a law that they might be equipped to ratify and implement several years hence, or as a substitute for national law. As such, they were in need of a code that, in and of itself, could change the relationship between suppliers and recipients of technology so as to aid developing countries' technological capabilities and potentials for economic development and export promotion. Many delegates from developing countries have come to believe that the code as it now stands does not satisfy these basic objectives. If work on the code is ever completed, most of the provisions of the code will be consistent with industrialized state anti-trust, industrial property, and commercial law. While this pleases group B, it is unsatisfactory to the Group of 77. In the chapter on restrictive practices, for instance, it appears that only 14 practices will be prohibited, not 40, thus giving weight to the idea that firms should be prohibited from practices that impede competition not that simply impede development. It seems fairly certain that developing countries will not get the overall prohibition on export restrictions that they would like.

This is not to say that the code will not help developing countries at all. The code does change the relationship between suppliers and developing country recipients, but in a way that is consistent with the underlying norms and philosophy of the 'old liberal international economic order' and the legal and economic systems of the West. Developing countries that did not have national laws, or were impeded in the enforcement of them, do have more 'power' than they had before: in situations where private transactions were not screened or regulated by the government, any instrument that the code legitimizes strengthens recipient governments. But, by specifying the precise nature of the regulation, the new power is considerably circumscribed.

In fact, in some chapters of the code, this circumscription has the effect of delegitimizing existing developing country technology transfer legislation or contradicting major tenets of the New International Economic Order and the Charter of Economic Rights and Duties. Regarding restrictive practices, industrialized states have been responsible for adding to each provision of the code a list of factors that should except a licensor from the provision. In their national legislation, Latin American states generally have no such list of exceptions. If licensors wish to bargain for exceptions, they must do so with the state. An internationally codified list of exceptions might have the effect of undermining developing countries' newly created bargaining power with supplying enterprises. A similar situation is created by the language in chapter 3 on national regulation. In this chapter, industrialized states have agreed that all states should have the right to screen and regulate technology transfer. However, also agreed upon was language to the effect that national laws should provide fair and equitable treatment to technology suppliers. The Charter of Economic Rights and Duties had given developing countries the right to ignore these standards; under a code, developing countries would be held accountable. Chapter 3 was completed in November 1979, but by the spring of 1980 the Africans began to express dissatisfaction with it, not only because of these standards, but also because of a clause on the renegotiation of contracts that the Africans believed would circumscribe some of their rights in this area.

That the code is in many ways a liberal document that seems more of an extension of the post-World War II Bretton Woods system rather than a harbinger of a new and different international economic order is supported by language in other chapters as well. While industrialized countries have agreed to the principle that the technological capacities of developing states should be strengthened, the measures suggested for doing so are consistent with Northern state technical assistance and foreign aid programs, and certainly do not reflect any redistributive principles advocated by the NIEO or CERD documents. In this same vein, developing countries have also been forced to abandon their position that the code should state that technology is the common heritage of mankind.

As developing countries have come to realize that the emerging code is quite different than their envisaged one, the character of the negotiations has changed. Those states that already have strong and effective national legislation have slowly begun to lose interest in the code. The code legitimizes the idea of national screening and legislation, but, by 1978, states began to recognize the possibility that a legally binding code could delegitimize regulation that is more restrictive than the code, or even force states to change their national legislation in a direction that is not necessarily beneficial to recipients or recipient governments. In addition, the code is a more balanced document than most national legislation, in that it recognizes the rights and obligations of suppliers, recipients, and governments. That year, those states with existing national legislation, and chiefly and most vocally Brazil, began to move away from the legally binding position.

If the code is not legally binding, there is no reason to believe that it would provide the kind of harmony of approach and substance that Latin American states and other countries with national legislation had hoped for. The substance of national law could vary in scope, restrictiveness and enforcement, and could vary over time because of changes in economic conditions in general, political regime, or reaction of technology transferors. Thus, suppliers could still choose locales for direct foreign investment and technology transfer according to, among other criteria, type of legislation on technology transfer.

It remains to be seen whether a code, legally binding or not, would much help those states that do not have national legislation. Since there is no provision for supranational enforcement of the code, states that have not been able to pass and implement legislation because of weak governmental bureaucracies or political instability would still face enforcement problems even with a code. The emerging code's value as a model law has diminished for those states that foresee the possibility of national legislation in this area within the near future; the code is not perceived by these states to be 'tough' enough to have much effect in the alteration of the relationship between suppliers and recipients.

It should not be surprising that these reactions have produced an internal split within the Group of 77. Many Latin American states have taken more moderate positions within the past three years; they have their national legislation and now perceive that the code should be a supplement to it, a seal of approval for the idea of screening and regulation. Some African states, however, are clinging to original hard-line positions, in the hopes of formulating either a strong substitute for national law, or a credible model law. This split, and certainly the position of some African states, has produced the current stalemate in negotiations.

In truth, an exercise that produces no code might be a limited victory for those states that already have national legislation, and afford the possibility of more freedom for those that do not. The original code offered by the Group of 77 was so restrictive that it probably would have diminished investment in and technology transfer to the developing world. The code as it exists now is so 'liberal' that it might delegitimize existing national legislation and make for a weak model law. But, during the course of negotiations, Latin American states and other developing countries have convinced the North that screening and regulation of technology transfer is legitimate, if only at the national level. Because of the publicity about the negotiations, some suppliers have already changed their behavior to conform to what now appear to be acceptable standards of conduct[72]. Perhaps this is all that can be realistically expected from this type of exercise.

6.3   Emerging trends and policy recommendations

Technology transfer relations were in a period of rapid transformation during the 1970s. Politicization of the issue was very high, and Latin American international aspirations and national successes in this area threatened the US and caused conflict. But US–Latin America conflict in this area may be more a problem of the 1970s than the 1980s, as new relationships stabilize and a new equilibrium is achieved.

The most striking example of this trend is Mexico. Under Echeverría, that country was a leader in international negotiations on the NIEO, a pioneer in adopting stringent legislation on technology transfer, and one of the initiators of the international negotiations on a technology transfer code of conduct. Although the law on technology transfer remains intact, Mexico has quietly stepped down from its position as leading spokesman for a code. The Director of the Technology Registry, Jaime Alvarez, who also represented Mexico in the UNCTAD negotiations, has been replaced. Miguel Wionczek has also been removed from the government by the López Portillo regime. The trademark bill has been at least postponed. Officials in the Technology Registry now confide that they do not think that a code, particularly a binding one, would necessarily be a boon for either Mexico or Latin America, especially in the relatively balanced form resulting from international negotiations with the United States.

Moreover, the spirit of regional cooperation that once existed in Latin America when technology legislation was formulated seems to have died down. As noted earlier, pressed by economic hardship (and a change in national regime), Chile withdrew from the Andean Pact. There have been reports that enforcement of Decision 24 in some states has been relaxed because of economic problems. Argentina has repealed its law on technology transfer. 'Free market' policies have gained some popularity in some of these states. Strong states like Brazil seem to have lost interest in regional and Third World cooperation on technology transfer. For example, Brazil has evidenced doubt about continuing to support the code in a strong way, and has also refused to participate in the formation of a Third World information bank on technology under UNIDO auspices[73]. Still, some stalwarts remain, like Venezuela. In general, though, the situation in technology transfer has stabilized and interest in technology transfer has waned.

What, then, should the United States government do to take advantage of this situation, to further its aims on technology transfer, and to promote better relations with Latin America in this area?

Regarding subsequent UNCTAD code of conduct conferences, the US might want to proceed as it has in the past. It is fairly clear that a code is not against the interests of the US. If a code is ever agreed to by the North and South, its ultimate effect may be to delegitimize restrictive national legislation on technology transfer and to provide for a stable climate for investment and technology transfer abroad.

Most of the efforts of the United States to improve relations with Latin America regarding technology transfer during the 1970s met with failure. The US offered to sponsor the creation of technology information banks, to enlarge its technical assistance programs, and to transfer more non-proprietary technology to developing countries. The creation of information banks on technology, first suggested by Henry Kissinger at UNCTAD IV, was probably a good idea. In a sense, it is a 'mid-way' policy. While technical assistance programs and transfers of non-proprietary technology to developing countries are straight aid programs, and a code of conduct is a market-restructuring program, information banks combine aspects of both types of programs. Banks make information about the existence and availability of technology accessible, and would also have the effect of clarifying, and thus to a certain extent restructuring, market conditions. In the Carter administration, the US government established the machinery for the Institute for Scientific and Technological Cooperation, which would have performed this kind of function, but Congress failed to fund it.

At the UN Conference on Science and Technology for Development in 1979, the US urged developing countries to consider a 'Basic Human Needs' approach to technology transfer. That is, it contended that because of the poverty that exists in the Third World, states should focus on acquiring mid-level technology that would help their poorer citizens, rather than attempting to acquire advanced technology that would not directly alleviate mass poverty. The US took this position possibly because it wanted to diffuse some of the Conference's attention on a code of conduct on proprietary technology, and because of certain humanitarian concerns as well.

Latin American states did not respond well to this suggestion. They suspected the motives of the US in promulgating its program and have grown disillusioned with technical assistance programs of this type[74]. US policy might have been more attractive to some of the least developed states in other areas, but a policy that substitutes programs encouraging the transfer of non-proprietary and middle-level technology for a restructuring of the proprietary technology market is bound to cause further friction between the US and Latin America.

The US cannot rely on its firms' bargaining strength in Latin America. That strength was based on a combination of overall US power, the firms' high market share in many sectors, and the absence of Latin American state intervention in the transfer process. During the 1970s, the two latter conditions changed, as was detailed in this chapter. In order to ensure the continuing profitability of US firms' activities in Latin America and to protect the proprietary nature of US technology, the US government, bilaterally or multilaterally, should stress the need for national technology policies that are equitable and consistent with the goals of all parties in this area. A set of Latin American laws that do not abrogate the industrial property rights of suppliers is bound to create a more stable climate for US business abroad. This is what the US has sought in the past and it may again be obtained in the future in Latin America.

The tasks for Latin America in harnessing technology for development purposes have just begun. As should be apparent by now, a code of conduct will have more costs than benefits to those states with strong national legislation. But even an 'ideal' code and effective national regulations are not a panacea for the technology problems of Latin America. Studies of the transfer process during the 1960s and 1970s pointed to three main problems, which were discussed earlier in this chapter: the high price of imported technology, the prevalence of restrictive business practices committed by suppliers, and technological dependence. The first problem would be somewhat alleviated by screening and regulation, but in order to combat high prices more effectively, more knowledge must be gained by recipients about the technology market. Information-sharing agreements and programs will help to restructure the technology market in that they would provide information about price and alternative suppliers, thus making the market more competitive. This should help to reduce the price of technology. If the market also becomes less concentrated during the next decade, all the better. An ideal code and national legislation would help but not completely solve the second problem.

Regulation alone does not scratch the surface of the problem of technological dependence. When developing countries enacted national technology transfer legislation they were, to some extent, emulating Japan, a country that screened and regulated technology importation as early as 1949. As is well known, after importing large amounts of technology, Japan's technological capacity grew dramatically and the country now exports much technology. Using screening and regulation, developing countries hoped to achieve similar results. However, screening and regulation of suppliers was only a part of Japan's economic development program. In addition, the government drew up lists of technologies it wanted to acquire and decided in which years firms would acquire them. Only particular firms were selected by the government to be recipients of technology, with the aim of creating monopsonies in each sector to countervail against the perceived monopoly power of suppliers. As imports grew, firms switched from importing 'finished' technology to technology that was still in its innovation stage where recipients would do the necessary R & D. In addition, a wide variety of international exchange programs for managers of firms and scientists were created and government sponsored R & D took place. Finally, as the Japanese economy developed, regulation of technology importation has decreased considerably[75]. Most developing countries have not emulated Japan. They have adopted screening and regulation, but have not engaged in comprehensive government programming as a follow-up. Some states have begun to realize that more than screening and regulation is needed. In particular, Mexico and Brazil are

> ... moving toward an emphasis on strategies which directly affect the capabilities of the country to develop and utilize technology ... [T]he majority of the strategies are aimed at the underlying constraints ... that affect the application of science and technology to development. The emphasis of these strategies is on applying and using technology efficiently while at the same time furthering national goals ... [T]hese programs do not relate to the control issue, but rather to the recognized problems of applying technology effectively ...[76].

National, or even ideal international, control systems should be thought of as only a first step in building up the technological capacity of Latin America and changing the relationship between suppliers and recipients of technology. Information about alternative suppliers is also a prerequisite. Ultimately, for Latin America to reduce its technological dependence on the United States and other industrialized countries, indigenous capabilities and comprehensive science and technology policies are needed. State regulation of technology suppliers may be a necessary step, but not a sufficient one, for producing development in Latin America.

Notes

1 Cited in Ulf Anderfelt, *International Patent-Legislation and Developing Countries*. Martinus Nijhoff, The Hague, 1971, p. 173.
2 For a discussion of the role of the national bourgeoisie in influencing policy on direct foreign investment, see ch. 2 in this volume.
3 As is evidenced, for example, by the fair number of patents taken out by Argentinians and Brazilians in the United States during the past two decades. See also Ernst B. Haas, 'Technological self-reliance for Latin America: the OAS contribution'. *International Organization*, 32 (4), 1978.
4 Francis Masson and R. Hal Mason, *Latin America's Balance of Payments on Technology Transfers*. Document prepared for the Organization of American States Specialized Conference on the Application of Science and Technology to Latin American Development, 12–19 May 1972, Brasilia, Brazil, p. 8.
5 ibid., p. 6.
6 ibid.
7 UNCTAD Secretariat, *An International Code of Conduct on Technology Transfer*. United Nations, New York, 1975, UN Doc. TD/B/C/AC.1/2/Supp. 1/Rev. 1, p. 3.
8 Constantine Vaitsos, *The Process of Commercialization of Technology in the Andean Pact: A synthesis*. Lima, October 1971, Andcom Doc. J/AJ/1, p. 13.
9 See, for example, UNCTAD Secretariat, *Major issues arising from the transfer of technology to developing countries*. United Nations, New York, 1974, UN Publications, Sales No. E.75.II.D.2.
10 UNCTAD Secretariat, *The Possibility and Feasibility of an International Code of Conduct on Transfer of Technology*. United Nations, New York, UN Doc. TD/B/AC.11/Rev.1, April 1974, p. 19.
11 Vaitsos (note 8), p. 27.
12 UNCTAD Secretariat (note 10).
13 UN Economic Commission for Latin America, 'The Expansion of International Enterprises and their Influence on Development in Latin America'. In ECLA's *Economic Survey of Latin America, 1970*. United Nations, New York, 1972, p. 283.
14 Albert O. Hirschman, 'Ideologies of Economic Development in Latin America'. In his *Latin American Issues: Essays and Comments*. Twentieth Century Fund, New York, 1961, p. 16.
15 ECLA (note 13), p. 265.
16 ibid., pp. 265–6.
17 See Paul Baran, *The Political Economy of Growth*. Monthly Review Press, New York, 1968, and Andre Gundar Frank, *Capitalism and Underdevelopment in Latin America*. Monthly Review Press, New York, 1967.
18 M. A. Trevor, 'Do MNCs really transfer technology?' In Babatunde Thomas and Miguel Wionczek (eds), *Integration of Science and Technology with Development*. Pergamon, New York, 1979, p. 73.
19 Alejandro Nadal, 'Multinational Corporations and Transfer of Technology: The case of Mexico'. In *Transfer of Technology by Multinational Corporations*, Vol. 1, Development Centre of the Organization for Economic Cooperation and Development, Paris, 1977, p. 233.
20 Lynn Krieger Mytelka, *Regional Development in a Global Economy: The Multinational Corporation, Technology and Andean Integration*. Yale University Press, New Haven and London, 1979.
21 See Fernando Henrique Cardoso and Enzo Faletto, *Dependency and Development in Latin America*. University of California Press, Berkeley and Los Angeles, 1979, pp. 175–6.
22 Peter Evans, *Dependent Development: The Alliance of Multinational, State and Local Capital in Brazil*. Princeton University Press, Princeton, NJ, 1979, p. 32.
23 Hirschman (note 14) pp. 20–1.
24 The UN General Assembly adopted on 1 May 1974 the Declaration and Programme of Action of the Establishment of a New International Economic Order. G.A. Res. 3201 and 3202, S-7, GAOR, Supp. (no. 1), 3,5,UN Doc. A/9559 (1974).
25 For the contents of some of these laws see UNCTAD Secretariat, *Selected legislation, policies and practices on the transfer of technology*. UNCTAD, Geneva, 28 August 1979, UN Doc. TD/B/C.6/48.
26 David R. Thomson, 'Imported Technology and National Interests in Latin America'. A case study for the 16th Session of the Senior Seminar in Foreign Policy, US Department of State, Foreign Service Institute, 1973/74, p. 8.
27 ibid., and Eduardo White, *Control of Restrictive Business Practices in Latin America*, UNCTAD, Geneva, 1975, UN Doc. UNCTAD/ST/MD/4, pp. 86–103.

28 See the US government's memorandum of 22 June 1977 on UNCTAD Principles and Rules of RBP's written by Walter Lockwood, State Dept EB/IFD/BP.

29 White (note 27), p. 87.

30 US State Department Memorandum of 7 December 1974 on UNCTAD Document TD/B/AC.11/L.12, *Draft Code of Conduct on Technology Transfer*, p. 1.

31 Lawrence F. Ebb, 'Transfers of Foreign Technology in Latin America: The Birth of Antitrust Laws?' In Barry Hawk (ed), *Annual Proceedings of the Fordham Corporate Law Institute, International Antitrust*. Matthew Bender, New York, 1974, p. 257.

32 'Multinationals, Host Governments and Regulation of Restrictive Business Practices'. Speech by Joel Davidow, Chief, Foreign Commerce Section, Antitrust Division, US Dept. of Justice, at 17th Annual International Studies Association Convention, Toronto, Canada, 28 February 1976, pp. 7–8.

33 Joseph S. Nye, Deputy to the Undersecretary of State for Security Assistance, Science and Technology, argued this in a speech delivered in Washington, DC, on 7 December 1977.

34 Cited in Henry R. Nau, *Technology Transfer and US Foreign Policy*. Praeger, New York, 1976, p. 30.

35 ibid.

36 Robert Gilpin, *US Power and the Multinational Corporation*. Basic Books, New York, 1975, p. 139.

37 Interestingly enough, US government policies on patents are not completely consistent with other trade and investment policies, which are usually characterized by a 'free market' ideology. As early as 1957, the US recognized that there existed a fundamental tension between the US foreign policy goal of an open, competitive system, on the one hand, and US patent laws that guaranteed and legitimized the granting of monopoly rights to inventors for their intellectual endeavors, on the other. In a 1957 study by the Senate Subcommittee on Patents, Trademarks, and Copyrights entitled 'The International Patent System and Foreign Policy', it is cautioned,

> When we are convinced that a mutual interest exists in having another nation grant exclusionary rights to foreigners, we should have no hesitation in trying to persuade it to our point of view. But we must always recognize the extraordinary nature of our demands, especially as seen through the eyes of nations which view the economic domination of foreigners in their internal economy as a real possibility. This point has special force ... in dealing with the new xenophobically tinged nations which have come into existence since World War II.

85th Congress, First Session, 1957, Committee Print No. 5, p. 34.

38 For the text of the Convention and the proceedings of the negotiations leading to its agreement, see Paris Union, *Procès-Verbaux des Séances de la Conférence Internationale pour la Protection de la Propriété Industrielle*. Imprimerie Nationale, Paris, 1880. For subsequent revisions, see Anderfelt (note 1).

39 See PCT/PCD/2, WIPO/BIRPI, 16 October 1970, *Summary and Advantages of the Patent Cooperation Treaty*, World Intellectual Property Organization, Geneva, 1970, paras 5–10. The Patent Cooperation Treaty allows a patentee to file one patent application, good in all of the states in which the patentee wishes his or her patent to be in force, and provides for an international search conducted by one of several national patent offices in industrialized states designated as an international search authority by WIPO that 'tries to discover any relevant prior art'. This ensures less paperwork and strong patents because of a thorough search procedure.

40 Franz Schurmann, *The Logic of World Power: An Inquiry into the Origins, Currents, and Contradictions of World Politics*. Random House, New York, 1974, p. 48.

41 US Dept. of Commerce, 'US International Transactions in Royalties and Fees: Their Relationship to the Transfer of Technology'. *Survey of Current Business*, Government Printing Office, Washington, DC, December 1973, p. 17.

42 Jack Baranson, *The New Generation of Technology Transfer Agreements: Implications for US Economic Strength*. Developing World Industry and Technology, Washington, DC, 18 June 1976, p. 4.

43 See Gilpin (note 36).

44 This is based on interviews I conducted with State Department officials in July 1978 and October 1980. Interviewees wish to remain anonymous.

45 Robert Rothstein's view of UNCTAD is typical of the State Department's view (Rothstein was a consultant for the Department). See his *Global Bargaining: UNCTAD and the Quest for a New International Economic Order.* Princeton University Press, Princeton, NJ, 1979.

46 ibid.

47 See WIPO Secretariat reports on the meetings and negotiations of the Ad Hoc Group of Government Experts on the Revision of the Paris Convention, WIPO Doc. PR/GE/1/4 through PR/GE/1/9 (1975); PR/GE/II/2, PR/GE/II/12 (1976); PR/WG/5A/1/3, PR/WG/5A/1/4, PR/WG/5A/1/6, Rev. (1977). World Intellectual Property Organization, Geneva.

48 See the Commission on the Organization of the Government for the Conduct of Foreign Policy, Government Printing Office, Washington, DC, June 1975, Vol. 1, Appendix B, 'The Management of Global Issues', and especially the articles by Victor Basiuk and Eugene Skolnikoff (This report is known popularly as the Murphy Commission report.)

49 Business International, *Transfer of Technology: A Survey of Corporate Reaction to a Proposed Code.* Business International SA, Geneva, April 1978, pp. 42–3.

50 This was reported to me by a member of the International Group of the American Chamber of Commerce in July 1976.

51 Vaitsos (note 8), pp. 32–3.

52 Mexico National Registry, *Informe Anual de Labores de la Direccion General Del Registro Nacional de Transferencia de Technologia.* Mexico City, 1977, pp. 6–8.

53 UNCTAD Secretariat, *Legislation and Regulations on Technology Transfer: Empirical Analysis of their Effects in Selected Countries; The implementation of transfer of technology regulations: A preliminary analysis of the experience of Latin America, India and Philippines.* UNCTAD, Geneva, UN Doc. TD/B/C.6/55, 28 August 1980, p. 36.

54 Joel Bleeke and James A. Rahl, 'The Value of Territorial and Field-of-Use Restrictions in the International Licensing of Unpatented Know-How: An Empirical Study'. *Northwestern Journal of International Law and Business*, 1 (2), Autumn 1979, p. 483.

55 See Business International (note 49).

56 Richard Armstrong, 'Suddenly It's Mañana in Latin America'. *Fortune*, August 1974, p. 216.

57 White (note 27), p. 87.

58 Executive Power of the Argentine Republic, Ministry of Economy, *Law No. 21,617, Transfer of Technology Law*, Buenos Aires, p. 1.

59 Jaime Alvarez Soberanis, 'The Law on Inventions and Trademarks and the Powers Granted to the National Registry of Transfer of Technology'. Unpublished Mexican National Registry memo (no date), pp. 19–20.

60 This was reported to me by officials in the Mexican National Registry in April 1978. Interviewees wish to remain anonymous.

61 See Gilpin (note 36), p. 110.

62 UNCTAD Secretariat (note 7), p. 2.

63 ibid.; see also Jaime Alvarez Soberanis, *The Need for the Formation of an International Code of Conduct for the Transfer of Technology.* Council of the Americas, New York, 1977, p. 27.

64 For a history of initiatives for the code, see UNCTAD Secretariat (note 10), TD/B/AC.11/22 and Corr. 1, pp. 87–99.

65 Pugwash conferences on Science and World Affairs, Report of the Working Group, *Working Group on Code of Conduct on Transfer of Technology.* PWG/CODE/5, 5 April 1974, pp. 1–2.

66 See UNCTAD Secretariat, *Report of the Intergovernmental Group of Experts on an International Code of Conduct on Transfer of Technology in its Third Session (TD/AC.1/9), July 25 to August 2, 1977*, UNCTAD, Geneva, 1977.

67 Mark R. Joelson, 'The Proposed International Codes of Conduct as Related to Restrictive Business Practices'. *Law and Policy in International Business*, 8 (4), 1976, p. 873.

68 See UNCTAD Secretariat (note 66).

69 ibid.

70 As of this writing, for the latest text of the code see UNCTAD Secretariat, *Draft international code of conduct on the transfer of technology.* UNCTAD, Geneva, 6 May 1980, TD/CODE TOT/25.

71 UNCTAD Secretariat, UNCTAD V, *Restructuring the legal and juridical environment: issues under negotiation*, Items 13(a) and (b): Main policy issues, Manila, May 1979 (TD/237), p. 9.

72 Miguel Wionczek has noted this. The code negotiations have thrust the issue of corporate conduct in this area into the limelight. During the late 1970s, at least 50 conferences sponsored by various private and semi-public groups were held on the

code and national regulation. Recently, both the World Intellectual Property Organization and UNCTAD have put out licensing guides for those who wish to transfer technology to developing countries that have national legislation. The idea of regulation in this area has gained an enormous amount of legitimacy during the past seven years.

73 A UN Industrial Development Organization official reported this to me in July 1978.

74 A consultant to the US government on the UN Conference on Science and Technology for Development has found this to be particularly true for Latin America, as evidenced by his discussions with members of science and economic ministries there. Personal communication, September 1978.

75 Terutomo Ozawa, 'Technology Transfer and Contról Systems: The Japanese Experience'. Paper prepared for the International Conference on Technology Transfer Control Systems, Phase II, Seattle, 6–7 April 1979 (mimeo).

76 Robert E. Driscoll and Harvey Wallender III, 'Control and Incentives for Technology Transfer: A Multinational Perspective'. Paper prepared for the International Conference on Technology Transfer Control Systems, Seattle, 6–7 April 1979, pp. 12 –14 (mimeo).

The costs and benefits of paying more attention to Latin America

Robert L. Paarlberg*

Latin American policy seldom receives the sustained attention of top political leaders in the US. This, in the mind of some policy critics, helps to account for the various ills that are said to afflict that policy: incoherence, inconsistency, inertia, and undue influence of corporate or bureaucratic interests, at the expense of the larger national interest. The recommended cure for these ills is to assign higher priority to Latin American policy, to lift that policy out of routine bureaucratic channels, to pay more attention to Latin America.

This chapter will investigate the supposed advantage to be gained from paying more attention to Latin America. The costs and benefits will be outlined first as theory, and second as a means to interpret past experience. Tentative conclusions drawn from the past will then be checked through brief reference to a more recent case study: US policy toward Jamaica and the Caribbean in 1977–78. Notice will be taken, throughout, of the unexpected advantages to be gained from conducting US policy in its subcontinent in routine fashion, without assigning high priority.

7.1   Costs and benefits of high priority

Critics of the US foreign policy-making process do not agree upon the costs and benefits of assigning high priority to a foreign policy issue. There is a dominant belief that policy in any given area will most likely improve if that area can attract sustained high priority treatment. This common preference for high priority is particularly notable among those who have taken interest in an area of relative neglect, such as Latin America. A minority will argue the opposite view – that the benefits of high priority are uncertain, that more can be gained through low-level, routine policy management. These contending views reflect more than the two sides of a single theoretical balance sheet. Each view is sustained by a separate logic, and each supports its own distinct interpretation of the past.

The benefits of paying more attention to Latin America

There are good reasons for most critics to believe that the quality of US policy in Latin America, or anywhere, will improve when priority is

* Department of Political Science, Wellesley College, and Center for International Affairs, Harvard University.

increased. This is because there are some things that only top leaders –
perhaps only the President – can do:

- resolve differences between competing executive departments;
- reduce the influence that corporate or bureaucratic actors may exercise
  over policy conducted in routine channels;
- persuade the legislative branch and the public at large to subscribe to a
  chosen policy;
- commit financial and administrative resources to support implementation of a chosen policy;
- persuade foreign governments of US determination to achieve policy
  objectives;
- change the policy of previous presidents.

Consider each of these supposed benefits briefly.

High priority treatment resolves differences between competing executive departments

Issues that are assigned only routine priority will be handled at the cabinet
level or below, frequently by more than one executive department. These
separate departments hold 'necessarily differing perspectives', and if left
alone are likely to pursue differing policy objectives[1]. Such differences
among departments, if they are ever to be resolved, require attention and
action from above. According to this view, when separate agencies fail to
reconcile positions, 'it will be by definition an issue worthy of Presidential
decision'[2].

High priority treatment weakens the influence of parochial bureaucratic actors who would otherwise exercise undue influence over policy

Even when separate agencies agree, priority treatment may be necessary to
ensure the pursuit of national rather than bureaucratic objectives. According
to this view, any policy choice that emerges from within the bureaucracy
will be biased in favor of routinized, parochial, working-level interests.
Presidential attention may not make bureaucrats any less parochial, but it
will restrict their freedom for independent parochial action[3].

The danger of bureaucratic parochialism is particularly evident in the case
of US policy in Latin America. Within the Department of State, personnel in
the Bureau of Inter-American Affairs suffer most from high rates of repeated
'in area' assignment[4]. Inter-American Affairs, more than any other bureau
in the Department, also has a reputation for placing its own interest in
'smooth relations' with Latin America ahead of wider or more important US
foreign policy objectives. Only when top executive officials pay close
attention to US policy can the influence of these parochial bureaucrats be
weakened[5].

High priority treatment weakens the influence of corporate actors who would otherwise exercise undue influence over policy

As with parochial bureaucrats, so with private corporate actors that do business in and with Latin America. Without the watchful involvement of top-level officials, US policy in Latin America will surely fall hostage to the multitude of commercial interest groups always eager to secure official backing for their own purposes in the subcontinent. US policy in Latin America is unusually susceptible to this defect. When top leaders stop paying attention to Africa, or to China, or to South Asia, a similar problem may not arise, owing to the modest volume of commercial interaction with these more distant regions of the world. But in Latin America, large numbers of ever-present US corporate actors (often seeking an alliance with ever-present bureaucrats), will immediately fill any void left by inattentive top leaders[6].

High priority treatment builds congressional and public support for policy

This is another general rule that applies with particular force to US policy in the subcontinent. Latin America has no large or active constituency within the US political system. Without the benefits to be gained from top-level executive interest and involvement, Latin American policy initiatives that require public or congressional support might fail.

High priority treatment commits financial and administrative resources to support the implementation of a chosen policy

Without sustained leadership attention, US foreign policy in Latin America might fail to receive an adequate share of the scarce governmental resources necessary for effective implementation. These resources are committed not at random, but with great selectivity, in response to the focus of leadership attention. The President can direct administrative resources at his own discretion, either toward or away from Latin America. Likewise, to secure a commitment of financial resources, in the form of program funding or foreign assistance, active presidential endorsement is at least a necessary condition. As is often noted, US aid to Latin America first increased in response to the onset of sustained presidential attention in the late 1950s, and declined in the late 1960s when presidential attention shifted away from Latin America, toward the war in Southeast Asia.

High priority treatment secures a more favorable response from foreign governments that are the object of US policy

In the eyes of any foreign government, presidential involvement in a foreign policy action will be read as evidence of greater US determination to secure its objectives, and as evidence that resistance to those objectives is less likely to be effective. Since Latin American governments may be prone to personalize the conduct of diplomacy, they will be particularly sensitive to the vicissitudes of presidential interest or neglect. They may resent the indignity of dealing with low-level functionaries who carry little weight and enjoy little reputation within the large US foreign policy community. To ensure a more compliant response from Latin America, top-level officials, including the President, must once again involve themselves more deeply in the subcontinent.

High priority treatment permits innovation

Innovation is one final benefit attributed to high priority treatment. Bureaucratic actors, naturally concerned with secure career advancement, have little incentive to fashion innovative or creative policies. Their own familiar routines become more important than larger policy objectives, and they may fail to react to rapidly changing external circumstances[7]. By contrast, top-level officials have both the authority and the incentive to innovate. They may even employ innovation as one means to establish their authority, or to distinguish themselves from their predecessors. In all, the likelihood of innovation will increase with the involvement of high-level officials. 'Although high-level attention at an early stage is no guarantee of success,' argues Robert Pastor, 'anything less appears to guarantee the status quo'[8].

These are the supposed benefits of high priority treatment. Together they appear to make a strong logical case for 'paying more attention' to a relatively neglected region such as Latin America. This case is further strengthened when the logic of high attention is used to explain past instances of foreign policy success in the subcontinent.

An interpretation of the past

These supposed benefits of assigning higher priority to US policy in Latin America are noted in one frequently encountered interpretation of the past. During one exceptional period, critics have argued, top US foreign policy leaders did pay sustained attention to Latin America. This period, the years 1960–65, is offered as a model of how US policy can be improved when the attention of the top leadership is engaged.

During the years 1960–65, Latin American policy issues were elevated by sustained presidential attention to the status of 'high politics', a status they had not enjoyed at any previous time during the post-war period, and a status that they have not fully regained. Measurement of leadership attention remains elusive to political science, but the impression that Latin America enjoyed very high priority during this brief six-year period tends to be substantiated by a count of foreign policy questions asked at presidential news conferences that made some reference to Latin America (*Table 7.1*).

Table 7.1 *Percentage of questions at presidential news conferences that make reference to Latin America*

Year	%	Year	%
1953	0.4	1969	3.0
1959	2.0	1970	0.0
1960	10.7	1971	1.9
1961	8.1	1972	0.9
1962	10.8	1973	0.0
1963	21.9	1974	1.3
1964	9.2	1975	1.3
1965	6.5	1976	3.7
1966	2.4	1977	3.7
1967	1.2	1978	5.6
1968	2.1		

Source: Questions posed at presidential news conferences,
Public Papers of the President, US Government
Printing Office, Washington, DC, 1953,
1959–1978. Inaugural years begin and end 20
January; 1963 ends 22 November; 1965 includes
only vol. 1; and 1978 includes only January–June.

During this period of high priority treatment for Latin America, the quality of US policy is alleged to have improved in some of the respects mentioned above. First, there was diminished bureaucratic influence over policies in the subcontinent. By one account, career diplomats were reduced to 'little more than bystanders' in the process of Latin American policy formulation during the early months of the Kennedy administration. Moreover, this reduced influence lasted only so long as the attention of top leaders remained engaged. 'As the President's own concern with Latin American issues diminished,' argues Abraham Lowenthal, 'so did the influence of his personal appointees relative to that of established bureaucrats'[9].

The high priority assigned to Latin America after 1960 also seems to have diminished the influence exercised by private corporate interests over the policy-making process. In the years before 1960, when the subcontinent received very little sustained leadership attention, US policy had been conducted with much deference to the private sector[10]. Only after Latin issues began to attract large quantities of leadership attention did commercial actors and interests begin to lose some of their influence. In 1961, for example, the Alliance for Progress was launched despite mistrust from the private sector. 'I cannot recall that businessmen played any role in the formulation of the Alliance,' says Arthur M. Schlesinger, Jr[11]. 'Far from reflecting big business determination of US foreign policy,' argues Lowenthal, 'the Alliance for Progress commitment emerged in part because of the unusual (and temporary) reduction of corporate influence in the foreign policy making process'[12].

The influence of private corporate interests in the subcontinent was eventually restored, but only after the priority assigned to Latin America had declined. According to Richard J. Bloomfield, 'once the threat of Castro-like upheavals in the hemisphere subsided and political attention in the US shifted to other areas, like Vietnam and the Middle East, the special interests began to eat up the Alliance like mice attacking cheese'[13].

An increased commitment of financial and administrative resources – specifically foreign aid – also followed from the 1960–65 increase in leadership attention. For more than a decade, Latin Americans had been calling for their own 'Marshall Plan', to no avail. Beyond the formation of a poorly funded Inter-American Development Bank, annual aid levels for the entire subcontinent remained well below $500 million until 1960. Only after leadership attention was engaged did US assistance grow to reach significant proportions. In the 1961 financial year, US loans and grants to Latin America more than doubled to reach $1.1 billion, and President Kennedy pledged a total of $20 billion in US aid before the end of the decade. Well before the end of the decade, however, leadership attention drifted away from Latin America, and so Alliance funding was never sustained at the promised level.

In addition, high priority treatment for Latin America is credited with having introduced a healthy measure of innovation into US policy in the subcontinent. After more than a decade of catering to Latin governments on the basis of investment climate or Cold War orientation, the US suddenly, in 1961, enunciated a favorable attitude toward the social and economic aspirations of Latin American regimes on the 'democratic left', and announced a policy of non-recognition toward governments established by military coup d'état. This new orientation was made possible by the involvement of the White House; it 'could never have come out of the State Department that Kennedy inherited from Eisenhower'[14]. Predictably, when presidential interest in Latin America later declined, these more innovative social and political aspects of US policy received reduced emphasis, and were implemented with less energy.

According to this rather conventional view of the past, assigning higher priority to Latin America was the key to improving the quality of US policy in the subcontinent. That policy, which had begun to meet repeated failure after more than a decade of presidential neglect, was redirected, and reinvigorated, by increased leadership interest and involvement. Then, following the Kennedy assassination and Johnson's growing preoccupation with Vietnam, Latin American issues lost priority once more. The result was a return to the purposes, the perspectives, and the policies of the earlier period. According to this view, so long as Latin America remains a low priority concern on the leadership agenda, the substance of US policy will remain captive of narrow corporate and bureaucratic interests, and will be crippled by inconsistency, incoherence, and inertia.

The costs of paying more attention to Latin America

A contrasting view can also be developed, one that sees costs that outweigh the benefits of paying more attention to Latin America. This alternative view is less familiar and less well formulated, but it may also be outlined, first as a series of general propositions, and then as a means to interpret past experience.

Upon reflection, a number of things can go wrong when policy decisions are taken at the highest levels of the government:

- banishment of expertise as top-level generalists take control of policy;
- improper linkage of unrelated issues on the leadership agenda;
- excessive intrusion of partisan or electoral politics into foreign policy;
- loss of executive branch control over policy management;
- damage done by subsequent loss of issue priority, and disengagement of leadership attention.

Consider each of these costs briefly.

Banishment of expertise

One cost of assigning high priority to any foreign policy issue is the 'banishment of expertise', which occurs whenever top-level generalists begin to replace low-level specialists around the decision table[15]. Foreign policy actions that are guided by officials at the highest level of the government, by political leaders and policy generalists, are less likely to be well informed.

Improper issue linkage

A second cost to anticipate when elevating the priority of any foreign policy issue is the likelihood of improper issue linkage. When unrelated issues happen to reach the President's agenda simultaneously, they run a much greater risk of being improperly considered in tight relation to one another[16]. One illustration might be the tight linkage that President Johnson drew, in April 1965, between US interests in the Dominican Republic and in Vietnam. Because these two diverse concerns came to the top of Johnson's agenda at the same time, they became excessively intertwined. (Johnson's decision to send troops to Santo Domingo was actually taken during a White House meeting that had been called to review the situation in Vietnam.) Johnson's later justification for the Dominican intervention was suggestive of this improper linkage: 'What can we do in Vietnam,' he said, 'if we can't clean up the Dominican Republic?'[17]

Excessive intrusion of partisan or electoral politics

Yet another cost of assigning high priority to a foreign policy issue derives from the frequent preoccupation of top leaders with partisan or electoral politics. Foreign policy decisions that are handled within the bureaucracy on a routine basis are often well insulated from short-run domestic political calculation. This insulation breaks down at the higher levels of the government, where issues are more often held hostage to purely partisan concerns.

Loss of executive branch control

Also, rather than imposing greater coherence or control on policy, priority treatment can produce quite the opposite effect. An issue assigned very high priority can seldom be contained within the executive branch of the government. Once an issue has escaped the executive branch, of course, presidential power to impose coherence or consistency on policy is greatly reduced: '...[T]he pattern emerges of a President who can make decisions within the executive branch on matters kept out of sight of Congress or the voters ... If the issue escapes the bounds of the executive branch, the process of bargaining begins'[18]. Any president seeking to gain control over policy by paying more attention actually runs a risk of losing control. He may inadvertently initiate a process of uncontrolled bargaining, in which aggrieved bureaucrats can resist a presidential decision by forming alliances with newly involved legislators, or newly attentive publics.

The inevitable disengagement of leadership attention

High priority treatment has yet another drawback: it can seldom be sustained. Some issues may be managed temporarily by top officials, but they will sooner or later be returned to the jurisdiction of career bureaucrats. Top officials will either be honestly distracted (by even larger concerns), or they will simply despair of quick success and lose interest. Issues that are forever gaining and then losing priority in this fashion will suffer from the familiar syndrome of aborted initiatives and broken promises.

These are costs that must be paid when any foreign policy issue receives high priority treatment. There are several specific features of US policy in Latin America, however, that may compound these costs of high priority treatment. First, US policy in Latin America can suffer when top leaders, as is their wont, seek to impose a single-minded sense of 'consistency' upon that policy. In the absence of a compelling security threat, US interests in Latin America will be impossible to arrange according to any single, agreed-upon formula of objectives. Many diverse and seemingly contradictory low-level goals must be pursued simultaneously. Top-level managers do not adapt well to such a task, which is perhaps a job for many low-level bureaucrats, loyal to diverse agency missions.

Second, top-level managers are likely to get involved in Latin American policy only when they sense that politico-military interests are somehow threatened. Or, once involved, they will then subordinate enduring social and economic interests in Latin America to often unfounded fears of ideological or security threat. This long-standing leadership preference for security concerns may be appropriate when dealing with East–West issues, with the Far East, with Africa, or with the Middle East, but it seldom suits the distribution of US interests in Latin America. Inevitably, Cubans in Nicaragua will receive more leadership attention than oil in Mexico, or manufactured imports from Brazil.

Finally, the opportunity cost of paying more attention to Latin America is especially prohibitive. In relation to other regions of the world, Latin America has lost importance since World War II[19]. In order to assign higher priority to Latin America today, foreign policy leaders would have to assign lower priority to other areas of the world, where the political, military, and economic interests of the US are under an even more visible strain. Alternatively, these same top leaders would have to assign lower priority to domestic policy issues. In neither case does Latin America emerge as the most worthy object of concern[20]. Not surprisingly, those who argue for more attention to Latin America, predominantly Latin Americans and Latin Americanists, do not bear the cost of diminished attention to other regions or to other issues.

Those who argue the case for 'routine treatment' of Latin America may concede that one supposed benefit does flow from an increase in issue priority: increased commitment of resources to support the implementation of policy. But this supposed benefit may be transformed into a serious cost if such resources are committed to a policy that has been earlier damaged by high priority treatment. The worst of two worlds may result: a policy that is *vigorously* misdirected.

This more pessimistic alternative view of what can happen when top leaders assign high priority to Latin America supports a very different interpretation of the past. The 1960–65 period of leadership interest in Latin America is viewed, from this second perspective, as a period of great risk, serious error, and unnecessary difficulty for US policy in the subcontinent.

A reinterpretation of the past

Reconsidering the 1960–65 period, the various costs associated with high priority treatment do appear to have increased alongside the benefits. First, it is clear that high priority policies toward Latin America did suffer from a considerable 'banishment of expertise'. Those who formulated the new US economic policies in the subcontinent during this period were not Latin Americanists. Both C. Douglas Dillon (under Eisenhower) and Lincoln Gordon (under Kennedy) were relative newcomers to Latin American policy. As veterans of the Marshall Plan, they were both inclined to hold an exaggerated view of what economic aid to Latin America could accomplish. These top planners found themselves under such pressure from the White House to work quickly, that their initial plans had to be built upon an inadequate base of economic data[21]. Still more telling was the scant knowledge of Latin American political realities that accompanied policy-making at the highest levels of the government. Top leaders decided in 1961 to build US policy upon the strength of an 'emerging democratic left' in Latin America. A succession of military takeovers in a half dozen key Latin American countries in 1962 and 1963 soon made a mockery of this leadership vision. It seems that Kennedy's belief in an emerging democratic left in Latin America was formed, in part, through the advice he received from Richard Goodwin, remembered by associates as quite the opposite of an expert[22]. Much of Goodwin's early knowledge of Latin American politics came from 'his friends among Latin American democratic exiles in Washington'[23]. It is perhaps understandable that professionals in the State Department 'mostly disdained the Alliance as a fantasy dreamed up by amateurs'[24].

High priority treatment for Latin America also linked US policy there to distant and weakly related priority concerns elsewhere. In early 1961, for example, US policy toward Cuba became linked, in Kennedy's mind, with US policy in Laos. During deliberations prior to the Bay of Pigs, according to one participant, 'Laos and Cuba were tied up with each other,' so that 'it was hard to know how one would affect the other'[25]. This dubious linkage between Latin America and Southeast Asia distorted policy at both ends. When the invasion plan failed in Cuba, Kennedy is said to have observed that 'because of the Bay of Pigs ... now we have a problem in trying to make our power credible, and Vietnam looks like the place'[26]. The link that later formed in Johnson's mind between Vietnam and the Dominican Republic has already been mentioned.

US policy in Latin America also suffered during this period from excessive exposure to partisan politics. Both of the major Latin American policy themes of the Kennedy administration – the Alliance for Progress and hostility to Castro's Cuba – emerged from promises made during the 1960 presidential campaign. Hostility to Cuba proved to be the more popular of the two, and came quickly to dominate US purposes throughout the subcontinent. Subsequently, during the Dominican crisis, it seems that Lyndon Johnson's fear of 'another Cuba on our doorstep' was more political than geopolitical in nature[27].

It can hardly be said that high priority treatment during this period introduced consistency into US policy in Latin America. A simultaneous pursuit of many divergent objectives continued throughout the 1960–65 period, only at a much higher level of energy. The Kennedy administration, from its first months in office, was in pursuit of two very different high priority policies at the same time: on the one hand, in a progressive vein, the reformist programs of the Alliance for Progress, and on the other hand, out of a very different mold, stepped-up efforts at counter-insurgency, covert intervention, and anti-Castroite paramilitary action. Throughout this period, overt US support for Latin leaders on the 'democratic left' was counterbalanced and often nullified by covert political action against leftist elements, or by support and training for military officers and police on the extreme right.

High priority treatment for Latin America during this period may have also contributed ultimately to a loss of executive control over policy. Having stimulated intense congressional interest in Latin American economic policy with his Alliance aid request, the President found himself accepting an unwanted aid termination provision in the form of the 1962 Hickenlooper Amendment. This same amendment tends to underscore another lesson: that private corporate influence over US policy in Latin America is not necessarily weakened by high priority treatment. Despite the modest role played by business interests in the early formulation of the Alliance, official support for corporate activities in the subcontinent was not demonstrably reduced in the implementation phase. Quite the opposite. With the Hicken-looper Amendment in place, the Alliance actually became a formidable instrument for investment protection, as increased US aid now only added to the anticipated pain of a mandatory aid cut-off. What is more, to protect itself from other congressional restrictions on its 'freedom of action', the executive branch began yielding to business interests. In 1963, US economic aid to Peru was cut off by the State Department in the mere anticipation of congressional displeasure over possible Peruvian actions against US investment[28].

High priority treatment for Latin America failed to weaken corporate influence in part because economic policy was not the primary focus of leadership concern. Top leaders in the executive branch were concerned, most of all, with eliminating the perceived security threat posed by Cuban communism. As a second order concern, economic policy came to be viewed as an adjunct to politico-military purposes, and as expendable for those purposes.

So a reinterpretation of the past indicates that high priority during the period 1960–65 did not significantly improve the quality or ensure the success of US policy in the subcontinent. We may reach this conclusion even if we view that policy entirely on its own terms. Neither of the two most clearly stated leadership objectives in Latin America – liberal reform together with the elimination of Castro's communist regime in Cuba – had been achieved by the time Latin America had lost its high priority status in 1965. In some respects, these six years of very high priority for Latin America had only amplified some of the more disagreeable or contradictory aspects of US policy in the subcontinent, at higher levels of cost and risk.

We are left, then, with contrasting prescriptions for US policy in Latin America. On the one hand, it is traditionally held that numerous benefits will derive from assigning higher priority to the hemisphere. Yet a reinterpretation indicates that paying more attention to Latin America may produce costs that outweigh the benefits. It is necessary at this point to move beyond these two rigid lines of argument. A prescription must be found that secures most of the benefits while containing most of the costs attributed to both high and low priority policy-making processes. Such a prescription will emerge during a brief review of a more recent policy-making case study – US policy in 1977 and 1978 toward Jamaica and the Caribbean.

7.2   The blessings of routine treatment: US policy toward Jamaica and the Caribbean, 1977–78

Bringing our perspective somewhat closer to the present, Latin America remained a foreign policy backwater for a decade after 1965, the year when the US military intervention in the Dominican Republic was completed. Lyndon Johnson's subsequent policy effort in 1967 to promote economic regionalism in the subcontinent was never more than a minor diversion from his deepening preoccupation with Vietnam[29]. Nixon made a *conscious* decision, in his first year in office, to pay little attention to Latin America – once again in favor of policy in Vietnam and relations with the communist world. When Nixon's Vietnam preoccupation finally came to an end in 1973, the vacant space on his foreign policy agenda was then filled by the Middle East. Despite Henry Kissinger's abortive effort, late in 1973, to launch a 'New Dialogue' with Latin America, policy in the subcontinent continued to receive only routine priority under both Nixon and Ford. This low leadership interest is indirectly reflected in the virtual absence of Latin American policy questions posed at presidential press conferences prior to 1976.

One Latin American policy issue did re-emerge during the 1976 election campaign as an object of keen presidential interest: the future status of the Panama Canal. Indeed, the Canal issue, together with a growing concern over Cuban troops in Africa, marked 1976 as a year of modestly renewed priority interest in the subcontinent. The Carter election then set the stage for what might have been a further revival of leadership concern for Latin America. Latin America was the only part of the world where Carter had done any significant travelling, and early in 1977 the new President told the Organization of American States (OAS), 'My heart and my interests to a major degree are in Latin America'. It appeared to some that Carter, like Kennedy 16 years earlier, was coming into office with an inclination to 'pay more attention to Latin America', and thus to repair the damage done by eight long years of Republican 'neglect'.

During his first two years in office, the period to be examined here, most of President Carter's attention to Latin America was actually focused upon Senate ratification of the Canal Treaties with Panama. The President also devoted bits of his time to a faltering effort to improve relations with Cuba, to human rights and reactor sales in Brazil, to a then emerging political crisis in Nicaragua, and to border relations and energy policy with Mexico. It would fall beyond the scope of this chapter to reconstruct the priority that President Carter assigned to each of these Latin American policy issues. Only US policy toward Jamaica and the Caribbean in 1977–78 is to be considered here. Carter administration sponsorship of a Caribbean Group for regional economic cooperation, together with renewed assistance for democratic socialism in the critical Caribbean island nation of Jamaica, were only a very small component of that administration's policy, and of modern US economic relations with Latin America. But they may nonetheless serve as a useful case study, to the degree that they illustrate the advantages to be gained today from assigning only routine priority to some kinds of Latin American policy issues.

US policy toward Jamaica and the Caribbean provides a useful glimpse at several important features of the contemporary Latin American policy-making process. First, the possibility of undue corporate influence over US policy in this region is very real, since the Caribbean basin presently contains more than \$4.3 billion in US direct investment – \$1 billion in Jamaica alone. The Overseas Private Investment Corporation (OPIC) has had its largest exposure in the world in Jamaica. Jamaica also supplies the US with more than half of its bauxite imports, and the US aluminum industry (led by Kaiser Aluminum, which still depends upon Jamaica for 70% of its bauxite) is highly sensitive to the politics of US–Jamaican relations. US policy in Jamaica and the Caribbean is also of interest because so many different agencies of the government are sure to be involved: the Treasury Department (EXIM credit ratings), the Department of Agriculture (sugar policy), the Civil Aeronautics Board (airline routes), and the International Trade Commission (trade issues), as well as the State Department, Defense, and CIA. The risk of an inconsistent or an incoherent US policy is thus very real. Third, it is of interest that several US policy objectives were in conflict in Jamaica and the Caribbean in 1977–78. Jamaica, since independence, has preserved its inherited tradition of press freedom and parliamentary democracy. Yet, during the period considered here, the Manley government in Jamaica pursued a socialist path to economic development, called upon the US to radically restructure its relations with the non-industrial world, and endorsed the policies of its Marxist neighbor, Cuba. Jamaica thus presented the US with an important litmus test of Latin American policy priorities. US hostility toward the Manley government would have been seen as reminiscent of US hostility toward democratic socialism in Allende's Chile, as a step away from the vigorous promotion of Latin American democracy, and as a rejection of one additional means to bridge diplomatic gaps between the US and Cuba.

Finally, Jamaica and the Caribbean are inviting case studies because of an impression, easily gained, that earlier patterns of US attention and neglect toward Latin America were repeating themselves in 1977–78. During its first year, the Carter administration appeared to be launching an ambitious and innovative Caribbean policy – not only a policy of regional cooperation and economic assistance to the Caribbean as a whole, but a policy of financial endorsement for democratic socialism in Jamaica in particular. This new policy seemed a significant break from the immediate past, and appeared to derive its energetic and innovative quality from high priority treatment, from direct presidential involvement in the policy-making process. When this new policy then began to encounter funding difficulties, late in 1977 and early in 1978, a lapse in presidential interest seemed the most obvious explanation. The view that sustained leadership interest would be essential to the improvement of US policy in Latin America was apparently confirmed.

In fact, as will be seen, the new US policy toward Jamaica and the Caribbean emerged under conditions of routine priority, without a large increase in presidential attention. Important policy changes were made through bureaucratic initiative. Moreover, when the President did focus bits of his attention on Jamaica and on the Caribbean, in 1977–78, the effect was not to energize so much as to constrain policy. In all, routine priority treatment yielded a US policy toward Jamaica and the Caribbean that steered neatly between two dangerous extremes: inflexible hostility on the one hand, and an overcommitment of bilateral assistance on the other.

To reach these and other conclusions, US policy toward Jamaica and the Caribbean in 1977–78 will first be described as a chronological sequence of actions taken at various levels and at various locations within the US foreign policy community[30]. Once the policy-making process has been described, the costs and benefits of routine priority treatment can be systematically assessed.

US policy toward Jamaica before 1977

When the Carter administration came to power in January 1977, both the US and Jamaican governments were seeking ways to end a difficult diplomatic impasse, which had been marked by escalating levels of acrimony and mutual disaffection. US–Jamaican relations had cooled following the 1972 election victory of Prime Minister Michael Manley's People's National Party (PNP). During the Jamaican election campaign, the US ambassador in Kingston, Vincent W. de Roulet, antagonized Manley by encouraging the Alcoa aluminum company to make an illegal contribution to the incumbent

Jamaican Labor Party (JLP). After the PNP victory, Ambassador de Roulet was declared *persona non grata*[31].

Soon thereafter, in 1973, Manley gave emphasis to his independent diplomatic style by flying to the conference of non-aligned states in Algiers with Fidel Castro in Fidel's private plane. Then in January 1974, Manley demanded renegotiation of existing contracts with the US-owned bauxite industry in Jamaica. Early talks failed when the industry refused a sharp tax increase. Manley then broke off negotiations and raised the bauxite levy unilaterally, by nearly 700%, with further increases scheduled for 1975 and 1976. All the while, Manley moved closer to Cuba. While on a state visit to Havana in 1975, he proclaimed, 'I walk hand in hand with Fidel Castro to lead our people to a common destiny'.

The US government did not hesitate to signal its disapproval of these developments in Jamaica. During the final days of the Nixon administration, the US suspended all new assistance to Jamaica, and put a stop on one Agency for International Development (AID) loan that had already been appropriated[32]. This aid 'embargo' was to remain in place for the next two years. Additional OPIC insurance in Jamaica was also terminated, pending settlement of the bauxite levy dispute.

US policy toward Jamaica remained essentially unchanged through the final months of the Ford administration. The Carter administration was later to take credit for modifying that policy (lifting of the aid embargo) and for the dramatic improvement in relations that followed. Yet the way for this policy change was prepared late in 1976, before Carter took office, by an important sequence of developments in Jamaica itself. In October 1976, Jamaica finally negotiated a satisfactory participation agreement with Alcoa (the largest of the US aluminum companies in Jamaica)[33], and the previously interrupted AID loan was reinstated, though the embargo on new lending remained in effect. Then in December, Prime Minister Manley won a decisive re-election victory. His PNP won 47 seats in the enlarged lower house, while the opposition JLP dropped to an all-time low 13 seats[34]. With the election behind him, Manley could now assume a far more flexible position toward the US. His frequent accusations that the CIA was seeking to destabilize his government were conspicuously discontinued, and he expressed hope that a new administration in Washington would open the way for reconciliation.

Manley's more flexible attitude was made necessary by the deepening distress of Jamaica's economy. Democratic socialism had proven costly and disruptive. Sharp wage increases had reduced competitiveness, and Jamaica's overall balance of payments deficit had grown from $82 million in 1975 to $268 million by 1976, despite expensive government subsidies for major export industries. These subsidies, on top of expensive efforts to reduce an unemployment rate running well above 20%, produced fiscal deficits as high as 18.5% of GDP. Price controls, designed to hold down inflation,

encouraged a rapid increase in consumption, accompanied by falling investment ratios, capital flight, and, finally, deep recession. In 1976, Jamaica's
real GDP *declined* by nearly 7%. Efforts at monetary restraint, tax
increases, and even devaluation, were inadequately implemented, and
overwhelmed by continuing fiscal expansion. The $102 million growth in
bauxite tax revenues between 1973 and 1975 was more than offset by a
simultaneous $129 million growth in oil import costs[35]. Late in December
1976, when gross official reserves fell to two weeks' worth of imports, the
foreign exchange market had to be closed altogether.

Manley was forced by this economic calamity to turn Jamaica back
toward the US and toward western financial institutions in search of
emergency balance of payments assistance. Even a very modest offer of
quick disbursing aid, at this point, could be enough to improve the badly
damaged state of US–Jamaican relations.

Launching a new US aid policy toward Jamaica

This opportunity to improve US–Jamaican relations was recognized and
seized upon by the Bureau of Inter-American Affairs, and by AID, within
the State Department. Immediately after the Carter inauguration, these
bureaucratic actors put forward a recommendation that the US provide the
Manley government with $31.5 million in Security Supporting Assistance
(SSA), quick disbursing aid that was well suited to Jamaica's immediate
problem – maintaining its needed level of imports[36].

Carter's top-level foreign policy team had not yet formulated a policy
toward Jamaica. Having criticized the US policy of 'destabilizing' democratic socialism in Chile, Carter was presumed to have at least an open mind
toward democratic socialism in Jamaica. Improved relations with Jamaica
might even be of some use in the effort then being launched within the new
Carter administration to build bridges of contact and communication with
Cuba. It was also significant that Michael Manley enjoyed a unique personal
tie to Carter's political entourage and to the Carter family: United Nations
Ambassador Andrew Young considered Manley a personal friend, and Mrs
Manley had at one time stayed with the Carter family while on a visit to
Atlanta.

Nevertheless, the Carter White House hesitated to approve large quantities of quick disbursing aid for Jamaica. The White House feared that any
bilateral balance of payments 'bail out' for Jamaica, even on a modest scale,
would entrap the new administration in an 'assistance–dependence' relationship of the kind it deemed no longer appropriate to modern US
economic relations with Latin America. The Carter White House was
actually looking forward to the day when the few bilateral aid projects left
over from the Alliance era could be terminated. This attitude grew out of a
belief that some in the Congress would use bilateral aid programs as a means

to attach undesirable political and economic conditions onto US policy in the subcontinent. Thus, early in February, the White House decided to ask Congress for only $10 million in immediate aid to Jamaica, just enough to signal some support for the Manley government, but not enough to constitute a US commitment to rescue Jamaica's troubled economy.

Even though the White House remained cautious and distant during the first months of 1977, those in the State Department anxious to improve bilateral relations and those in AID eager to launch a new development project, continued to think in more ambitious terms. On 3 March, Jamaica's Foreign Minister, Percival J. Patterson, met with Secretary Vance at the State Department, expressed his hopes that US–Jamaican relations might improve, and mentioned Jamaica's interest in economic assistance. Vance agreed that a joint technical committee should be formed to study Jamaica's needs. He then accepted Patterson's invitation to visit Jamaica 'at the earliest possible opportunity', and even promised to try to arrange a meeting between Manley and Carter at a mutually convenient date. Within a month, having received and accepted Jamaica's 'terms of reference' for the joint study effort, the Assistant Secretary of State for Inter-American Affairs, Terence A. Todman, requested that Deputy Assistant AID Administrator Donor M. Lion lead the first US study team to Jamaica. At this point, Lion foresaw 'a multi-year assistance effort' involving PL 480 Title I ('Food for Peace' food aid), Security Supporting Assistance, and Housing Investment Guarantees, as well as development loans and grants. His study team travelled to Jamaica in late April, followed up by a technical team in early May.

State Department and AID enthusiasm for an expanded aid effort in Jamaica continued to build during the month of May. Mr William Luers, former acting Assistant Secretary of State for Inter-American Affairs, who participated in the study effort, announced publicly upon his return to the US that 'There is no country that qualifies more for US aid than Jamaica'. He told the Black Forum in Washington that it was 'time we got on with the job of improving relations with Jamaica'[37].

The White House was no less anxious to improve US relations with Jamaica, but remained skeptical of bilateral aid as the instrument best suited to that purpose. In June, while both Secretary Vance and Assistant Secretary Todman were publicly endorsing more financial aid to Jamaica, Rosalyn Carter's Latin American tour took her to Kingston, where she left Manley with no explicit pledge on aid, only an invitation to pay an 'informal' return visit to Washington later in the year. This was less than Manley had hoped for, particularly since he had agreed to lift a state of emergency and to release 17 opposition political detainees just before the First Lady arrived[38].

White House anxieties about the likely congressional response to an expanded Jamaican aid project proved well founded. Even the much-reduced $10 million request for emergency Security Supporting Assistance to Jamaica, when it came up for approval in June, provoked a hostile reaction from conservative ranks in the Senate. Senator Orrin G. Hatch (R–Utah) introduced an amendment on the floor to delete all assistance to Jamaica. Hatch, who was supported in floor debate by Senators Helms, Curtis, and Randolph, argued that the US ought not to support Manley, because he had become 'a logical extension of Cuba'[39]. Senators Case, Javits, and Humphrey defended Jamaican aid, but without adequate preparation and with a clear lack of conviction. They sensed confusion within the executive branch and had expressed puzzlement over the request in their Committee Report on the bill[40]. The Hatch Amendment was defeated, 30–57, but congressional doubts and opposition to expanded Jamaican aid had been demonstrated.

One important group that did not raise significant opposition to an expanded Jamaican aid program was the US aluminum industry. By June 1977, almost all of the large US companies taking bauxite and alumina out of Jamaica – including Kaiser, Alcoa, Reynolds, and Anaconda – were learning to live with the Manley government. After the agreement signed with Alcoa in October 1976, Manley had gone on to sign an equally generous participation agreement with the industry leader, Kaiser Aluminum, in early February 1977. Under the terms of this agreement, Kaiser would sell to the government of Jamaica, at book value, 51% of its mining assets, as well as its extensive bauxite lands, resettlement lands, and other property not required for plant operation. In return, Kaiser obtained a mining lease for adequate supplies of bauxite (sufficient to operate two Louisiana aluminum plants for the next 40 years), and a reduction of the bauxite levy from 8% to a maximum 7.5% through 1983. As evidence of its satisfaction with this arrangement, Kaiser dropped its proceedings against the government of Jamaica before the Center for the Settlement of Investment Disputes[41]. In March, Jamaica signed a similar agreement with Reynolds. *Business Latin America* viewed this series of participation agreements as 'one more positive sign' that the Manley government was now ready to deal responsibly with US investors[42].

Under these new conditions, the US aluminum industry was quite willing to see certain kinds of US economic assistance reach the Manley government. Project aid to improve Jamaica's deficient industrial infrastructure was viewed most favorably by these companies, which now believed that they would be remaining in Jamaica for some time to come. The US aluminum industry had long since taken care to cut back on its own new investments in Jamaica, as well as on procurement of Jamaican bauxite[43]. But, if the US government wished to pay the bill, there would be no serious objection to a lifting of the aid embargo[44].

Persistent State Department efforts to secure presidential approval for a substantial economic aid package finally bore fruit in July. The President approved $63.3 million in aid for Jamaica as soon as he learned that Jamaica had reached a two-year standby loan agreement with the IMF. The Treasury Department had insisted upon this linkage between US aid and an IMF loan. Once the loan was secured, added assistance in several forms simultaneously became available, including an unusual $30 million World Bank balance of payments loan, as well as smaller loans from Venezuela, OPEC, and the EEC. Moreover, the US EXIM Bank agreed, following the IMF deal, to review Jamaica's 'D' credit rating[45].

Caribbean policy overtakes aid to Jamaica

In retrospect, President Carter's approval of the $63.3 million Jamaican aid package in late July represents the high water mark of State Department influence over US policy toward Jamaica. From that point forward the hopes of the State Department for a generous bilateral aid policy toward the Manley government met increased resistance, primarily on substantive grounds from the National Security Council (NSC), and on budgetary grounds from the Office of Management and Budget (OMB).

This resistance was first manifest in a White House decision to postpone the public announcement of the $63.3 million aid package, in view of a visit that Fidel Castro paid to Jamaica in October 1977. The White House, which had become increasingly concerned with the growing presence of Cuban troops in Africa, decided that it would be inappropriate to announce the assistance package at the very moment that Manley was reaffirming his ties to Havana. The announcement was postponed until November.

More important than this, the efforts of the State Department to expand bilateral aid to Jamaica were being overtaken in the summer of 1977 by a separate policy initiative, one that the White House momentarily came to view as more nearly its own. This was a Caribbean policy initiative, based more upon a vision of multilateral 'regionalism' than upon bilateral relations with individual Caribbean nations. This Caribbean policy emerged from more than one location within the foreign policy community. Indeed, one of those with a strong claim to authorship was not even a member of the administration. Representative Dante Fascell (D–Fla), a member of the House International Relations Committee and chairman of the Subcommittee on International Operations, had been speaking in support of a new policy for the Caribbean region since 1973. Fascell was active during the Carter transition period, pressing Vance and others to endorse regionalism on America's 'third frontier'. A parallel impetus to place Caribbean assistance into a 'regional' context came from the Senate, recalling the June 1977 Foreign Relations Committee report to that effect. Multilateral institutions and procedures were also strongly favored by the NSC, which was seeking to move US policy in Latin America beyond the bilateral assistance –dependence syndrome of the past. Finally, it was significant that the new Assistant Secretary of State for Latin America, Terence Todman, had been born in the Virgin Islands and was particularly knowledgeable on the Caribbean region. This combination of favorable circumstances led to the creation of a Caribbean Task Force within the State Department by the middle of 1977. The recommendations of this task force reached the White House by early September.

The President's review of Caribbean policy options produced a decision in early September to approach the region primarily through multilateral channels. Simply on the merits of the case, there seemed no other sensible way to deal with the 25 or more separate entities, spread among hundreds of separate Caribbean islands, few of which could hope for economic or political viability except in cooperation with the rest. To encourage such cooperation, the President decided that the economic assistance that was already coming to the region from many separate donors should be coordinated and channeled through common facilities (including international financial institutions already operating in the region, such as the World Bank, the Inter-American Development Bank, and the Caribbean Development Bank). This aid should also be disbursed contingent upon consultation and cooperation among recipients. The institutional vehicle for this new Caribbean policy was to be the Caribbean Group for Cooperation and Economic Development (CGCED), an entity launched under World Bank chairmanship at an international conference held in Washington, DC, 14–15 December 1977[46].

The President's new Caribbean policy created momentary problems for some within the State Department. First, this multilateral Caribbean initiative complicated the task of managing bilateral relations with Jamaica. Prime Minister Manley had expressed a total disinterest in Caribbean 'regionalism'. The thought that aid to Jamaica would now be contingent upon coordination and cooperation with lesser Caribbean neighbors was unwelcome to Manley, who stated as much in a personal letter to Carter late in the year. As if to make his feelings on the matter clear, Manley then presented Carter, in December 1977, with an unacceptable request – that Cuba be welcomed into the new Caribbean Group, to receive assistance along with Jamaica. In the end, Manley's resistance did bring some reward. Jamaica bargained to establish a special 'sub-group' within the CGCED, which would allow it to use CGCED funds without real obligation to coordinate policies with neighbors in the region. This was only a small victory for Jamaica, however, as it soon became clear that the President did not consider his new Caribbean policy to be the occasion for any further increase in US assistance to the region.

Clarification of White House priorities

It had finally come down to money. The bilateral and multilateral assistance policies, which were developing somewhat at cross purposes in late 1977, ran into this common obstacle. The President refused to recommend any major new funding initiative in the Caribbean, be it a bilateral bail-out for Jamaica, or a multilateral, multi-donor 'Marshall Plan' for the Caribbean as a whole.

Between September and December 1977, following the routine of the annual budget cycle, assistance policies toward Jamaica and the Caribbean finally came under the scrutiny of the Office of Management and Budget. The full cost of pursuing these policies was assessed for the first time, and weighed for the first time against competing claims on the federal budget. Proposals from the State Department and the Agency for International Development for expanded assistance to Jamaica and the Caribbean in the financial year of 1979 were cut sharply. AID and State recommended another $10 million SSA for Jamaica, and a $123 million economic aid package, not including PL 480, for the Caribbean as a whole. OMB rejected *all* SSA for Jamaica and cut the Caribbean economic aid request back to $87 million. The economic aid request for Jamaica alone in the financial year of 1979, including PL 480, was cut back to $46.8 million, well below the $63.3 million total of the previous year. The President upheld these OMB cuts, despite appeals from the State Department.

The combined effect of these OMB cutbacks on US policy was clearly visible by mid-December. The US delegation to the World Bank Conference on the Caribbean was instructed to back-pedal, not to promise expanded US financial commitments to the new Caribbean Group. Likewise, when Prime Minister Manley arrived in Washington for his long-scheduled informal visit with President Carter, the atmosphere was cooled somewhat by knowledge on both sides that US bilateral assistance programs in Jamaica would not continue to expand.

The State Department was greatly disappointed by this turn of events. It had considered its aid plans for Jamaica and for the Caribbean to be more than just another wishful budget request. It trusted that these programs had attracted special presidential interest and had received presidential endorsement. The OMB cutback left it with a sense of having pushed forward the President's policy, only to run into an indiscriminate budgetary barrier.

This State Department view was sadly mistaken. State and AID had never received any clear presidential endorsement for an expanded aid program, either in Jamaica specifically, or in the Caribbean more generally. The desire to spend more money was theirs and theirs alone. Throughout the year they had sought by various means to secure a firm presidential commitment to a policy of expanded aid, and they erroneously believed that the President's acceptance of a $63.3 million Jamaican aid package in July marked his acceptance of their anticipated 'multi-year effort', whereas the President seems to have been thinking only of a 'one-shot' or at most a 'year-by-year' effort.

OMB had good reason to believe that the President would support its cutback on aid requests for Jamaica and the Caribbean. First, the President himself, as early as April 1977 (speaking to the OAS), had endorsed 'directing more and more of our bilateral economic assistance to the poorer countries'. Jamaica, despite its financial distress, is by no means a poor country by world standards. In contrast to the nations of South Asia and Africa, it enjoys a $1200 per capita GNP, and rates at least an 'upper middle-income' classification. Second, in December 1977, OMB sensed that the President's foreign assistance priorities were being shaped by urgent security contingencies in Africa, both in Zaire and in the Horn of Africa. The Caribbean, especially when compared to Africa, was for that brief time losing much of its salience. Moreover, the President's residual interests in the Caribbean were now focused more clearly on the problem of Cuba, and Manley's support for Cuba made Jamaica a less favored object of presidential policy. Finally, Jamaica had compromised its own aid-worthiness early in December 1977 by failing to meet one of the performance targets (the domestic assets test) that had been imposed under the terms of the IMF loan received earlier in the year. Jamaica failed the test by only a small margin – $9.1 million – but automatically lost its IMF loan. The Jamaican government had to agree to enter into negotiations for a new balance of payments loan in 1978, under the Extended Fund Facility (EFF), which could provide a more generous three-year period for stabilization goals to be met.

Developments early in 1978 confirmed that the US was pulling back on expanded assistance for Jamaica and the Caribbean. When the newly formed CGCED finally began to function on 1 July 1978, with the establishment of a Caribbean Development Facility (CDF), the US was prepared to pledge only $20 million (in reprogrammed 1978 financial year funds), $12.5 million of which was earmarked for Jamaica. Financial year 1979 funding for the CDF was omitted, and further US contributions were reserved for the uncertain future.

The Jamaicans had hoped for much more, particularly since they had agreed, in May 1978, to the strictest possible terms for the $240 million EFF loan from the IMF. Manley had agreed to a massive 30% devaluation of the Jamaican dollar, while accepting stringent controls on imports, together with a series of big tax increases on manufacturing and on tourism, higher interest rates, limits on credit expansion, and a tight ceiling on workers' wage increases. It was expected that this IMF 'shock treatment' would produce a net 15% drop in the standard of living, a temporary inflation rate of 30–40%, and no immediate relief from the chronic 30% unemployment rate[47]. The once proud Manley government was now close to abandoning its domestic social policy, cutting back on public services, and placing itself at the mercy of western financial institutions. Yet the Carter administration, with its continuing reluctance to increase bilateral aid, and with its very small $12.5 million pledge to the CDF, held fast to a policy of low commitment.

It was significant that this period through June 1978 was one of heavy leadership preoccupation with two Latin American policy issues that did not bode well for aid to Manley's Jamaica: the Canal Treaties ratification process and the alleged Cuban role in the Shaba Province incident. Conservative congressional elements had to be pacified on both Panama and Cuba, requiring further retreat from any expensive aid initiatives in Jamaica or the Caribbean.

As the Congress moved to complete action on the President's aid requests for the 1979 financial year for Jamaica and the Caribbean, and as the State Department and AID prepared to submit their financial year 1980 requests to OMB, further aid cutbacks were in the making. Left holding onto an underfunded policy, the State Department and AID complained that top leadership had once again betrayed Latin America, by raising expectations with rhetorical initiatives early in the first year of the new administration, and then by failing in the second year to 'put their money where their mouth was'. This was not a fair assessment of what had taken place. The State Department and AID, not top leadership, had pressed most vigorously in 1977 for expanded assistance to Jamaica and the Caribbean. Top leaders had paid only scant attention to the issue, tentatively endorsing bureaucratic initiatives so long as commitments remained limited and costs remained low. When a routine budget review was conducted at year's end, leadership priorities were registered in a decision to limit aid both to Jamaica and to its neighbors in the Caribbean.

Analysis

US policy toward Jamaica and the Caribbean in 1977–78 evolved under conditions of routine priority. It was certainly not the least important of President Carter's Latin American policy concerns, but it ranked below the Canal Treaties, Cuba, and US relations with several other nations, including Mexico, Brazil, and Nicaragua. In any event, there is no evidence that President Carter ever involved himself on more than a routine basis in the management of US relations with Jamaica, or in the related question of assistance to the Caribbean. On those infrequent occasions when the question of US policy toward Jamaica did reach the President's desk, it did so in routine fashion, as in the form of an inter-agency recommendation, a brief visit requested by Manley, or as a part of the State Department's annual budget request.

In my view, this assignment of routine priority did not prevent the US from fashioning an appropriate policy toward Jamaica and the Caribbean. The sustained interest of top leaders was not required, in this case, to ensure the effective pursuit of leadership goals and interests. Most of the supposed costs of low priority treatment were never felt, while some of the benefits usually associated only with high priority were nonetheless realized.

I assume that one goal of the US foreign policy leadership was to improve bilateral relations with the Jamaican government, while another goal was to limit bilateral aid commitments and to move Caribbean aid policy into a multilateral (and hence multi-donor) context. Both of these goals were successfully pursued in 1977–78, with a minimum of effort and at very low cost. This was possible because working-level officials responded well to changes in the policy environment. Routine bureaucratic procedures did not preclude the timely initiation of policy change. Without any assignment of high priority, the aid 'embargo' was lifted, a rapprochement between the US and the Manley government was effected, and the formulation of a new regional policy in the Caribbean was accomplished. In each case, a healthy mix of low-level as well as high-level policy perspectives was preserved, ensuring that actions taken would be tolerable to the wide range of actors involved.

Routine priority status did not prevent working-level officials from responding quickly to the opportunity presented by Jamaica's need for economic assistance early in 1977. An inter-agency mission was constituted, State and AID expertise was brought to bear, and a proposed assistance package was ready for the President's approval by early summer. This was a timely, innovative, and adequately coordinated change of policy, accomplished by professionals at the working level without the benefit of intense leadership concern or involvement. Despite low-level management of this issue, evidence of undue private or corporate influence over the policy process is entirely absent. The modest degree of leadership involvement that proved necessary to place appropriate limits upon new aid commitments to Jamaica was also accomplished in routine fashion, primarily through the OMB budget review process. While paying scant attention to Jamaica, the President and his agents were nevertheless in a position to place effective limits on bureaucratic action. The President's preference for multilateral assistance projects in the Caribbean was imposed upon reluctant AID and State Department officials, and to some degree upon Jamaica as well, even while the issue was losing ground as a priority concern.

Not only were leadership goals effectively pursued, and leadership interests protected, under conditions of routine treatment. Had higher priority been assigned to US policy in Jamaica and the Caribbean, that policy might have been adversely affected in a number of ways. Speculation is dangerous, but much deeper White House involvement in US policy toward Jamaica, in 1977–78, probably would have exposed that policy to a tightened linkage with other high priority Latin American issues, most likely Cuba. It is my view that US relations with Jamaica had sufficient weight and substance to be managed on their own terms; policy toward Jamaica should not rise and fall with the tide of policy toward Cuba. Had Jamaican policy been managed at higher levels within the government, issue separation would have been more difficult to maintain. The links to Cuba that did tend to form whenever the White House looked at Jamaica would have hindered the process of improving relations with the Manley government.

This danger was manifest to some extent in the years following 1978. Quite suddenly, in 1979, the Caribbean region did become a matter of higher priority on the US foreign policy agenda. In one single eight-month period in 1979, a revolutionary government came to power in Grenada, the Sandanistas finally toppled the Somoza government in Nicaragua, issue was made of a Soviet 'combat bridge' based in Cuba, and further unsettling developments were signaled by a coup in El Salvador. Anxieties about Cuba and the Soviet Union, strongly felt by Congress and by the President's National Security Advisor, were now injected directly into US policy in the area, overwhelming the priorities of those who had earlier managed policy in the State Department. One US policy response was to increase its military presence in the region, and to expand by several orders of magnitude its military as well as its economic assistance programs.

While not entirely excluded from these aid increases, the Manley government in Jamaica was dealt with in less generous fashion than most of its neighbors, despite its acute economic crisis (continued negative economic growth, plus new difficulties in securing IMF assistance). Congress declined to vote substantial new assistance funds for Jamaica until after the election there in October 1980, in which Manley was at last soundly defeated by Edward P. G. Seaga, leader of the more conservative Jamaican Labor Party, and an outspoken anti-communist with close ties to the US. Only following that election did Congress vote to provide Jamaica with an additional $40 million in economic aid. Additional US assistance, plus a new line of IMF credits, were talked about in January 1981, when Prime Minister Seaga arrived one week after the inauguration as the first official foreign guest of the Reagan administration.

The election victory of Prime Minister Seaga in 1980 may itself illustrate another virtue to be found in the routine treatment of this particular Latin American policy issue during the early years of the Carter administration. Had the US assigned higher priority to its relations with the Manley government, involving itself ever more deeply in Jamaica's economic problems, and in Jamaica's highly personal political wars, it doubtless would have found itself (as in 1976) a central issue in the Jamaican election. Had the outcome of that election then turned on relations with the US (rather than upon domestic problems, or external relations with the IMF), Seaga's victory would have been less likely, or the legitimacy of that victory would have been more open to challenge by those fearful of US domination.

Wherever the complexion of a government is prone to sudden change, an overly energetic US policy carries risks. There is first the risk of making too great an investment in a government soon to fall. And if such an investment is not made, or if it is seen as inadequate, there is the opposite risk of seeming responsible for a fall. Better not to appear to care too much about political dynamics that are beyond one's effective control. Better to cushion US relations with such changeable governments by assigning no more than routine priority to those relations.

Several other risks that might have been associated with assigning higher priority to Jamaica in 1977–78 come to mind. High priority treatment might have inspired an effort to introduce greater 'consistency' into US policy toward Jamaica and the Caribbean. This drive for consistency, or apparent consistency, which more often emerges at the highest levels of the government, might have then forced a number of unwanted exclusive choices onto US policy. For example:

- The US praised the Manley government for its democratic institutions, while remaining critical of its close relations with Cuba. It would have been more difficult to maintain, and to express, this sort of mixed approval in the politicized atmosphere of high priority policy-making procedures.

- The US continued to provide bilateral assistance to Jamaica, even while publicizing its goal of multilateral coordination among aid donors and recipients in the Caribbean. High priority treatment would have made this necessary inconsistency in US policy more obvious.

- The US asked Jamaica to remain a functioning parliamentary democracy, but simultaneously insisted upon Jamaica's acceptance of IMF austerity measures that democratic governments cannot easily enforce. The luxury of doing both might be lost for the US if the issue had been assigned very high priority.

- The US constructed some foreign policies that were specifically designed to help Jamaica, but also took policy actions harmful to Jamaica (such as the 1977 increase in the price of sugar imported into the US, which effectively eliminated Jamaica's price advantage in the US market) whenever its own domestic interests were involved. Of course, doing inconsistent things to Jamaica may have been perfectly consistent with the interests of the US. But if Jamaica were assigned very high priority, a policy based upon exclusive choice would have been more likely to emerge, if only in response to pressure from newly alerted policy critics in Congress, whose critical interest is always aroused by a perceived inconsistency in presidential policy.

Finally, deeper leadership involvement in US policy toward Jamaica in this case might have become subversive of the leadership's own interest in caution, frugality, and low commitment. An assignment of higher priority to Jamaica would have further stimulated a bureaucratic search for 'solutions' to Jamaica's current difficulties. The White House would then have been faced with an array of ambitious and expensive bureaucratic proposals to bail the island out of distress. Much higher expectations would have been raised in Jamaica, only to be disappointed, in all likelihood, under the glare of much greater publicity.

7.3   Conclusion

In all, top leaders had less to gain than to lose by increasing the priority of US policy toward Jamaica in 1977–78. Routine priority treatment was more than adequate to secure US policy objectives. It introduced balance and caution (if not beauty or drama) into US policy, protecting the US (and perhaps Jamaica as well) from the worst case of a policy built upon inflexible or single-minded top-level commitment.

Routine treatment, in this case and perhaps others as well, may even gain for the US a certain tactical advantage. So long as top leaders can remain somewhat aloof from the policy process, working-level officials can more easily hold out to foreign governments a hope that policy is soon to improve. In 1977, Jamaica was lured into a more agreeable relationship with the US in just this fashion. Routine treatment helped to contain Jamaica's disappointment in US policy by encouraging a hope that US policy might yet take a more generous turn, if the President himself could ever find time to get involved.

The surest means to maximize the benefits of 'routine treatment' is to adjust and to improve the routines that govern the policy-making process[48]. Even then, some matters will defy routine treatment. But they will do so out of a special need for deep political commitment, or out of urgency or novelty, and not simply because of their importance. Policy issues do not require management at the highest level of the government merely because important interests are at risk or merely because divergent views exist within the bureaucracy. Particularly when disagreement exists, or when the stakes are high, time-tested working-level policy routines become a valuable means of protection against haste, oversight, and distortion, which can accompany decisions taken by partially informed generalists in a highly politicized atmosphere.

In the case of US policy toward Jamaica and the Caribbean, the many blessings of routine or low priority treatment were realized. US policy elsewhere in Latin America may also do better under the low light of routine professional treatment, than under the bright glare of constant leadership involvement and concern. In El Salvador today, and perhaps in Guatemala tomorrow, the dangers of excessive top-level attention are clearly visible. Leadership participation in the day-to-day policy-making process has weakened a much needed appreciation for local conditions that are sufficient by themselves to generate revolutionary pressures in Central America, entirely apart from the designs of Moscow and Havana. The 'high priority' recently assigned to Central America has mostly served to activate crude geopolitical instincts and atavistic ideological anxieties among top leaders within the executive and within the Congress. The better informed and more nuanced viewpoints of policy professionals at the middle level have been overwhelmed. If the US soon finds itself burdened by an irreversible 'high priority' commitment to preserve an unsustainable status quo in Central America, an unfortunate leadership decision to pay too much attention to the region may be in part to blame. The routine priority that is so frequently assigned to US policy in Latin America ought not to appear a burden on the policy-making process. The costs of paying more attention to Latin America too often outweigh the benefits.

Notes

1 Commission on the Organization of the Government for the Conduct of Foreign Policy. Government Printing Office, Washington, DC, 1975, vol. 1, p. 31. Latin American observers probably see very little genuine conflict on matters of policy substance among the various executive departments of the US government. They see primarily technical or jurisdictional differences over *how* US influence in the subcontinent is to be preserved.

2 Commission on the Organization of the Government for the Conduct of Foreign Policy, vol. 1, p. 62.

3 Stephen Krasner, 'Are Bureaucracies Important?' *Foreign Policy*, 7, Summer 1972, p. 168. See also Yale H. Ferguson, 'Through Glasses Darkly'. *Journal of International Studies and World Affairs*, 19 (1), February 1977, p. 18.

4 See Harry Weiner, 'Some Suggestions for Improving the Organization of the Bureau of Inter-American Affairs'. In *Appendices*, Commission on the Organization of the Government for the Conduct of Foreign Policy (note 1), Vol. 3, p. 274.

5 Christopher Mitchell applies this rule of attention to more than just the State Department. See Mitchell, 'Dominance and Fragmentation in US–Latin American Policy'. In Julio Cotler and Richard R. Fagen (eds), *Latin America and the United States; The Changing Political Realites.* Stanford University Press, Stanford, Calif., 1974, p. 201.

6 See Gregory F. Treverton, 'United States Policy-Making Toward Peru: The IPC Affair'. In *Appendices*, Commission on the Organization of the Government for the Conduct of Foreign Policy (note 1), Vol. 3, pp. 210–11.

7 This, once again, is particularly true within the Bureau of Inter-American Affairs. See Weiner (note 4), p. 275.

8 Robert Pastor, 'US Sugar Politics and Latin America: Asymmetries in Input and Impact'. In *Appendices*, Commission on the Organization of the Government for the Conduct of Foreign Policy (note 1), Vol. 3, p. 231.

9 Abraham F. Lowenthal, '"Liberal", "Radical," and "Bureaucratic" Perspectives on US–Latin American Policy: The Alliance for Progress in Retrospect'. In Cotler and Fagen (note 5), p. 231.

10 Jerome Levinson and Juan de Onis, *The Alliance That Lost Its Way.* Quadrangle Books, Chicago, 1970, p. 5.

11 Arthur M. Schlesinger, Jr., 'The Alliance For Progress: A Retrospective'. In Ronald G. Hellman and H. J. Rosenbaum (eds), *Latin America: The Search for a New International Role.* John Wiley and Sons, New York, 1975, p. 67.

12 Lowenthal (note 9), p. 232.

13 Richard J. Bloomfield, 'Who Makes American Foreign Policy?' Harvard University Center for International Affairs, Cambridge, Mass., April 1972, p. 112.

14 Schlesinger (note 11), p. 65.

15 James C. Thomson, Jr., in Richard J. Pfeffer (ed), *No More Vietnams?* Harper and Row, New York, 1968, p. 45.

16 I. M. Destler, *Presidents, Bureaucrats, and Foreign Policy.* Princeton University Press, Princeton, 1972, p. 60.

17 John Bartlow Martin, *Overtaken By Events*. Doubleday, New York, 1966, p. 661.

18 Jessica Einhorn, *Expropriation Politics*. Lexington Books, Lexington, Mass., 1974, pp. 128–9.

19 See Ernest R. May, 'The American Commonwealth'. In *Appendices*, Commission on the Organization of the Government for the Conduct of Foreign Policy (note 1), Vol. 3, pp. 280–5.

20 This is true unless high priority treatment is judged to be so damaging to policy that its appropriate focus becomes, by a reverse logic, the least important area of concern.

21 Levinson and de Onis (note 10), p. 63.

22 Arthur M. Schlesinger, Jr., *A Thousand Days*. Houghton Mifflin Co., New York, 1965, p. 200.

23 Schlesinger (note 11), p. 61.

24 ibid., p. 65.

25 Schlesinger (note 22), p. 232.

26 David Halberstam, *The Best and the Brightest*. Random House, New York, 1972, p. 28.

27 Lyndon B. Johnson, *The Vantage Point*. Holt, Rinehart, and Winston, New York, 1971, p. 198. See also Jerome Slater, *Intervention and Negotiation*. Harper and Row, New York, 1970, p. 199.

28 Treverton (note 6), p. 207. 'To the extent that high-level government officials were attentive to the issue,' says Treverton, 'their actions served as signals which reinforced the inclinations of the operating officials to began a pre-emptive aid embargo.'

29 Schlesinger (note 11), p. 83.

30 Much of the information provided in the case study section of this work was gained from confidential personal interviews, conducted in August 1978, with officials and staff in the US Senate, the House of Representatives, the State Department, the Agency for International Development, the Office of Management and Budget, the National Security Council, and with Washington representatives of US business firms operating in Jamaica.

31 J. Daniel O'Flaherty, 'Finding Jamaica's Way'. *Foreign Policy*, **31**, Summer 1978, p. 153. I am most grateful to Daniel O'Flaherty for his perceptive work on US–Jamaican relations, as contained in *Foreign Policy*, and as shared with me directly.

32 ibid., p. 154.

33 *Iron Age*, 24 January 1977, p. 27.

34 *Latin America Political Report*, **X** (50), 24 December 1976, p. 1.

35 'The Cartel That Never Was'. *Forbes*, 1 March 1977.

36 The somewhat unlikely proposal that SSA be extended to Jamaica was made necessary by those provisions added to the Foreign Assistance Act in 1973 and 1975 that prohibit the use of economic aid for balance of payments purposes. Jamaican officials were later forced to explain to their own people that the term 'Security Assistance' in fact carried 'no connotation of assistance in terms of military hardware or the like'. *Jamaican Weekly Gleaner*, 17 November 1977, p. 29.

37 *Jamaican Weekly Gleaner*, 17 May 1977, p. 1.

38 *Latin America Political Report*, **XI** (22), 10 June 1977, p. 176.

39 *Congressional Record*, Senate, US Government Printing Office, Washington, DC, 15 June 1977, pp. S9895–S9896.

40 ibid. The Senate Foreign Relations Committee endorsed aid to Jamaica, but expressed 'concern' about the use of SSA, in the absence of a credible security threat, about the obvious disparity between the scope of Jamaica's needs and the modesty of the dollar figure involved, and finally about the lack of any larger 'Caribbean' policy context for the request. The Committee report urged the administration to 'consider these concerns in developing next year's program'.

41 *Chemical Marketing Reporter*, 7 February 1977.

42 *Business Latin America*, 13 April 1977, p. 116.

43 Kaiser had accelerated its procurement of Australian bauxite, and Alcoa, which relied upon Jamaica for 84% of its alumina in 1972, had reduced that figure to less than 40%.

44 The exception to this rule is Revere Copper and Brass, which shut down its bauxite operation in Jamaica in 1975 and instigated action to collect $66.5 million from OPIC under the expropriation clauses of its insurance contract with that agency. In early 1977, Revere's claim was pending before the American Arbitration Association, and that company, seeking a means to extricate itself from what had always been a bad investment in Jamaica, was less favorably inclined to a warming of relations between the two governments. See *American Metal Market*, 8 February 1977.

45 See *Jamaican Weekly Gleaner*, 14 October 1977, p. 32. Not only the World Bank but the IMF itself may have been more generous than otherwise in 1977, owing to US plans to extend aid to Jamaica. The 'surprising mildness' of IMF conditions on Jamaica's loan package has been attributed by some to the parallel interest and influence of the US government. See *Latin America Political Report*, XI (30), 5 August 1977, p. 329. See also column by Charles Bartlett, *Washington Star*, 15 October 1977, p. 11.

46 Andrew Young, US representative to the World Bank Conference, 'Remarks Before the World Bank Conference on the Caribbean', unpublished speech, 14 December 1977.

47 *Latin America Political Report*, XII (19), 19 May 1978

48 See, for example, John Odell's proposed change in those routine standards and procedures that govern applications of countervailing duties to Latin American exports.

Index

agenda
  national foreign policy, 4
  North–South, 142
  President's, 214
  US–Latin America, 1, 4, 14, 209
  US–Mexico, 69, 100
agriculture, 17, 20–23, 100, 179
  exports, 146–147, 154, 158, 165 n7
Alemán, Miguel, 47, 78–79
Algeria, 196–197
Allende, Salvador, 32, 220
Alliance for Progress, 212–213, 217–218, 223
  and Hickenlooper amendment, 218
aluminum and bauxite exports, 118, 125, 220, 222–223, 225
  see also mining
Aluminum Company of America (Alcoa), 221–222, 225, 236 n43
Andean Pact, 39–40, 60, 86, 115, 120, 122–123, 134, 176, 186–189, 201
Anti-trust laws, 176–178, 182, 191, 196–197
Argentina, 3, 4, 13, 17, 19–21, 34, 40–46, 51, 59–60, 65 n61, 70, 143, 147, 150, 152, 157, 159, 171, 173, 176, 186, 188–190, 201
  manufacturers in, 16, 94, 154–155
  opinions in city of Buenos Aires, 26–29, 41
armed forces
  Argentina, 45–46
  Brazil, 52
  officers in, 22, 24, 26, 59
  US, 3
authoritarian regimes, 3–4, 31–32, 52–53, 150
Avila Camacho, Manuel, 78

balance of payments, 23, 37, 79, 81, 92–93, 95, 101 n6, 125, 132, 147, 157, 222–223, 229
  and foreign exchange, 30, 38, 46, 53, 94, 171–172, 223
banks, 20, 32, 34, 39, 62, 75, 122, 126–128, 140 n56, 154
  central, 127, 176
  of information, 201–202

bargaining
  internal, 6, 25, 70, 82, 88–91, 95–96, 99, 109, 215
  international, 5, 11, 13, 99, 111, 113, 142, 143, 146–147, 149, 151, 155–156, 159, 161–162, 175, 183, 188, 193, 198, 202, 227
  and obsolescent bargain, 121
  see also product cycle
benefits, 11–13, 22, 31–32, 34, 36, 43, 45, 47, 49, 60–62, 83, 89, 92, 94, 109, 112, 117, 121, 135, 137, 150, 152–153, 169–170, 184, 189, 192, 202, 208–211, 214, 216, 219, 221, 234
Betancourt, Rómulo, 112
Betancourt doctrine, 134
border industries, 75, 147, 220
Brazil, 3, 4, 13, 17–20, 52–60, 67 n100, 70, 94, 109, 116, 127–128, 136, 143, 146–148, 150–152, 154, 156–158, 161, 166 n7, 166 n19, 169, 171, 176, 186–188, 199, 201, 203, 216, 220, 230
  attitudes in urban, 26–29, 53
Brazilian Capital Goods Manufacturing Association (ABDIB), 55–57
  see also business federations
budget, 2, 137 n8, 222, 226, 228, 230
bureaucracies, 8, 11–12, 76–77, 80, 88, 90, 98, 128, 137, 149, 151, 159, 187, 193, 199, 208, 209–212, 214–215, 221, 223, 230–231, 233–234
business coalitions
  general, 3–4, 10, 13, 67 n100, 91, 178
  national bourgeois, 10, 14, 16, 24–26, 31–32, 34–62, 74–75, 77, 119, 122–123, 126, 169
  small businessmen, 10, 24, 29, 31–32, 35, 38–41, 43, 45, 47, 49, 51, 53, 59, 64 n36
  statist, 16, 22–24, 26, 29–34, 35, 37, 45, 48, 51–52, 58
  transnational, 10, 16–17, 22, 24, 26, 29–34, 35, 37–40, 43, 46–47, 48–49, 51–52, 54, 58–59, 80

business federations
  in Brazil, 54–57
  in Chile, 30, 32
  in Colombia, 38–39
  in Mexico, 47, 51, 80–81, 105 n53
  in Peru, 33–34
  in US, 157, 184–186
  in Venezuela, 35, 122, 125

Caldera, Rafael, 117
Calvo Doctrine, 197
Canada, 35, 36, 97, 115, 117, 133, 149,
  155–156, 159, 173
capital resources, 21, 23, 97, 123, 125, 127,
  175, 223
capitalism , 2, 16–17, 25, 35, 37, 43, 49–50,
  58, 61, 65 n61, 74–76, 83, 96, 102 n16,
  110, 120, 125, 169, 174, 181
  and capitalists, 22, 25, 45, 109
  and mercantilism, 107, 135
Cárdenas, Lázaro, 20, 78
Caribbean, 3, 86, 119, 135, 147, 152, 160,
  208, 219–221, 226–234
Caribbean Group for Cooperation and
  Economic Development, 220, 227–229
cartels, 108, 119, 129, 181
Carter administration, 126, 129, 134, 147,
  153, 162, 201, 219–234
Central America, 4, 5, 86, 147, 160, 234–235
Chile, 3, 17–20, 23, 29–32, 35–36, 46, 58–59,
  173, 176, 189, 201, 220, 223
  and opinions in city of Santiago, 26–29
Citibank, 122, 154
clients
  firms, 115
  states, 2, 89–91, 99, 114
coffee, 38, 145, 153–154, 157
Cold War, 1, 4–5, 213
Colombia, 17–21, 34, 38–40, 116, 147,
  150–151, 153, 158–160, 171, 173, 176,
  185–186, 188
  and Bogotá, 38–40, 153
  and Medellín, 38–40
communism and anti-communism, 2, 4, 35,
  54, 61, 145, 218, 232
competition
  advantages of, 111–112, 177–178
  edge in, 23
  industrial, 6, 10, 22, 24, 31, 35, 37–39, 46,
    47–48, 53, 55, 57–60, 71, 80, 91, 173
  and international competitiveness, 26, 32,
    81, 93, 96, 119, 142, 181, 187, 189, 222
  non-manufacturing, 30
  political, 34
  restraints on, 173, 195–196, 197, 202
  unfair, 118, 143, 146
  with US producers, 142, 146, 152–154,
    156–159, 165 n6, 180

Congress
  in Chile, 30
  in US, 117, 130, 143, 152–153, 167 n26,
    167 n31, 181, 201, 215, 218, 223–226,
    230, 232–233, 235
constraints, 69–70, 74–77, 80, 90, 96, 98,
  110, 121, 203, 221
corruption, 90–91, 221–222
costs, 4, 11–12, 22, 37, 56, 60, 73, 79, 87, 92,
  95, 101 n6, 109–110, 113, 121, 132, 135,
  162, 170–172, 184, 189, 202, 208,
  214–216, 218–219, 221, 231, 233–234
countervailing duties, 143, 146, 150,
  152–153, 156–158, 160–161, 165 n6
  and injury tests, 143, 161–162, 165 n7
  see also trade
coups, military, 30, 33, 54, 59, 213, 217,
  232
Cuba, 1–3, 23, 58, 65 n61, 134, 141 n83, 146,
  152, 155, 159, 179, 213, 216–223,
  226–227, 229–234

Data General Corp., 56
debt, 5, 11, 26, 45, 75, 96, 127–128, 140 n65,
  147, 149, 154, 156
Dedini, 55–56
democracy, 108–109, 112, 132, 134, 153, 220,
  233
  and democratic socialism, 220–223
dependency and autonomy arguments,
  12–13, 16–17, 37, 67 n100, 73–74, 76,
  81, 97–98, 109–110, 117–118, 120,
  132–134, 137, 149, 159, 166 n9,
  169–170, 174–175, 189–190, 192,
  202–203, 223, 226, 232
development and underdevelopment, 3, 23,
  32–33, 48, 53, 55, 60, 67 n100, 73–76,
  78–79, 81, 87–88, 93–94, 96, 98, 100,
  108–109, 113, 120, 132–133, 147,
  169–171, 173–175, 177, 179, 183,
  188–189, 192, 197, 202–203
  see also modernization
Díaz Ordaz, Gustavo, 80
discrimination, 6, 10, 24–26, 31–34, 36–37,
  40–41, 43, 45–46, 47, 52, 56, 58–59,
  61–62, 65 n61, 80, 83, 90, 94–95, 98,
  109, 114, 120–122, 160–161, 174, 177
disputes and conflicts, 6, 10–11, 13–14, 17,
  24–26, 49, 60–61, 74, 81–83, 87, 91,
  108–109, 111, 114, 116, 129, 136,
  142–162, 170, 181, 183, 197, 200, 234,
  235 n1
Dominican Republic, US intervention in, 1,
  3, 134, 214, 217, 219
Dow Chemical, 45
dumping, 32, 146–147, 155, 165 n6, 167 n31
  see also trade, countervailing duties

Echeverría, Luis, 47, 49–52, 81–83, 87–89, 91, 93–94, 98–99, 187, 200
Ecuador, 39, 146, 160, 173, 176, 184, 188
efficiency, 26, 38, 46, 57, 60, 81, 93
Eisenhower administration, 213, 216
El Salvador, 1, 4, 7, 134, 232, 234
electricity, 20–22, 51, 57, 80–81, 118
  see also utilities
elites, 8, 16, 21–22, 37, 39–40, 48, 50, 61, 74, 98, 110, 121, 173
  opinion of, 8–9, 16, 35–36, 38–39
Elliott, 55–56
energy, 3–4, 97, 100, 118–119, 134, 220
  and coal, 39
  and oil-producing countries, 3, 108, 117, 129, 149
  and prices, 4
  see also oil
Europe, East, 97, 155, 178
Europe, West, 1–4, 9, 97, 116, 173, 177, 179, 188, 191
  and European Economic Community, 195, 226
expertise, 7, 12–13, 56, 76, 81, 94, 97, 98, 103 n19, 113–114, 123, 125, 135, 174, 187, 214, 217, 231, 234–235
  see also technical strategies
export promotion strategies, 74, 81, 83, 89, 92–96, 117–119, 142–162, 172–174, 176, 185, 187, 194–195, 197–198, 222
  see also manufacturing, trade
expropriation of firms, 10, 18, 20, 22–23, 26–29, 37–38, 41, 48, 54, 61–62, 78, 108, 115, 117, 120–123, 129, 139 n39, 155, 181, 191
  and nationalization, 21–23, 53, 58–59
  and socialization, 21–24, 29–34, 35–36, 45, 49, 51, 58

Fascell, Dante, 226
Fedecámaras, 35, 122, 125
  see also business federations
Figueiredo, João, 57
Ford administration, 129, 147, 165 n6, 165 n7, 219
foreign aid
  from Mexico, 135
  from US, 178–179, 210, 213, 217–218, 220–234, 236 n36
  from Venezuela, 135
  multilateral, 226–231, 233
  and technical assistance, 171–172, 178–179, 199, 201–202
foreign investment, 2–3, 5–6, 8, 10–11, 13–14, 16–17, 19–62, 69–100, 104 n40, 108–109, 114, 119–126, 135, 139 n45, 168, 174, 176, 178–180, 186, 188, 199

foreign investment (*cont.*)
  US-based, 9, 12, 17–20, 61–62, 70–75, 86, 123–126, 133, 218, 220, 225
  see also multinational enterprises
France, 56–57
Frei, Eduardo, 31

Germany, West, 56–57, 119, 127, 133, 188
Grenada, 1, 232
gross domestic product (GDP)
  of Jamaica, 222–223, 229
  of Venezuela, 113, 119, 135
Guatemala, 2, 234
guerrillas, 4
Guevara, Ernesto (Che), 1

hegemony, 2–3, 149
Herrera Campíns, Luís, 37, 120, 124, 128, 134, 137 n9, 138 n10
host governments, 21–26, 30, 40, 46, 51, 58, 99, 109, 120–121, 175, 177, 179–180, 188, 225
  officials of, 22, 24, 26, 30–31, 35–37, 81, 88, 95
  see also states
human rights, 3, 134, 220
  and human needs, 201

ideology, 3, 6, 8, 13, 16, 26, 32–33, 48, 77, 96, 150, 175, 183, 190, 205 n37, 216–218, 235
  conservative, 225, 230
  liberal, 6, 111, 178, 218
  and organizations, 13, 209, 211–212
Illia, Arturo, 45
imperialism, 12, 14, 16, 66 n89, 109–110, 148
implementation, 70, 78, 80, 82, 88–91, 95–97, 99, 124, 188, 191, 195, 199, 209–210
import substitution strategies, 74, 78–79, 81, 92–93, 95, 118–119, 173–174
  see also manufacturing
India, 192–193
Industrial Development Council (CDI), 54–56
inflation, 2, 43, 56, 60, 81, 96–97, 100, 157, 222, 229
intellectual property, 169
intellectuals, 22, 24, 26, 30, 59, 168, 175
  and university professors, 35, 49
  and university students, 31, 35–36, 49–50
Inter-American Development Bank, 135, 171, 213, 227
inter-American relations, 1–6, 8, 10–12, 14, 16, 169, 183–184, 219, 226
Inter-American Treaty of Reciprocal Assistance, 1
interest groups, 13, 33, 35, 102 n16, 152, 180

interests, 10, 12–13, 17, 22, 25, 35, 39, 49, 52,
    54–56, 58, 61, 81–82, 89, 108–110, 117,
    120, 123–124, 132, 134, 136–137, 142,
    151, 153–154, 160, 178, 189, 201,
    208–209, 214–216, 219–220, 224,
    228–229, 231, 233–234
International Business Machines (IBM), 56
international economic
    order, 2–4, 9, 14, 61, 67 n100, 107–108,
        117, 119, 135, 142, 168, 173, 176, 181,
        183, 194, 198–200
    regimes, 3, 5, 9, 14, 160–162, 168, 192–200
    rules, 2–3, 5, 11, 81, 169, 175, 192–193
international financial system, 4, 96,
    126–128, 135–136, 223
    and internal impacts, 126–127, 229
    see also debt
international monetary system, 2–3, 151
    and devaluation, 2–3, 82, 87, 105 n41, 108,
        126–127, 223, 229
    and International Monetary Fund (IMF), 2,
        45, 135, 226, 229, 232–233, 237 n45
international organizations, 11, 13, 169–170,
    182, 195
    see also United Nations, Organization of
        American States
International Petroleum Company (IPC), 33
international system, 1, 3, 6, 10, 12, 110–111,
    148–150, 159, 198
    and global issues, 5, 7, 9, 151, 162,
        168–169, 178
iron ore exports, 115–116, 118, 119, 123,
    139 n39
issue areas, 6–8, 9–10, 12, 14, 99–100, 120,
    214

Jamaica, 12–13, 134, 208, 219–234, 236 n36,
    237 n45
Japan, 1, 3, 4, 9, 36, 56–57, 97, 108, 115, 119,
    127, 151, 176, 188, 191, 193, 203
Johnson, President Lyndon B., 3, 213–214,
    217, 219
joint ventures, 14, 20–21, 24–26, 31, 36, 40,
    43, 45, 50, 55, 57, 59, 67 n100, 75, 81,
    118, 124

Kawasaki Heavy Industries, 55–56
Kaiser Aluminum, 220, 225, 236 n43
Kennedy administration, 212–213, 216–218
Kissinger, Henry, 152, 155, 181, 183, 201,
    219

labor
    attitudes of manual workers, 26–29, 35, 41,
        47–48, 53, 64 n36
    control over, 74, 87
    force, 97

labor (cont.)
    leaders, 49
    legislation, 34
    wages, 22, 45, 87, 95, 104 n39, 222, 229
    see also unemployment
Latin America, 1, 5, 9–10, 107, 114, 119, 159,
    197–200, 203
    objectives of governments in, 10–11, 13,
        142
    relations with the US, 1–4, 8, 12, 134, 136,
        147–149, 156, 162, 169–170, 183–184,
        190–192, 200–203, 208–219, 234–235
Latin American Economic System (SELA),
    115, 134
Latin American Free Trade Association
    (LAFTA), 60, 115
Latin American Integration Association, see
    Latin American Free Trade Association
law firms, 156–158, 167 n31
learning and innovation, 21–26, 50, 76, 81,
    98, 113, 135, 202, 211, 213, 221, 231
legitimacy, 77, 83, 96, 108–109, 112, 129,
    134, 176–177, 192, 196–197, 199–201,
    232
levels of power
    presidential, 7, 12–13, 77, 90, 98–99, 136,
        159, 208–219, 221, 224, 226–230,
        232–235
    sub-presidential, 7, 12, 61, 136, 147, 152,
        156, 165 n6, 215–216, 219–221,
        223–224, 230–232, 234–235
leverage, 6, 25
linkages, 7, 12, 16, 35, 75, 83, 89, 92, 97–98,
    214, 217, 231–232
López Mateos, Adolfo, 76, 89, 92
López Portillo, José, 50, 52, 82–83, 93,
    97–98, 200

management, 21, 23, 69, 75, 90–91, 97–98,
    121, 123–126, 180, 187, 203, 231, 234
    foreign-born, 30–31, 36, 38, 43, 50
    and managers, 30–31, 35, 43, 46, 49–50,
        53, 98, 215
Manley, Michael, 134, 220–233
manufacturing
    exports, 3, 5–7, 9–12, 71, 83, 95, 118,
        142–162, 173
    firms, 23–26, 38, 46, 55–56, 58–60
    imports, 117, 119, 216
    industrialization, 6, 9–10, 38, 73–74,
        78–79, 81, 96, 108, 147, 157, 159, 168,
        170, 173, 175, 189
    infant industries, 2, 59, 78, 113
    investments in, 19–21, 23–26, 32, 59, 97
    US investments in, 17–20, 30, 34, 37, 40,
        52–53, 70–71, 73, 100 n3, 123–124
    see also manufacturing sectors

manufacturing sectors
  automobiles, 45, 51, 78, 80–81, 83, 91–96,
    116, 123, 143, 146, 152, 155, 165 n6,
    180
  capital goods, 24, 52, 54–55, 57–58, 60, 71,
    147
  chemicals, 45, 51, 71, 81, 180
  consumer electronics, 40, 180
  data processing, 56
  food industry, 71, 81
  footwear, 147, 150, 152–154, 157–158,
    161, 165 n7
  leather products, 153–154, 158
  steel, 24, 45, 81, 125, 146, 151, 158, 162
  textiles, 39, 119, 153, 155–156, 162
  see also manufacturing
markets
  internal, 22, 24, 55–56, 59, 61, 67 n100,
    78–79, 86–88, 90, 94, 96, 112, 122,
    147, 150, 177, 187–189
  international, 21, 23, 50, 60, 83, 86–87, 92,
    97, 112, 117, 130–131, 139 n39, 142,
    146–148, 151–152, 157, 159, 172–173,
    175, 180, 183, 201–202
  share of, 142, 151, 158–159, 170
masses, opinion of, 8–9, 16, 36, 48, 210, 215
Mexico, 3–4, 5, 8, 9, 11, 13–14, 17–21, 23,
    47–52, 58–59, 69–100, 116–117, 128,
    136, 142, 147–148, 150, 158–162,
    165 n7, 167 n31, 171, 173, 176, 185–188,
    189, 191, 193–194, 200, 203, 216, 220,
    230
  foreign policy of, 73, 155
  opinions in Mexico City, 26–29
migration, 75, 97, 100
military relations, 1–2, 4, 6, 8, 149, 178, 218,
    232, 236 n36
mining, 17, 19–23, 33, 60, 78, 80–81, 113,
    121, 225
  copper, 18, 23, 30–32, 35, 38
  sulphur, 51, 155
  see also aluminum and bauxite exports
mobilization, 11, 35, 60, 77, 149
  of international allies, 149, 151–154, 156,
    158–159
modernization, 17, 21
  see also development and
    underdevelopment
multinational enterprises, 2, 5, 6, 9–11, 14,
    16–18, 20–21, 23–24, 29–62, 67 n100,
    69, 76, 80–83, 86, 88–89, 91–94, 97,
    101 n6, 105 n51, 108–109, 120–122, 124,
    149, 170, 174–175, 177, 179–180,
    182–190, 192–199, 202, 209–210,
    212–214, 218, 220, 231
  subsidiaries of, 6, 22, 24–52, 75, 90, 171,
    173, 187, 195–196
  see also foreign investment

National Association of Industries
    (CONCAMIN), 47
  see also business federations
National Association of Manufacturing
    Industries (CNIT or CANACINTRA),
    47, 51
  see also business federations
National Confederation of Chambers of
    Commerce (CONCANACO), 47, 51
  see also business federations
National Economic Development Bank
    (BNDE), 54–55
national, private business, 2, 5–6, 9–10, 14,
    16–17, 20, 22–26, 29–32, 35–62, 69,
    73–75, 79–81, 83, 94, 97–98, 101 n6,
    102 n16, 121–122, 125, 127, 133, 134,
    177, 196
  see also business coalitions
national security, 3, 22, 59–60, 121, 215–216,
    218, 236 n40
nationalism, 11–12, 16, 21, 26, 37–38, 53, 55,
    58–60, 65 n61, 99, 107–114, 116,
    120–121, 123, 126, 128, 133–136
  and denationalization, 71, 81
  and nationalists, 22, 30, 45, 47, 49, 61,
    77–78, 80
natural resources, 10, 22–24, 29, 31, 33–34,
    50, 58–59, 124
  see also agriculture, mining, oil, aluminum
    and bauxite exports
Nicaragua, 1, 4, 134, 160, 216, 220, 230, 232
Nixon administration, 117, 129, 143, 151,
    219, 222
North–South international relations, 5, 8–9,
    13, 109, 119, 142, 156, 162, 168–169,
    174, 189, 192–201
  see also international economic

oceans, negotiations governing, 2–3
oil, 11, 14, 17–18, 21, 23, 35–38, 45, 55, 74,
    96–100, 101 n7, 108, 111, 113, 115–117,
    119–123, 125–126, 128–136, 216, 223
  embargo, 117
  see also energy
oligopolies, 24–26, 54–56, 58–59, 61, 202
  and monopolies, 172, 203
Onganía, Juan, 45
Organization of American States, 1, 4, 162,
    219, 229
Organization of Petroleum Exporting
    Countries (OPEC), 108, 115, 126,
    128–130, 135, 181, 183, 226
  and Organization of Arab Petroleum
    Exporting Countries (OAPEC), 117
Orinoco heavy oil belt, 133–134, 141 n82
outcomes, 10–14, 111, 121, 133, 135, 142,
    146, 148–159, 161, 169

Panama
  Canal, 1, 153, 183, 219–220, 230
  country of, 39
Paraguay, 57, 160
Paris Convention on Industrial Property
  (1883), 169, 179, 191
parties, political, 30, 35, 41, 77, 137 n9,
  214–215, 217
  in Jamaica, 222, 232
patents and trademarks, 82, 92, 169, 173, 175,
  178–179, 181, 183, 191, 193, 200, 204 n3,
  205 n37
  and Patent Cooperation Treaty (1970), 179,
  205 n39
Pérez, Carlos Andrés, 119–120, 123, 137 n9
Pérez Jiménez, Marcos, 111–112, 137 n8
Peronists, 41, 45–46
  and Isabel Perón, 46
  and Juan Perón, 154–155, 157
Peru, 17, 19–20, 23, 29, 33–34, 58–59, 171,
  173, 176, 186, 218
Petrobras, 55–56
Petróleos de Venezuela (PDVSA), 125
planning, 6, 76, 88, 98, 108, 115, 124, 133,
  147, 174, 203
policy-making, 7, 10, 12, 56–57, 69–70, 74,
  76, 78, 83, 109, 137, 147, 159, 166 n19,
  168, 182, 235
  in private firms, 25
  styles of, 11, 70, 77, 88, 90–91, 96, 98–99,
  124
  see also levels of power, presidential terms,
  bureaucracies
politicization, 6, 12–13, 126, 168, 180–181,
  200, 233–234
presidential terms, 11, 13, 20, 50, 70, 76–83,
  87, 89, 91, 94, 98–99, 134
  and presidential authority, 209–219, 221,
  225–226, 228–230, 233
  see also levels of power
prices, 23, 46, 50, 52, 54, 56, 60, 83, 93–95,
  103 n19, 108–109, 119, 128–130,
  132–133, 143, 146–147, 157, 162,
  172–173, 185–186, 197, 202, 222, 233
priorities and attention, 7–8, 12–13, 61, 142,
  208–221, 229, 232–235
product cycle, 21–26
  see also bargaining
proprietary technology, 168, 178–181, 192,
  198, 201–202
  see also technology, patents and trademarks

railroads, 21, 56–57
Reagan administration, 4, 7, 141 n74, 232
regulations and state interference, 11, 22, 30,
  39, 47–48, 51–52, 56, 58, 61, 69–70,
  74–77, 79–83, 88–91, 96, 98–99,
  104 n33, 112, 114, 119, 142, 160, 168,
  170, 172, 181
  on credit, 24, 34, 54–55, 57, 59, 61, 229

regulations and state interference (*cont.*)
  on equity of firms, 14, 24, 38–39, 45–46,
  49–50, 56–57, 78, 80–83, 93, 95, 97,
  104 n32, 122, 176, 226
  and local content, 14, 52, 56–57, 60, 92–95
  on purchases of goods, 24, 39–40, 52,
  54–55, 59, 61
  on technology, 172–174, 176–178, 180,
  184–194, 198, 200, 202–203
revolution
  in Central America, 234–235
  in Cuba, 3
  in Grenada, 1, 232
  in Mexico, 51, 77, 101 n7, 102 n10
  in Nicaragua, 1, 232
  in Venezuela, 109
Reynolds Aluminum, 118–119, 123, 125, 225
Ruíz Cortines, Adolfo, 78–79, 103 n19

Saudi Arabia, 126, 129
Seaga, Edward, 232
Singapore, 7
social classes, 16, 26–29, 30–31, 35, 41, 43,
  48, 101 n6
South Korea, 7
Southeast Asia, 3, 8, 217
Soviet Union, 2, 4, 149, 232, 234
Spain, 115
special relationship, 8–9
stability and instability, 87–88, 91, 100, 123,
  126, 187–188, 195, 199, 202, 222–223,
  229
state enterprises, 9, 14, 20, 36–37, 46, 55,
  57–59, 61, 108, 112–113, 125
states
  internal action, 3, 5–6, 9, 11, 22, 26, 41,
  45–46, 47, 51–53, 58, 67 n100, 69–71,
  74–75, 80–81, 90–92, 99, 102 n16,
  109, 112–113, 125, 169, 171, 176–178,
  184–191, 201, 203, 225
  international action, 3, 5, 14, 112, 135, 142,
  143, 148–149, 159, 161, 170, 173–174,
  176, 183–200
  and state capitalism, 74
strategies
  international, 170–171, 175–176, 189,
  192–200, 203
  national 170–171, 175, 184–190, 193,
  199–201, 203
  protests, 150–151
  yielding, 150, 157, 218
  see also mobilization, threats, technical
  strategies
subsidies, 46, 57, 108, 113, 117–119, 143,
  146, 148, 150, 156–162, 222
suppliers, 11, 59, 92, 94–95, 114–115, 119,
  122, 129, 136, 148, 151, 168–169, 172,
  175–176, 194–195, 197–198, 200, 202–203
  and security of supply, 129–130, 132, 225
symbols, political, 14, 136, 148

Taiwan, 7
taxes, 22, 31, 34–36, 45, 57, 59, 75, 80, 83,
    90, 95, 117, 129, 143, 152, 157–158, 179,
    222–223, 225, 229
  and incentives, 10, 40, 54–55, 61, 79, 118,
    157
technical strategies, 11, 13, 76, 145, 151,
    156–160
technocrats, 52, 156–160
technology, 4–6, 8–11, 13–14, 21, 23–24, 43,
    50, 55–56, 60, 69, 81, 88–90, 92, 95–96,
    98, 108, 121, 124–126, 133–134, 136,
    149, 168–203
  codes on transfer of, 13, 81–83, 89, 97,
    175–176, 180–181, 192–202
  license and royalties over, 82, 171–172,
    176, 185, 187
  registries for, 82, 176, 185–187, 192, 200
theoretical perspectives, 12–13, 16–17,
    109–111, 148–151, 159–160
Third World, 8, 73, 94, 99, 108, 117–119,
    129, 136, 192, 201
threats and retaliation, 11, 36, 79–80, 108,
    110–111, 118–119, 123, 136, 149–151,
    154–157, 159, 200
Todman, Terence, 224, 226–227
trade
  access to raw materials, 124–125
  agreements, 115, 142, 143, 146
  direction, 75, 114–117, 136, 138 n17, 147
  exports, 36, 56, 60, 142–162
  General Agreement on Tariffs and Trade
    (GATT), 2, 56, 143, 160–162
  industrial, 11, 13, 142–162
  multilateral negotiations, 143, 152,
    160–162
  non-tariff barriers, 56–57, 78–80, 89–90,
    92, 94–95, 129, 146, 154, 156, 160, 162
  orderly marketing agreements, 151, 161
  pattern, of, 3–6, 8, 10–12, 17, 20–21, 90,
    93, 97, 100, 108, 114, 116, 120,
    130–131, 134–135, 178
  protection against, 2, 5–6, 10, 38, 59, 61,
    75, 79, 92, 95, 122, 142, 146, 159, 161
  special preferences, 117–118, 128, 136,
    146, 162, 233
  tariffs, 2, 32, 46, 59, 78, 80, 94–95, 98,
    118–119, 143, 147, 151, 155, 160–162
  US Trade Act (1974), 117, 130, 136, 143,
    151–152, 183
  US Trade Agreements Act (1979), 160, 162
  see also dumping, countervailing duties
Trinidad and Tobago, 113

Unemployment, 43, 81, 87, 96–97, 100, 222,
    229
  and employment, 75, 113
  see also labor

United Nations, 2
  Conference on Trade and Development
    (UNCTAD), 119, 169, 171–173, 176,
    181–183, 186, 193–196, 200–201
  Economic and Social Council (ECOSOC),
    181
  Economic Commission for Latin America
    (ECLA), 112, 162, 173–175, 193
  General Assembly, 13, 169, 181, 193
  Group B, 193–195, 197–198
  Group D, 193–195
  Group of 77, 182, 193–200
  Industrial Development Organization
    (UNIDO), 169, 201
  Intergovernmental Group of Experts
    (IGE), 193–194
United States
  government, 6–7, 11, 56
  objectives, 10, 13–14, 110, 148–150, 159,
    178–183, 201–203, 220, 234
  policies, 10, 12, 14, 17, 61–62, 76,
    152–153, 176, 181, 191–192, 195, 197,
    205 n37, 208–219, 220–234
  relations with, 97, 99–100, 107–137,
    157–162, 168, 208–234
  relative power, 3, 9, 14, 76, 128, 148, 159,
    170, 184, 188, 202, 216
  trade with, 75, 114–120, 127, 130–132,
    143, 147–162, 180
  views abut, 35–37, 43, 48, 65 n61, 73–74
  see also Latin America
Uruguay, 3, 150
US Agency for International Development
    (AID), 171, 222–224, 228, 230–231
US Central Intelligence Agency (CIA), 220,
    222
US Department of Commerce, 160, 166 n7
  Patent Office, 182
US Department of Defense, 165 n7, 220
US Department of State, 117, 151–152, 155,
    157, 165 n7, 181–182, 213, 217–218,
    220, 226–228, 230–232
  Bureau of Inter-American Affairs, 209,
    223–224
  Bureau of International Organization
    Affairs (IO), 182
  Bureau of Oceans, International
    Environmental and Scientific Affairs
    (OES), 182
  Economic and Business Bureau (EB), 180,
    182
US International Trade Commission (ITC),
    147, 154, 165 n7, 220
US National Security Council, 151–153, 226,
    232
US Office of Management and Budget
    (OMB), 226, 228, 230–231
US Overseas Private Investment Corporation
    (OPIC), 179, 220, 222, 236 n44

US Steel, 45, 115
US Treasury Department, 143, 146–147,
    152–153, 156–158, 165 n7, 220, 226
utilities, 10, 17, 20–24, 33–34, 51, 58, 81
    see also electricity

Velasco Alvarado, Juan, 33
Venezuela, 4–5, 9, 11–14, 17–21, 23, 31,
    34–38, 40, 58–59, 70, 146, 160, 176,
    185–186, 201, 226
    foreign policy of, 107–137

Venezuela (*cont.*)
    opinions in city of Caracas, 26–29, 35,
        64 n36
Videla, Jorge, 46
Vietnam, effects of, 213–214, 217, 219
    and effects of Laos, 217

Wionczek, Miguel, 193, 200
World Bank, 171, 226–228, 237 n45
World Intellectual Property Organization
    (WIPO), 169, 179, 205 n39
World War II, 1, 78, 107, 169, 178, 216